On Falcons' Wings

✦

AN INTREPID GENERATION

John C. Scharfen

D1280100

iUniverse, Inc.

New York Lincoln Shanghai

On Falcons' Wings
AN INTREPID GENERATION

Copyright © 2006 by John Cole Scharfen

iUniverse books may be ordered through booksellers or by contacting:

iUniverse
2021 Pine Lake Road, Suite 100
Lincoln, NE 68512
www.iuniverse.com
1-800-Authors (1-800-288-4677)

ISBN-13: 978-0-595-37174-7 (pbk)
ISBN-13: 978-0-595-67468-8 (cloth)
ISBN-13: 978-0-595-81572-2 (ebk)
ISBN-10: 0-595-37174-4 (pbk)
ISBN-10: 0-595-67468-2 (cloth)
ISBN-10: 0-595-81572-3 (ebk)

Printed in the United States of America

On Falcons' Wings

For the residents of Falcons Landing—past, present, and future.

IN MEMORIAM

Helen D. Schulz

James C. Irvine

Lt. Gen. Edward Bronars, USMC

Gen. Kenneth McLennan, USMC

Col. George C. McNaughton, USMC

B. Gen. Ernest R. Reid, USMC

Col. Wendell N. Vest, USMC

Donald J. Gordon

Kevin O'Shea

Mary McVay Spaulding

Contents

Preface

The telephone call was unexpected. It was an offer of a duplex unit at Falcons Landing, the Air Force retired officer continuing care community in Potomac Falls, Virginia. Even though we had been on a wait list for such a unit for four years, we were number six on that list and expected that we had at least another year's wait. My wife, Nancy, and I did not hesitate. We gave a provisional acceptance to Carolyn Hill, marketer for Falcons Landing. The following day, we drove the twenty-eight miles from Alexandria, Virginia, to Falcons Landing, and inspected the 1,464-square-foot unit, with attached, single-car garage. The units are smaller than the twenty detached Manor houses, but to secure one of these larger units would have extended our wait for years. We had elected not to put our names on the list for one of the 239 apartments that range in size from 815 to 1,834 square feet. Our good health and age did not warrant consideration of the assisted living and nursing accommodations that are part of the Falcons Landing continuing care contract. However, the availability of those facilities in future years made our decision to join the community seem prudent.

We were ecstatic with the offer. We conducted but a cursory inspection, because we had visited the facility often and had close friends already in residence. We accepted the unit and initiated contract formalities. We still had to provide results of a physical examination and undergo a mental/psychological screening, but we were confident on both scores. Ninety days later, we were at Falcons Landing unpacking our household effects.

As this is being written, it has been over three years since we made the move that is one of many we have made after a thirty-year career in the Marine Corps. That's right—the Marine Corps. Retired military officers from all uniformed services, their spouses, and their unremarried surviving spouses are eligible to apply to this community.

When Falcons Landing was only partially completed, the eligibility criteria were temporarily extended to include federal retirees closely affiliated with the military, such as the Department of Defense, the Central Intelligence Agency, the Federal Bureau of Investigation, the Department of State, and others. In 1998, when the community reached 90 percent occupancy, the eligibility criteria was limited to commissioned officers of the uniformed services with at least twenty years of active duty who were entitled to retired pay, including reservists. As of this writing, this community includes members of the Marines, Army, Navy, Air Force and Coast Guard, as well as diplomats, senior federal executives, and their spouses. There is at least one exception allowed by the board of governors for a widow who had lost her youngest son in Vietnam. Notwithstanding the current diversity, the character of the community is U.S. Air Force. It was born of the inspiration and raised with the labors of active-duty and retired Air Force officers. We are grateful for their enthusiasm, their dedication, and their acceptance of fellow officers and civilian counterparts.

I welcome this opportunity to acknowledge my debt to all whose assistance has been critical in this project. I especially want to thank those who have been profiled or who make a cameo appearance in these pages as they have given much time and their confidences to the writing of their stories. As always, my wife, Nancy, has been a bedrock of support. Notwithstanding all of the assistance I have received in this work, errors or omissions found herein are mine alone.

1

Overture

Falcons Landing
Photo by Lloyd Hill

In writing of Falcons Landing, one has several choices. The history of its inception, the challenges, and the vision of its creators are all fascinating stories. The tale of the available facilities and opportunities for continued intellectual, physical, and spiritual growth is intriguing. But it seems that the most interesting stories are those that deal with the lives and accomplishments of the many distinguished and less well-known members of this community who have served their country well over many years, in crucial times, in so many different ways. In a few personal profiles I hope to capture the character of this beautiful community, composed of such remarkable, intrepid Americans. Along the way, I will salt the profiles with information about the nature and activities of the community, but the focus will be upon its citizens.

There are many more heroic, comic, compelling stories than there is space in this volume. I regret that the sample is so limited. There are some 450 residents here at Falcons Landing, and there are some 450 stories worthy of inclusion in these pages. Would that they could all be told.

Here are sketches of some of the stories that have not been told:

Lt. Col. Floyd Sweet, USAF (Ret), has an International Soaring Pilot rating, with certificate number 45 in the United States, signed by Orville Wright. He earned his rating on Columbus Day, 1932. When the new Smithsonian National Air and Space Museum's Steven F. Udvar-Hazy Center was opened in December 2003, Floyd was one of twenty-five pioneers chosen to represent the history of flight.

Gen. David C. Jones retired from the Air Force on July 1, 1982, and moved to an apartment at Falcons Landing with his engaging wife, Lois, in 2004. David was chief of staff of the Air Force from 1974 to 1978 and chairman of the Joint Chiefs of Staff from 1978 to 1982, serving as the senior military advisor to the president, the National Security Council, and the secretary of defense.

Maria-Theresa "Resi" Steeg was born in Bitburg, Germany, and was an Air Force pilot's widow before marrying George Steeg. Resi earned diplomas in English and French and a bachelor of arts in German. She served as a translator, interpreter, and administrative assistant with British, French, and American government agencies in Germany. She has a facility with languages that served her well while working as a bilingual legal assistant for the German consulate in Detroit, Michigan. George graduated from Rensselaer on the G.I. Bill and pioneered systems for radar, electronic warfare, and intelligence. He is a true defense electronics boffin, a World War II term coined by the father of radar, Sir Robert Watson-Watt, for engineers and scientists who "are at home on the tarmac as well as in the laboratory." He taught electronic warfare systems at UCLA and authored the electronic warfare technology section of Brassey's "International Military and Defense Encyclopedia." The secretary of defense awarded George the Department of Defense's second highest civilian award. The Steegs' entrée to Falcons Landing is unique in that it was sanctioned by Resi's Air Force association rather than George's military affiliation. Their backgrounds make them intriguing dinner companions.

Retired Brig. Gen. Bain McClintock of the Marine Corps is a chemical engineer by schooling, a master cabinetmaker by avocation, and a member of the Purdue University NROTC Hall of Fame. A man of action, Bain eloped with

Charlotte McClintock from their Indiana homes a half century ago—now, that's a story.

Janet Goldfogle can tell a story of what life was like being reared on a family farm in Nebraska during the 1930s—the challenge and joys of living without electricity or indoor plumbing, of being schooled in a one-room schoolhouse that had all eight grades, walking two miles to school, the party-line telephone, the threshing season rituals, the dust storms, and the Saturday night trips to town.

The life of Gen. Lew Allen, USAF (Ret.), is worth a biography. He served as director of the National Security Agency (1973–1977), chief of staff of the United States Air Force (1978–1982), and, upon retirement from the Air Force, director of the jet propulsion laboratory at the California Institute of Technology in Pasadena, California. He earned a doctorate in physics from the University of Illinois (1950–1954). He and his wife, Barbara, lead active, social lives at Falcons Landing. Lew, from Gainesville, Texas, heeds his mother's advice never to ask a man where he is from. *If he comes from Texas, he will tell you. If he doesn't, don't embarrass him.*

A former employee at Falcons Landing, Gail Rainbow walked across the United States with her family, which included a six-month-old daughter. Their walk took them from Berkeley, California, to Cape Henlopen, Delaware. The walk lasted fourteen-and-a-half months.

The late Buford Kelly Meade (known as B. K.) lived to be ninety-four. He was a geodesist whose specialty was measuring the size and shape of the earth. One of his professional feats was the recalculation of the lay of the 1764 Mason Dixon Line. His calculations redefined the boundary between Maryland and Pennsylvania. Gifted with a marvelous mind, he entertained by reciting all the names of the presidents in order, recited the alphabet backwards, or stated the twenty significant digits of pi (3.14159265…). B. K. was considered to be the last survivor of the Golden Age of geodesy at the Coast and Geodetic Survey. For most of B. K.'s forty-four-year career at C&GS, that agency dominated the geodetic scene in this country, and B. K. was an essential component of that dominance. While the field of geodesy is replete with mystery for the layman, in semi-technical terms, geodesists improved the national horizontal and vertical control networks that are essential for all surveying and scientific positioning measurements. B. K.'s research and leadership in the field resulted in vast improvements in the art so that the distance between two points on the globe could be known to one part in a million. B. K.'s efforts led to a tenfold improvement in accuracy, a truly monumental accomplishment. He was the recipient of many awards and was elected a fellow of the American Geophysical Union, an honor limited yearly to one-tenth of 1 percent of the membership.

Brig. Gen. Sally Wells, USAF, is one of about two dozen women of Falcons Landing who served in or with the U.S. armed forces. Three of the women, including Sally, retired after serving full careers in the military. Sally served as chief of the United State Air Force Nurse Corps from 1979 to 1982.

The late Janie Arison was a lady of great high spirits and talent who could recite spoonerisms at length. Spoonerisms are speech patterns in which letters or syllables are swapped either accidentally (such as, tips of the slung), in humor, or because of a speech disability. These verbal somersaults are termed "spoonerisms" for their eponymous sovereign, the Rev. William Archibald Spooner (1844–1930), an Anglican priest and scholar and dean and warden of New College, Oxford. Spooner is reported to have admonished a student who had been absent from one of his history sessions, "You have hissed my mystery lecture," and, "You have tasted two worms." But this is about Janie, not the Rev. Spooner, for it is Janie who could recite the story of Cinderella in "Spoonereeze," which she did elegantly on the Falcons Landing closed-circuit television show *Backfire Boys*, directed by resident Ray Goelz. Here are some excerpts of her February 2004 filmed performance:

> Here is a tale to make your cresh fleep. It will give you poose gimples.
>
> It's the story about Cinderella who lived in a big hark douse with her mean old mep-strother and her two sisty uglers. And they made Cinderella do all the worty dirk while they sat around cheating ocolates and maging readazines....
>
> So, the next day the pranssome hince went from house to house, and soon, he came to the Cin where housederella lived and docked on the noor. And who should answer but the two sisty uglers. He said, "I'm looking for the woman whose soot this flipper sits. Well, of course, their beet were too fig!
>
> But then it was Cinderella's turn and the flipper sitted perfectly, they were married and they happed lively ever after.

There is the story of Maj. Jim Evans, USAF (Ret), who at the age of nineteen, as a pathfinder from the 502nd Parachute Infantry Regiment of the 101st Airborne Division "Screaming Eagles," parachuted into France in a midnight drop on December 1, 1944, to disrupt the German lines of communication before the assault on the Normandy beaches. He subsequently made two more World War II jumps in the European Theater and fought in the Battle of the Bulge, earning four Bronze Stars.

Lt. Gen. John S. Pustay, although a 1954 graduate of the Naval Academy, was commissioned in the Air Force. He spent most of his distinguished career in intelligence, psychological warfare, strategic planning, and nuclear and military policy development. He served as a White House fellow, military assistant to the secretary of state, Air Force deputy assistant chief of staff for Intelligence and director of Strategic Concepts and Doctrine, the commander of Keesler Technical Training Center, assistant to the chairman of the Joint Chiefs of Staff, a member of the deputies group of the National Security Council, and president of the National Defense University. Notwithstanding the demands of John's Air Force career, he somehow found time to author the book *Counterinsurgency Warfare* and earn a master's and a doctorate degree in international relations. He didn't slow down after retirement. He became a member of the Nunn-Lugar Commission on Soviet-U.S. Confidence-Building Measures, a member of the secretary of defense's Special Operations Advisory Council, a member of the Council on Foreign Affairs, a member of the board of visitors for the Joint Military Intelligence College, and executive vice president of the Analytical Services Corporation. All that energy and intellect will be put to good use at Falcons Landing.

Joy Arant on a stallion in Libya.

Joy Arant, wife of Air Force Col. Rock Arant, is a Texan's Texan. She spent much of her youth on the back of a horse in Center, Texas, before she met and married Rock. They met in Hondo, Texas, where Rock was stationed and Joy was secretary to the base commander. Center is a small town of about five thousand, the county seat of Shelby County, about as far east as you can get in Texas, bordering on Louisiana. Joy's father, James T. Booth, was a veteran, having fought in Germany and France in World War I. Booth owned a ranch near Laredo, Texas, on the Rio Grande.

While stationed in Tripoli, Libya, Joy demonstrated her prowess as an accomplished horsewoman. (Joy would resent being called an equestrienne—too elitist.) In an effort to improve relations with the Libyans, the local commander decided to stage an American-style rodeo bringing riders, mounts, and other livestock to Tripoli for the event. Sheiks came out of the desert to witness the contests and riding demonstrations. Joy and Rock had their two young children with them as they watched the British and Arabs demonstrate their horsemanship skills before the start of the rodeo. One sheik had a beautiful black stallion with a saddle that Joy described as having so much silver on it that, "Its value could have paid for the tuition of our two children through college. As it turned out, the horse that I admired so much belonged to the leader of the tribe that our houseboy Ali belonged to. Through Ali, I asked the sheik's permission to ride his horse. Ali said that was impossible, that the sheik would never allow it. I insisted. The sheik finally agreed, being quite assured that I wouldn't be able to ride the spirited mount. Well, I approached the beautiful animal and he shied and danced. I held out my hand and was able to steady and reassure him enough for me to get into the saddle. He immediately reared and tried to throw me, but he was fitted with a hackamore bit, and I pulled back on it hard to get his feet on the ground. Well, I ran that horse a good quarter of a mile until he was under control, and brought him back to the sheik's party as pretty as you would like. The sheik was so impressed that he offered a fortune in Libyan currency, that is, livestock, goats, horses, cows, camels, and such for my services. So as not to offend the sheik, Rock asked Ali to say that, as a young mother, I could not leave my baby son."

With such neighbors, dining mates, and friends as these, how can life be anything but interesting at Falcons Landing?

2

Clement I. Irons

Ask almost any of the Falcons Landing residents where they were, what they were doing, or what their reaction was to the bombing of Pearl Harbor on the seventh of December 1941, and you will get an interesting anecdote. When the question was asked of Air Force retiree Ed McManus and his German-born wife, Rosemarie, Ed replied:

---

1. This account is based largely on briefings prepared and recorded by Clem Irons and an interview conducted December 1, 2004. Background material was also found in: Shannon Sollinger, "From Cockpit to POW," *Loudoun Times-Mirror*, June 9, 2004, A9.

"Early on a pleasant Sunday afternoon, we four friends were sitting in a row in the mezzanine of the Loew's State Theater, Broadway, near Times Square, in New York City. We were absorbed in the movie when suddenly the screen went blank. The lights came on, and we heard the voice of the president, Franklin D. Roosevelt, as he announced the attack by the Japanese upon Pearl Harbor and that a state of war existed between the United States and Japan. What followed was remarkable. I will never forget the scene. There was dead silence in the theater as it emptied without a word being spoken or a sound made, other than the movement of the crowd down the aisles, filing out onto the city streets. The group was solemn, and there seemed to be a collective realization that we were part of a great calamity, and that this was truly a day of infamy."

Rosemarie, then living in a different time zone, in Germany, said:

"I remember December 8, 1941, as being a cold, clear day in Ruedesheim, Germany. My family and I were returning home from Mass as it was the Feast of the Immaculate Conception, a holy day in this Catholic part of Germany. I could hardly wait to get home, eat *mittagessen*, and meet with my friends for a day of sledding. When we opened the front door, we were greeted by the delicious smell of my Omie's sauerbraten, and the radio was at full pitch, which was unusual. The radio was in the kitchen where Omie was sitting at the table with her head in her hands. She looked up at our entrance and stared at us, placing a finger to her lips signaling silence. The radio announcer was reporting that the Japanese had bombed the American fleet at Pearl Harbor, and that Germany had declared war on America, and that America, in turn, had declared war on Germany.

"Uncle Jakob, my mother's youngest brother, had been drafted into the German army and was home on leave for a few days. As Jakob listened to the broadcast, he walked to the window and hit the sill with his fist muttering, "Oh *scheisse!*" The announcement was followed by the German National Anthem, and as the first notes of the Nazi hymn sounded, my mother turned off the radio. We were all stunned. My mother made the sign of the cross and said, 'Now things are going to be very bad for us. America is a mighty nation. May God help us all.'"

On that fateful day, just two weeks before his twentieth birthday, Clement I. Irons was socializing with other students at the Art Institute of Pittsburgh. He recalled:

"Several of us students were discussing some serious financial matters as to how we could have a champagne New Year's Eve celebration on our Coca-Cola resources. Someone yelled, 'Listen to the radio.' The news was that Pearl Harbor had been bombed. In the next few days, I got my uncomplicated affairs in order and within a month, on 7 January 1942, I enlisted in the Army Air Corps. My battle cry was, 'I'm here Uncle Sam—the war is over.' But not quite. It took three-and-a-half years, which entailed a lifetime worth of adventure and tribulation before it was."

Clem was not alone in rallying to the flag after Pearl Harbor. There were 16.5 million men and women who served from 1940 to 1947, which included one-third of all males over the age of fifteen. Seventy-three percent of them served overseas, and 407,000 of them died in the service. As of 2005, the average age of the surviving World War II veterans was 82 years.

Col. Clement I. Irons, USAF (Ret.), was born in 1921 in Mount Vernon, Ohio. He grew up in Linesville, Pennsylvania, a small town south of Erie. He graduated from the small Linesville-Conneaut High School where he was president of his junior and senior classes, which had an enrollment of only thirty-six students. There are only sixteen survivors of that high school class, and Clem is the only male survivor, despite the hard life he lived in the latter years of World War II. From an early age, he was fascinated with the graphic arts and the printing process and had ambitions to be a commercial artist. His older brother was a printer by trade, and there would be days when Clem, still in a high chair, would watch his brother setting type as a linotype operator at the local newspaper.

His college education spread over seventeen years of night school at such institutions as Hofstra College in New York, the University of Alabama, and Arizona State University, wherever his Air Force assignments took him. His diligence and aptitude finally earned him the credits to graduate from the University of Maryland while he was stationed at the Pentagon. His college grades were consistently A's until he took a take-home final examination for one course. In his characteristic zeal, he wrote a treatise rather than the several-page blue book anticipated and desired by the professor. His zeal earned him a "C" from a professor who was displeased at having to read Clem's lengthy discourse. He and his wife, the former Betty Dolores Terrill of Conneautville, Pennsylvania, subsequently earned master's degrees in educational administration from Virginia Polytechnic Institute and State University.

In 1945 his sister-in-law had arranged a meeting and date for him with Dolores. In five weeks, they were engaged. The next week, on July 21, 1945, they were married. One might think that such a whirlwind romance would forebode a rocky marriage, but it was a strong, happy union of fifty-four years. They had two children, a son, C. Charles Irons of Herndon, Va., and a daughter, Deborah, of Suffolk, Va. Clem has two grandchildren, Chris and Melanie, courtesy of his son Charles and daughter-in-law Linda.

After Clem's enlistment in the Army Air Corps, he spent a year in Puerto Rico before becoming an aviation cadet. He was not destined to fly as a pilot but was commissioned as a second lieutenant navigator and assigned to Avon Park, Florida, to join a B-17 air crew. Assignments were democratic, that is, by alphabetical order. He recounts his experiences:

> We were lucky as we wound up with four compatible crews. Each crew member had trained with his counterpart—pilots with pilots, navigators with navigators, and so forth—and we were good friends.
>
> We sailed to England on the Queen Elizabeth with fifteen thousand other troops and arrived at our first operational duty station in March 1944, where we were assigned to the 385th Bomb Group and its 548th Bomb Squadron. I had waited two years to get into combat, and my hopes were about to be fulfilled. Our crew was named the "Jeanne Rickey," after our pilot's wife and son. The four commissioned officers of the crew were the pilot, the copilot, the navigator, and the bombardier. The six non-commissioned officers who made up the crew were the engineer/top turret gunner, the ball turret gunner/assistant engineer, the two waist gunners, the radio operator, and the tail gunner.
>
> On the seventh of May, I flew with this crew in an old clunker of an aircraft. As we crossed the German border, I discovered that we were almost out of oxygen, and so we aborted the flight. Now, aborting a flight without a very good reason was not looked upon with favor, and so we returned with an intact aircraft to some cold, fishy stares. The following day, the same crew, in the same aircraft, set out on a mission to Berlin—without me. They ran out of oxygen again. However, this time, they went on to the target. They could not maintain altitude at twenty-one thousand feet without oxygen for the crew, so they had to drop out of formation and try to make it home alone.
>
> They were attacked by German fighter aircraft and were badly shot up. Fred Ihlenburg, one of the best natural pilots I ever flew with, got them back to our base in England but not without some terrible damage. Both the ball turret gunner and engineer lost an eye from flying flak or Plexiglas. The radio operator was wearing a flak vest, but still his arms and legs were badly riddled. When Ihlenburg braked after landing, the left wing collapsed, and he passed out. But they were safely back on the ground, and then they were told that I had been shot down on another flight.
>
> Forty years later, I felt vindicated in my 7 May reporting of oxygen failure aboard that aborted flight when, at a reunion, the maintenance chief of that aircraft told us that there had been a problem. He told me that when the crew chief filled his walk-around oxygen bottle, the valve froze open and the oxygen bled out. After forty years of wondering, I felt better about the incident.
>
> The four compatible crews wound up in the same squadron. Let me tell you what happened to them, to put this type of combat, just before D-Day, into perspective. Within three months, of the sixteen officers in the four

crews, one navigator was killed by flak, thirteen of us became prisoners of war, and only two—my pilot and copilot—completed the requisite twenty-five missions to be eligible for rotation. During the air war over Germany the Army Air Forces flew over a million and a half sorties, 89 percent of which were determined to be effective, with some thirty-two thousand aircraft, of which over half were lost in action. On the plus side of the ledger, almost thirty thousand enemy aircraft were destroyed. We had nearly ninety-five thousand American combat air casualties, of which thirty thousand were killed in action, and fifty-one thousand were missing in action or were POWs and internees. [The internees were those who had crashed or landed in neutral countries.]

I had been checked out as a lead navigator so that on my eighth mission, on May 8, I was flying with the deputy group lead on what would turn out to be my longest mission. We'd dropped our bombs on Berlin and were on our way home when our number three engine ran away.

The prop broke off from the vibration and clipped a couple of cylinders off the number four engine and came through the side of the plane behind me, cutting the electrical systems that led to the nose. We dropped out of formation and could maintain air speed of only about 120 miles per hour. We were alone.

We'd been above the clouds all day, and I hadn't seen the ground, so I was navigating by dead reckoning. We had a P-51 escort named Dumb Dora with us for awhile, but then he called over that he was going to leave us as he was running low on fuel. He thought things looked pretty quiet and assumed that we were going to be okay. I spotted a railroad junction through a hole in the clouds and was looking for it on my map, when, from out of the sun at twelve o'clock high, four German FW-190s hit us in a hail of bullets. It was a classic attack that shattered our plane. Our aircraft started to spiral down, and when in that mode, in a big plane, you are going to have difficulty bailing out. We learned later that our pilot had expertly put it into a spin (out of the spiral) to give us a better chance to leave the aircraft.

Navigators get in the habit of timing everything. I bailed out at about twelve noon, and it took me seventeen minutes to come down from twenty-one thousand feet. I had planned to drop several thousand feet before pulling the rip cord. However, I had barely cleared the plane when my chute blew open. I had a chest pack, and the rip cord should have been in my right hand, but it was in the left, which meant that I had snapped the chute on upside down. In a daze, I transferred the cord to my right hand where it belonged.

I was wounded. I had flak in my wrist, and my eyes were flash-burned, so that it was months before I could stand bright sunlight. There were tiny bits of metal in my face that gradually worked themselves out.

I landed hard in a field near a railroad station. Of course, I didn't have the slightest idea of where I was, other than that I was near Bremen in Germany. I spilled the air out of my chute and wrapped my helmet and equipment in it. Then, with my head down, hoping to avoid detection, I crawled toward some trees. I had just reached the tree line and was starting to hide my chute and gear in a ditch when I heard a noise and looked up into the barrel of a rifle, the bore of which looked to me like an 88 mm cannon. It was actually an old rifle being held by a little guy in a leather coat and cap with a Hitler-style moustache. He told me that the "Krieg was Kaput!" for me. I crawled through the barbed wire fence that separated us, and he indicated that I should pick up my gear and move out. He must have been given instruction on the Geneva Convention and concluded that POW officers were not required to work, so he asked, "Officer?" I showed him my shiny second lieutenant bars and answered, "Yah, lieutenant." He then relieved me of the burden of carrying my gear by loading it all on the back of his bicycle while an assemblage of women, children, and soldiers watched.

Off we went, with me in front and him carrying his rifle and pushing the overloaded bicycle. We stopped at a nearby antiaircraft artillery battery, and he attempted to turn me over to them, but they wanted no part of me. However, they did want to take photos of the *"mordflieger"* or *"terrorflieger"* as we had been labeled by Mr. Goebbels's propaganda machine. I was then transported to Bremen where I rejoined the rest of our crew. The pilot had been wounded in the hand and told me that the instrument panel and bulkhead between us had exploded from hits by penetrating 20 mm shells from the fighter attack.

In his book, *Stalag Luft III, The Secret Story*[2], Arthur Durand, a retired U.S. Air Force colonel, studied the differences between the airman and his ground- and sea-based counterparts once they fall into the hands of the enemy. He pointed out that Army and Navy personnel usually fall into the hands of the enemy as a group. In contrast, airmen most often are taken prisoners as individuals who must face the hazards of their capture by themselves. Once on the ground, it was highly uncertain what kind of a reception they would receive from either civilian crowds or ill-trained militia who may not know or care about the protection prisoners are afforded under the Geneva Conventions.

In the first few minutes of his capture, Clem was quite aware of the dangers involved:

> In my case, only minutes before, I had been dropping bombs on these people who had captured me, and now I was at their mercy. We had heard stories of airmen being attacked by angry, merciless mobs. I was fortunate. The worst thing that happened to me when I was captured was that one of the women in the crowd spat in my face. We Americans, except for Pearl Harbor and 9-11,

---

2.   Arthur A. Durand, *Stalag Luft III, the Secret Story* (New Orleans: Louisiana State University Press, 1999).

have never been attacked directly on our home turf. I have often wondered what our citizens' reactions would be here in the States if an enemy flier had been shot down and captured, given similar circumstances.

Once you are captured, you worry about how your family is going to get the news. It becomes important to you to have them know that you are still alive. Their not knowing means that you have lost part of your identity. My parents received a telegram on 21 May that read, "The Secretary of War desires me to express his deep regrets that your son has been reported missing in action since the 8th of May over Germany." The telegram was followed by letters on 24 May and 21 June. Finally, on 11 July, after two anxious months, they received a telegram that the International Red Cross had established that I was still alive and confirmed my status as a prisoner of war.

My first stop, once I got into the POW processing system, was in Oberursel, the Dulag Luft interrogation center near Frankfort. When we arrived there, we were given a bogus Red Cross form that asked for a lot of intelligence information on our unit. I gave my name, rank, and serial number and my home address, with the latter provided in the hopes that my parents would be notified sooner.

Initially, I was kept in solitary confinement in a room about five-and-a-half by ten-and-a-half feet, which contained only an army cot and a small stand for a water bottle. I was permitted to leave the room only for interrogation or trips to the latrine. I was fed four thin slices of black bread per day with some ersatz margarine or jam spread thinly between the slices, and some ersatz tea.

About every third day I would be called in for an interrogation session. The standard German technique was to tell you that if you couldn't properly identify yourself—that is, give them the information they wanted—they would have to consider you a spy and shoot you. When you refused to give them the information they wanted, they sent you back to your solitary confinement cell to think about it—and you would.

We all think that we are important to someone in this world. Here, at the age of twenty-two, you realize that they could kill you, and no one would be the wiser. Oh, of course, your family would miss you, and there is the remote chance that, after a few years had passed, an old friend might hoist a drink and comment, "Too bad about old Clem," sip, "How'd the Yankees do today?" You realize, while sitting in a POW cell, that if your life ended in that second, the world would keep spinning. It's a real jolt to recognize, so young, how insignificant you are in the big scheme of things. Under other circumstances, at this tender age you would be basking in the young man's hubris of immortality.

One day, I managed to open the frosted window of my cell and saw some Russian prisoners working in the courtyard. One came over, and I managed to impart to him that I was an American, and that I had bombed our common enemy. He liked that, grinned, and took off. A few minutes later he tapped on the window and pulled a loaf of bread from under his coat that he had stolen from the officers' mess.

One evening, I heard a hauntingly beautiful melody drifting across the courtyard from that same officers' mess. I later learned that it was "Lili Marlene" which was to become the universal lament of every soldier, sailor, airman, or Marine separated from his sweetheart waiting for him at home.

To keep busy, I laboriously broke straw into little pieces and played tic-tac-toe on my bunk. On the tenth day, the interrogator showed me a notebook on my group with comprehensive information about our officers, plane numbers, and the like. It was an accurate representation, but about a month out-of-date, which, of course, I didn't tell him. The German said, "See I've already got the information. We don't need you." So the next day, they sent me to the transient camp at Wetzlar, where I received a Red Cross issue of clothing and a much-needed pair of shoes.

On Sunday morning, we prisoners, without any planning, gathered around for an informal religious service. It was an epiphany of sorts for us. In my case, an airplane propeller had torn through the fuselage of my aircraft less than three feet behind me. The bulkhead at my rear had been riddled with bullets, and I had bailed out of a dying airplane and landed with only minor wounds. It couldn't have been just luck. I believed that there was a divine intervention, and I could tell that the others sensed the same. There we stood under a Nazi flag, dreaming of home and saying our thanks to God while one of the men who had a New Testament read a few verses.

From Wetzlar, I was sent to Stalag Luft III near Sagan, Poland, one hundred miles southeast of Berlin. There I joined thousands of other allied *"kriegies"*—our abbreviated version of *kriegsgefangenen* or prisoners of war.

Shown in Figure 2–1 are some of the more interesting souvenirs saved by Clem. The German identification card prepared when he arrived at Stalag Luft III cites his barracks and room numbers. It is difficult to see, but the photo shows the beginning of a handlebar moustache that reached nine and a half inches from tip to tip before an unknown prankster cut one end off while Clem was sleeping. Clem's POW number "5084" appears on the card and is also on the German dog tags. You will note that there is one American dog tag missing. It had been sent to the American authorities in accordance with international requirements. Clem's Caterpillar Club card and pin for having survived a parachute jump under lifesaving conditions is also shown. Clem made the navigator's clipped wings with ball and chain by pouring lead from a tin can into a sand mold. This was the *kriegie* symbol of "The Chained Bird." The Stalag III sketch in Figure 2-2 shows Clem's barracks number 167 (highlighted) in the west compound. The west compound was the last of five to be opened on April 27, 1944.

Clem tells about his days in Stalag III:

Stalag III, more properly Oflag III or Officers' Lager, opened in April 1942. The first British POW in the camp was Wing Commander "Wings" Day who had been shot down at the start of the war in Europe in October 1939. The first American guest at the camp was Navy Lt. Comdr. John Dunn who was shot down on April 14, 1942. By January 1945, there were over ten thousand Allied flying officers of which 6,844 were Americans. The buildings consisted of prefabricated sections that were bolted together. The roofs leaked, and winter winds found every crack. There were thirteen rooms in each that housed an average of 140 men per barracks. In our room, number three, we had twelve officers in approximately twenty square feet per man for all our needs—eating, sleeping, and everyday life. We had triple-decker bunks, and there were four of them that had burlap mattresses filled with straw or wood shavings. Each of us had two thin German blankets and one U.S. Army blanket. Each bed had precisely nine bed boards, which were counted regularly to prevent their use in shoring up escape tunnels.

We had some books from the YMCA and maintained our own camp bulletin board for news. A Catholic chaplain had been shot down and taken prisoner, so we had church services. We organized a theater and had *kriegie*-produced plays, and there was some athletic and sports equipment. Some of my roommates played bridge and fought constantly over the details of the game.

Clem kept busy at Stalag III reading, walking, and drawing an occasional cartoon for the small camp newspaper, the *Kriegie Klarion.*

"Mail was the life-blood of *kriegie* morale," Clem recalled. "Outgoing mail was limited to three letter forms and four cards per POW per month. Each sixty days, a POWs next-of-kin could send a package of clothing or food or other items not forbidden by either government. Incoming mail was generally unlimited, but all mail was censored on both ends."

Mail wasn't always good news. There was the occasional "Dear John Letter. This apocryphal letter form a girl back home lives in infamy.

"Dear Johnny: You have been gone a long time and I have been so lonesome. I couldn't wait, so I married your Dad. Love, Mom"

Food was a concern to the prisoners. Clem said:

The Germans provided one loaf of sour, black *swartzbrot* (war bread) per man per week. We were sure it was made from sawdust and gas. About four hundred grams of potatoes or kohlrabis per week, soup—usually green death or barley (with protein)—three times per week, ersatz jam, cheese, and sometimes salt and sugar. The books say we got meat, but I don't remember any except the time a horse got hit outside the camp. We also got *blutwurst* (blood sausage), which few Americans would eat. What really saved us were the Red

Cross parcels, usually one per man per week unless the hosts thought we should be punished for something, then it was half-parcels. A typical Red Cross parcel would include Spam, corned beef, salmon, or tuna, klim powdered milk ("klim" is milk spelled backwards), cheese crackers, sugar, juice, raisins or prunes, instant coffee, soap, and cigarettes. The German rations were cooked at a central kitchen, but we shared our parcels in our rooms, and our "chef" would prepare the meals for everyone. Unfortunately, the Germans punctured the meat cans so they couldn't be stored for escapes, so we sealed them with margarine so they'd last a little longer.

The barracks were on cinder blocks, so guards—we called them "ferrets"—could crawl under the buildings looking for tunnels and listening to our conversations. [Figure 2–3 is a sketch Clem drew of a "ferret," with the ferret's tunnel-probing prod slightly exaggerated.]

We were locked in at night and during air raids. Guards patrolled with dogs. Guard towers with searchlights and machine guns were spaced around the camp, which was surrounded by two barbed wire fences, about nine feet high, with concertina wire between. Thirty feet inside the fence was the trip-wire, and anyone who stepped over it would be shot.

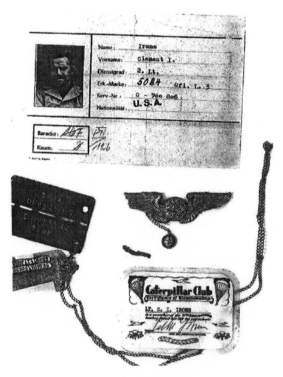

Figure 2–1
Clem's POW keepsakes

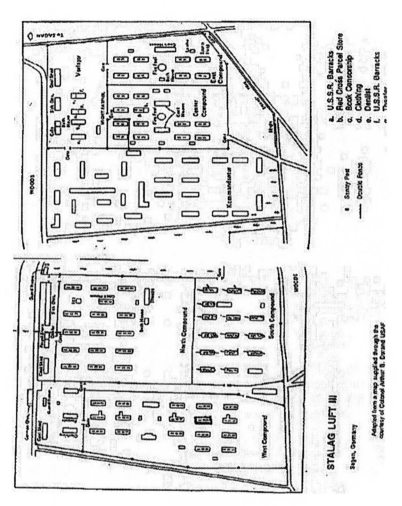

Figure 2-2
Stalag Luft III

Figure 2-3

Clem arrived at Stalag Luft III about two months after the "Great Escape," a story later told in a movie by that name and in a stirring book by Paul Brickhill. ("Stalag Luft" was short for the German term "*Stammlager Luft*," meaning permanent camps for airmen.) Under the moderate German kommandant, Oberst (Colonel) Friedrich-Wilhelm von Lindeiner-Wildau, prisoners were treated quite fairly, abiding by the Geneva Convention. The German Luftwaffe was responsible for Air Force prisoners of war and afforded a degree of respect for the fellow airmen whom they guarded. They were not the SS or the Gestapo. Security was tight, confinement was miserable, and there were discomfort and hunger, but the situation was not intolerable at Stalag Luft III.

Squadron Leader Roger J. Bushell of the Royal Air Force was one of the ten thousand Allied POWs in the camp and leader of the "Great Escape." He had escaped from another facility and was hiding in Prague when he was recaptured. Members of the family that had hidden him were executed, leaving Bushell with a deep-seated hatred for his captors. He was determined to organize a massive escape from Stalag Luft III.

Bushell assembled and trained a corps of master tunnel engineers, forgers, tailors, intelligence personnel, and navigators intent on making an escape with the objective not of returning to Allied lines, but once free, to harass and wreak havoc on the German infrastructure. Escape kits were made and issued to those who were designated as escapees. Compasses were fabricated using fragments of bakelite phonograph records and tiny magnetized needles made from slivers of razor blades. The bottom of the devices were stamped with the words, "Made in Stalag Luft III—Patent Pending."

Clem said:

> I understand that the movie that told the story of the Great Escape was quite accurate, accurate except for Steve McQueen dashing around on a motorcycle, and I don't believe that there was a blind man among the escapees. There were three tunnels dug, named "Tom" "Dick" and "Harry." Considering the circumstances and the tools at their disposal, it was a marvel of engineering. The entrance of "Harry" was through a trapdoor beneath a stove in Block 104 of the North Compound [Figure 2–2]. The tunnel shaft went

down thirty feet to escape sound detectors. An air pump with a bellows was made, and a railway tram ran the length of the tunnel to transport men and dirt. It was more than three hundred feet long and took about ten months to dig, under the supervision of the escape organization headed by Squadron Leader Bushell. The original plan was for two hundred men to make the breakout through the tunnel on the night of 24–25 March. Actually, seventy-six men got away before the last four were discovered. Three men—a Dutch pilot serving with the RAF and two Norwegians, all proficient in the German language—escaped to England. At a POW reunion in Norfolk in 1990, one of these men met two German women who had been mail censors and were in the train station that night. They had pointed out to the local guards two men whom they considered to be suspicious. But the escapees convinced the guards that they were laborers who had missed their train—the guards helped them get on the next one. Of those seventy-three who were recaptured, fifty were executed by firing squads on direct orders from Adolph Hitler. To circumvent the provisions of the Geneva Convention, the Germans claimed that they were shot trying to escape again. However, that was a fiction. What happened was plain murder by the Gestapo.

When Clem arrived at Stalag Luft III, the poster at Figure 2–4 warning POWS against trying to escape was posted around the camp.

"As the war on the eastern front came closer to our camp, I could stand outside the barracks and watch the tremendous air show as every aircraft in the German air force flew overhead, from the tiny Storch to the giant transport glider with twelve engines, as they flew to the west as part of the German retreat from Russia," Clem recalled.

"In January 1945, in anticipation of a difficult forced march, our senior officers ordered us to walk the three-quarter mile perimeter of our compound ten times a day for a total of seven and a half miles."

It was a prudent exercise, because soon the POWs survival would depend upon their stamina and fortitude to march through the bitter-cold German countryside. On January 27, Hitler ordered that the prisoners in Stalag Luft III should be moved to a compound to the south to ensure against their liberation by the advancing Russians, and so they couldn't be used as hostages.

Clem recalled:

According to Durand, Glenn Infield related in a book *Eva and Adolph*[3] that Hitler had decided late in the war to use thirty-five thousand of us as hostages until he could obtain a truce that was satisfactory to Germany. He

---

3.   Durand, op.cit., pp112-113.

ordered General Berger of the Waffen SS, who was in charge of the administration of the Allied POWs, to take us to the mountains. If war termination
negotiations with the Allies were unsuccessful, we were to be executed. Eva
Braun, we are told, arranged for Hitler to give the signed order directly to
Berger, because she knew that he would stall and would not kill us, whereas
another SS factotum might.

On the night of 27 January, we could hear the Russian artillery a mere
twenty to thirty miles away. At the order of our senior officers, the South
Compound moved out into the winter night at 11:00 PM, and the rest followed, with the last group leaving at 6:00 AM. There was a line of ten thousand struggling POWs that stretched for more than twenty miles making its
way toward Muskau and Spremberg. There were two thousand of us from the
West Compound who left at 12:30 AM in a blinding blizzard at near zero temperatures with six inches of snow on the ground and with a wind-chill estimated to be a minus ten degrees.

Figure 2–4

We weren't out of the compound long when we heard gunshots, and we scrambled into a ditch. Apparently, the home guard (Volksturm) panicked on hearing our advance through the woods and fired into the air. The guards shot back, but evidently no one was hit or injured. We plowed on.

Each of us took what we could in packs we made of shirts or trousers, including Red Cross parcels if we had them. As I trudged along, I learned to appreciate the lowly prune by sucking on them for hours at a time. The sugar gave me energy and sucking on the prune kept my mouth moist. It also gave me something to do to keep my mind off my misery.

While en route, the senior *kriegie* of the South Compound, Colonel Goodrich, passed word down the line giving permission to escape if the situation permitted. Some thirty-two *kriegies* did make the attempt, and all were recaptured within thirty-six hours. Clem remembers:

> For fifty years, I had harbored a memory of circling a town and seeing signs that read "3 km to Muskau" over and over. It must have been a hallucination, because when we went back for a visit in 1995, the road was fairly straight, and there were no such signs.
>
> With ten-minute stops each hour and one two-hour rest, we walked thirty-four and a half miles in twenty-nine hours to arrive at Muskau where we were sheltered in a tile factory.
>
> Many of our guards were older and not in very good shape. It was not unusual to see a *kriegie* and a guard sharing a sled made from bed boards and, once or twice, a *kriegie* carrying a rifle for a weary guard. While I didn't see anyone die on the march, others did, and it has been called a "death march." British paratrooper chaplain Murdo MacDonald wrote that he was summoned to the side of an All-American football player who had decided to die. He stayed until the man passed away, closed his eyes, and ran to catch up with the rest of the South Compound column. He attested to the number that died when he wrote, "The summons came again and again."[4] I do know that, generally, those who fell out were picked up by German wagons and taken to a safe haven.
>
> It seems that no matter how bad things can get, there is someone else worse off. And so it was with us during that miserable march as we watched the refugee families from the east, fleeing the Russian advance, struggling through the same blizzard with their meager belongings and no place to go. We POWs never had any doubt that eventually we would get home. But these German refugees were aimlessly fleeing the Russian armies without objective or purpose but survival.

---

4.   Association of Former Prisoners of Stalag Luft III, op.cit.,p.21

We stayed in Muskau for about thirty hours in the tile factory before we set out again with an objective of Spremberg, another fifteen and a half miles. This would bring our trek on foot, through this awful weather, to a total of fifty miles. At Spremberg, there was a railroad yard where we were crowded into "40 & 8s." (You remember the World War I stories of those French rail cars that had a capacity of forty men or eight horses.) But we had fifty-four men and a guard in each car, and the guard kept an area clear about him by swinging his rifle butt. We couldn't stand or sit, except toboggan style, stacked in rows. Every hour or so, we would stand, turn and face the other way to stretch our limbs. We spent one night in the marshalling yards at Chemnitz in those unmarked rail cars and later learned that we just escaped a heavy Allied bombing the following night.

The map at Figure 2–5 traces the route taken by the POWs by foot and by train.[5]

---

5.   Bob Neary, *Stalag Luft III* (North Wales, PA, 1946) p.29.

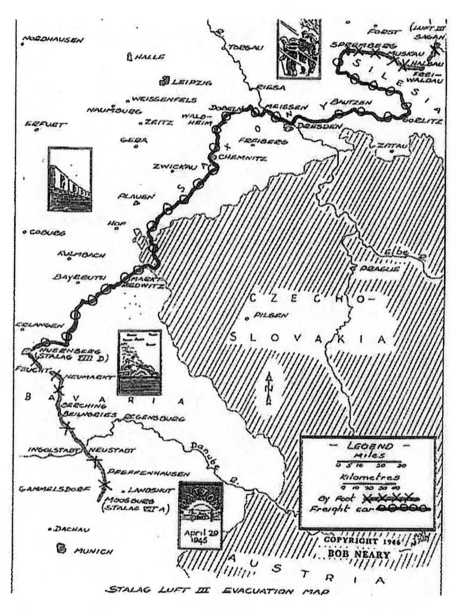

Figure 2-5

After three miserable days in the box cars, we arrived at Stalag XIII-D at Nuremburg. The conditions were deplorable. We were within three kilometers (1.86 miles) of some major marshalling yards which, as prime targets for Allied bombings, were bombed day and night. During these raids, we were held indoors at gunpoint in direct violation of the mandates of the Geneva Convention. Our POW senior officer, Colonel Darr Alkire told the *kommandant* that if they were going to shoot his men, they'd have to shoot him first. The *kommandant* relented to the extent of allowing us to dig protective slit trenches alongside the barracks but issued us only two shovels. We were too weak to use the shovels for any more than a few minutes at a time. Using tin cans and bed boards, we eventually dug enough trenches to provide a modicum of protection from the flak and debris that fell during the raids. We finished the trenches just in time, for the bombardments and answering antiaircraft fire were ferocious and spectacular.

One night the RAF flew over to lay down a line of flares between the marshalling yards and our camp. We knew the Brit bombers would bomb on one side or the other of that line, but we didn't know which side it would be. Fortunately, they hit the marshalling yards. The night sky was afire with bursting bombs and burning oil tanks, buildings, and railroad cars. Overhead, shone the twinkling stars of flak and planes caught in the searchlights. As we huddled in our new slit trenches covered only with blankets, hoping they might protect us from the falling shrapnel, we heard the death-scream of a Lancaster bomber as it came to earth, barely missing our camp before it exploded.

By day, the American bombers came with thousand-plane raids with beautiful silver formations and contrails overhead as they used our camp as a turning point. We cheered them on!

The barracks at Stalag XIII-D in Nuremberg were badly overcrowded with quadruple triple-decker bunks. We averaged nineteen square feet of floor space and 119 cubic feet of air space per man. Even with that, 1,246 of us had to sleep on the cold, damp floors.

Food was scarce in Germany at that time. The rations issued to us were about 300 grams of black bread, 250 grams of potatoes, and wormy, dehydrated vegetables. We all lost a great deal of weight. I found my ribs for the first time. When you are as hungry as we were, all you can think about is food. We spent hours of our boredom naming candy bars and food dishes, and we wrote the names down on paper on the inside of cigarette packages or on the backs of letters from home.

Clem has over a thousand foods listed on the backs of Lucky Strike cigarette packages and on the letters he received from home. (See Figure 2–6 for his pork entries.)

Further describing conditions during the march and at the new prison camp, Clem said:

Figure 2-6

We had no heat, no laundry, or bathing facilities. From 27 January to March, I had one shower and could not change my underwear. We had two outdoor faucets for 250 men, and we were buried in filth and vermin. We had outside latrines for use during the day, but at night we had one five-gallon bucket for two hundred men, and it was usually overflowing. One of the more pitiful sights I recall was a man who previously had been held prisoner in a stone jail in Budapest when it was bombed, and he was trapped as the building collapsed around him. During the air raids over Nuremberg, he would sit by the slop bucket in a fetal position and shake.

On 28 February, our senior officer, Colonel Alkire, wrote a detailed letter enumerating and protesting our conditions. He described all the violations of the Geneva Convention and, as a result, we did get some relief, especially through the Red Cross parcels which arrived in a "Great White Fleet" of American trucks on loan to the International Red Cross. Of course, when we received the parcels, we all pigged out and made ourselves sick from the rich food.

On 4 April, we took to the road again, heading for Stalag VII-A at Moosburg, about forty kilometers (twenty-four miles) north of Munich and a hundred miles from where we started in Nuremberg. This time we weren't rushed, and it took us ten days to complete the journey (about ten miles per day). We were allowed to trade our Red Cross cigarettes or chocolate to the German civilians in exchange for food. We considered white bread to be our cake, and we got some eggs and fresh vegetables. We slowly started to regain some strength.

The party crossed the Danube at Neustadt, and we noted that the bridge was mined with two five-hundred-pound bombs and that there were eighty-millimeter cannons lined along the river, waiting to engage the American forces that were advancing. One time, while we were on an elevated field beyond the town, we saw some P-47s dive-bombing the railroad yards below us. They banked in our direction, and we knew that if their noses dropped, armed with all those guns, we would be done for. Within seconds, POWs who had white items had laid them out in a pattern to spell out "POW." I was taking as much cover as possible, which was not much. The wingmen turned, and the leader came across our position, wagging his wings in greeting. We could breathe again.

Stalag VII-A was another disaster. Fortunately, we from the West Compound were only there two weeks. Other compounds from Sagan had gone there directly and suffered longer. It was built to hold 14,000 prisoners in barracks. It swelled to 130,000, with many of us living in tents by the end of the war. Everything was in short supply, especially fuel. We tore apart wooden buildings to get wood shavings for our tin can cookers, and, as we were late arrivals, we lived in tents which weren't as crowded as the barracks, but they afforded less shelter.

There were again wild rumors as to what Hitler planned to do with us. One rumor had it that we were to be put in cages on the *Unter den Linden* (Berlin's most beautiful street, lined with linden trees) to inhibit Allied bombings. An order was actually given to move us farther south, but Supreme Headquarters Allied Expeditionary Force reached an agreement with the Nazis to leave us in place. And, in turn, no more German captives would be removed from the continent.[6]

On 29 April 1945, we heard gunfire outside the camp and saw a long line of American tanks and armored vehicles coming down a hill toward the camp. About noon, one of the tanks from the Fourteenth Armored Division of Patton's Third Army rolled over the fence, and we were free. A friend of mine has written about, "The day I saw 10,000 men cry." I think it was more like a 130,000 men of all nationalities that cried as we saw the most beautiful sight in the world as Old Glory replaced the swastika flying over the compound. Two days later, General Patton appeared in a jeep with his four stars and ivory-handled pistols.

During our march from Nuremburg to Moosburg, the local Germans had expressed fears that the Russians might get there first. They asked us what they should do if the Americans came. We told them to "just do what they ask of you and don't resist." Our armored forces went through that area like a hot knife through butter, and I've often wondered how much our advice to the German populace helped.

After the war, Clem returned to duty in the States and continued his career in the Army Air Force. He attended a graduate navigation instructors' course at Ellington Air Force Base in Texas. Later at Ellington, he was given an assignment to write and illustrate a textbook on aerial navigation. The project turned out to be the precursor for a number of tours of duty that involved production of professional textbooks. In one assignment, from 1947 to 1955, Clem, as chief of a development and production unit, estimates that he must have produced 120 textbooks, with two million copies printed, along with related audio-visual mate-

6.   Durand, op. cit., p. 347.

rials. The texts were used to train more than a half million students, mostly Air Force ROTC cadets at 206 colleges. In 1960, as an outstanding graduate of the Air Force Command and Staff College, he was selected for the U.S. Air Force speakers program, making appearances before about thirteen thousand people in major cities across the country. By 1963, he had joined the Headquarters U.S. Air Force Military Assistance Program, which led to his being the project officer for training German air force pilots. Being a former POW in camps controlled by the German air force presented an irony that was not lost on him.

Clem retired from the Air Force in 1965 and embarked on a second career with the Agency for International Development, training AID employees preparing to serve in Vietnam and ultimately serving in Management Operations as chief of the policy and procedures staff of the Agency for International Development's overseas missions. Clem retired from AID in 1985. He and Dolores moved to Falcons Landing in 1997. Dolores died on Clem's birthday in 1999.

As he reflects on his two careers spanning more than forty years, Clem notes that every job he held after his World War II wartime experiences, whether in education or training, support services or management planning and operations, involved problem solving to help people work together through improved knowledge, skills, and processes that led to enhanced effectiveness, morale, and welfare. His hard work and creative solutions earned two Air Force commendation medals, as well as AIDs Management Improvement and Equal Employment Opportunity awards.

Clem said:

> In 1995, about 250 of we former POWs and our wives toured all the areas where we had been held. On 29 April, we ended up at twelve noon in Moosburg, fifty years to the day and almost to the minute of our liberation. The city fathers held a special service at a memorial at the former camp site to memorialize all the former prisoners. The service was followed by a luncheon and a banquet in the city hall for us Americans and a group of French ex-POWs. Back In the States, we held a fiftieth reunion party in Cincinnati. It was a great party financed by many patriotic citizens in the area. There were thirteen hundred of us at the banquet and our guest speaker was the astronaut Neil Armstrong. Our celebration took us to the Air Force Museum at Wright-Patterson Air Force Base where we dedicated a plaque depicting a magnificent eagle breaking loose from its chains. The plaque told our story. The theme of our reunion was that all of us had passed through the "eye of the needle,"[7] that indescribably small window between life and death that all of we downed fly-

---

7.   Durand, op.cit, p4.

ers had to squeeze through on our brutal journey from a dying aircraft through gruesome captivity to eventual freedom.

During our 1995 trip, we visited the murderous Dachau, as well as the site of kangaroo courts and killing chambers in Berlin. We saw the graves of the fifty murdered airmen who had been recaptured after the "Great Escape." We saw the evil that the Nazis, who were the terrorists of their day, had wrought.

But let's put all this in context. As prisoners, we had suffered through abysmal conditions and were subjected to many violations of the Geneva Conventions. However, to be fair, particularly during the last few months of the war, we must remember the conditions in Germany were miserable for the Germans as well. The Allies dominated the air, and transport within Germany was most difficult either by train or truck. Even our camp honey wagon (human waste disposal wagon) went out one day and never made it back. The air raids over Nuremberg were near constant. We were so edgy that if someone dropped a shoe on the floor we all took cover. Despite all this, we thanked God that we were under the protection of the German *Luftwaffe* (air force). On more than one occasion, that saved our lives, in spite of direct orders from Adolph Hitler or Heinrich Himmler, the *reichsfuhrer* of the Nazi SS.

I made another trip to Germany in 1964, a trip that demonstrated to me how little personal animus I felt toward our *Luftwaffe* captors. I was working in the U.S. military assistance program, and the German air force had asked us to expand their training program in this country to a complete program, from primary to advanced combat crew training, and I had the good fortune to be the project officer for the program. In November of that year, I was sitting in my cubicle in room 5B-461 in the Pentagon—a room of some notice years later, since it was in the area of the 9-11 crash into the Pentagon. I was working on a brochure for my presentation to the German air staff in Bonn that was to be made in a few days. I thought of the irony that here I was, this former *kriegie*, now working with the Germans to train the new *Luftwafffe*. I realized that, after twenty years, I had no bitterness or resentment over the years of my captivity. I was working as hard as I could to make the pilots we trained to be as good as the German pilots who had shot us down. Only now I wanted them to be on our side.

Clem's survival as a prisoner of war was a tribute to his physical and mental stamina and a dose of good luck. There were about 130,200 American prisoners of war taken during World War II, and almost one-third of them died in captivity.

"I think that the insignia designed by Walt Disney for the Americans in Stalag III sums it up beautifully as Donald Duck laments through prison bars, 'I wanted wings.' We all wanted wings, and we used them for a while."

3

Francis X. Riley

Official Coast Guard photo

There is a small but distinguished coterie of the United States Coast Guard living at Falcons Landing. There is Marjorie Hirshfield, widow of Vice Adm. James Hirshfield, former assistant commandant of the Coast Guard. Marjorie was widowed in 1993 and moved to Falcons Landing in October 1996 from their home in Rancho Santa Fe, California. During his thirty-eight-year career in the Coast Guard, Jimmy was awarded the Navy Cross and the Purple Heart while in command of the U.S. Coast Guard *Campbell* on North Atlantic Convoy duty in 1943. From 1950 until he retired in 1962, he served on the board of the U.S. Naval Institute. Following his career in the Coast Guard, Admiral Hirshfield

---

1.   This account is based on a series of interviews with Commander Francis Riley commencing in October 2004, and from his personal papers.

became president of Lake Carriers Association in Cleveland, Ohio. Jimmy was the uncle of another resident, Denise Munchmeyer.

Denise is the wife of retired Coast Guard Comdr. Fred Munchmeyer. Fred is a World War II veteran of the Pacific campaigns. He retired early from the Coast Guard after having a heart attack and launched a notable career as an academician. (See profile of Denise Munchmeyer.) There is Bert Putnam, the widow of Comdr. Robert E. Putnam who served fifteen months aboard ship in the Pacific during World War II. Frank Riley and Fred Munchmeyer were classmates at the Coast Guard Academy in the class of 1943 and were commissioned in 1942 from one of the wartime classes that finished their schooling in three rather than the peacetime term of four years.

Frank Riley was born in 1919 in Brooklyn, New York, where he attended Bishop Loughlin High School. He was attracted to a seagoing career from early years. After serving in the Reserve Officer Training Program at City College of New York, he was selected to attend the Coast Guard Academy. (There are no congressional nominations or geographic quotas for the Coast Guard Academy. These appointments are made by the commandant of the Coast Guard, based on a national competitive examination.) Frank met Rosemary Dedrick at Rockaway Point, New York, when the two of them were sixteen. They were married the day after his graduation and commissioning as an ensign. Within six months of their wedding, they were separated for nearly two years as Frank sailed to the North Africa and the European combat theaters.

Ensign Riley's initial assignments out of the academy were brief and unremarkable. His first assignment was to a training ship for merchant marine seamen, the *Empire State*, which was home-ported in Saint Petersburg, Florida. The ship was used to train merchant seamen survival skills for their hazardous trips across the Atlantic. After a brief tour with the *Empire State*, he was assigned to duty as commanding officer of a small training station in Laporte, Texas, outside of Houston.

In one of these initial billets, Frank was temporarily assigned to the command of the captain of the Port of Galveston and placed in charge of the horse and dog patrol that was tasked with securing the island coast against German infiltration. In hindsight, this seems an implausible mission, yet one must recall that there had been two such infiltration attempts by German saboteurs before the summer of 1942. Patrolling coastal areas for infiltrators was taken seriously. Frank recalled:

So there I was, a kid from Brooklyn, in charge of a stable of horses and a kennel of dogs patrolling the shoreline of Galveston Island. I thought that if I wanted to work with horses, I wouldn't have joined the Coast Guard, I would have joined the cavalry.

Nevertheless, one night, when I was the duty officer, I received a phone call from the chief petty officer who was in charge of the Coast Guard station at the west end of the island who was in contact with the beach patrols. He told me that one of the patrols had reported that their horses had been "spooked" and implied that there may be some cause for concern, which, of course, given our mission, meant that we should be on the alert for infiltrators. I called the commanding officer for instructions. He told me to do what I thought was necessary. So I did. I first ordered the available boats to patrol around the entire island. We had some one thousand Coast Guardsmen billeted in a Galveston hotel awaiting assignment that I mobilized to cordon off the island and search for any suspicious activity. I instructed them to search every house on the island outside the city of Galveston to look for and bring in any suspicious persons. There were no weapons with which to arm them. Just in case, I had checked with the local Army organization and was informed that they didn't have any available rifles. Well, those one thousand men did try to enter every house on that beach for a distance of twenty-five miles. I had created quite a stir, and there were a lot of unhappy Texans and threats of lawsuits for trespassing and the like.

Fortunately, I soon had orders to leave that command to go to a sea-going billet, and I escaped the consequences of my island search. In retrospect, I would have been mighty unhappy if I had taken no action, and it was later determined that saboteurs had actually landed there.

Frank learned that a flotilla of Landing Craft Infantry (Large) (LCI [L]) was forming in Galveston with Coast Guard crews. He volunteered for assignment to the organization and was accepted into "Fighting Flotilla Four" in February 1943. Little did he know that this marriage to the awkward, flat-bottom craft would take him across the Atlantic twice and through four major campaigns for a year and eight months. The craft was armed with four twenty-millimeter guns, had a five-foot draft, and two variable pitch propellers. It was manned by a crew of four officers and twenty enlisted men. The craft was designed so that it could be beached at the bow and backed off again after the infantry had disembarked. At the front of the craft were two ramps that could be dropped to load and unload troops. They were designed to carry and land two hundred troops in an amphibious assault.

Frank was assigned duties as executive officer of the USS LCI (L) 323, an assignment in which he served for about eight months. Not everyone believed that the flat-bottomed LCIs were seaworthy, and their first transits out into the open seas gave some of the crew serious doubts, as they suffered through incessant pounding, pitching, and rolling. Many of the men suffered seasickness. Probably half of the crew had never before been to sea, and this was a dismal introduction to being a sailor.

LCI (L) 323, as part of the twenty-four-craft flotilla, spent over a month preparing for deployment to the war zone across the Atlantic. By March 1943, there was an urgent need for landing ships for the impending invasion of Sicily.

At dawn on April 1, the flotilla sailed for North Africa, making a stop at Bermuda. They joined a seventy-five-ship convoy for an eighteen-day sail to Port Lyautey, Morocco, where they spent several weeks conducting beaching drills. They then put in to Gibraltar and to a number of Mediterranean ports until they reached Bizerte, Tunisia, a strategic port, because it was the nearest good port to Sicily. At Bizerte, they staged, trained, and equipped for the amphibious operation against Sicily, often under aerial assault by German and Italian aircraft and some misdirected friendly fire. It was not a pleasant stay. Frank described it:

> After our three-month voyage from the States, to include mooring and training at more than a half dozen ports, we were knocking on the back door of the Axis. They meant to beat us back through air attacks before we launched our assault against their underbelly at Sicily, Italy. We were subjected to three months of air raids, three to four a week. The raids were among the most intense the Germans and Italians were to launch against us anywhere we deployed, including the invasion beaches of Italy and Normandy.
>
> We had searchlights and anti-aircraft guns all around the perimeter of the bay. The first warning of an air raid would be the sound of the guns, followed by the searchlights scanning the skies. The bombers always came from the northeast, and soon one of them would be caught in the beam of a searchlight, then suddenly, there would be many searchlights coming from all directions. In about half of these cases, once the planes had been lit up like that, they were goners and were shot down.
>
> The first major air raid we witnessed at Bizerte seemed exciting, thrilling, spectacular. We were so green; we cheered as if we were at a sporting event when the home team scores. However, I soon realized that I was never really going to like this game.
>
> I remember the first plane I watched being hit. It was afire as it came over the center of the bay. Smoke poured out as it was being pounded by the anti-aircraft guns. It seemed that it would crash into our ships. When it did crash in the sea, it erupted into a giant fireball. One of the German crew did bail out and was saved. We cheered when the plane was destroyed, but we never cheered again. We soon realized that it was a horrible experience, and that we were in just as much danger as the enemy, for during these raids there were would be fifty to a hundred bombers. However, more American casualties

resulted from our friendly fire and the falling shrapnel than from the enemies' bombs. One night, our friendly fire injured one hundred and eight Americans without downing a single enemy aircraft.

The Coast Guard craft of the Fighting Flotilla Four came under the operational control of the Navy.

"The Navy used the Coast Guard LCI flotilla and other Coast Guard units interchangeably with comparable Navy units in war operations," Frank said. "When we were matched with Navy ships, if their crews were less experienced, it was only logical that we got the more difficult and hazardous assignments, as we did in the Normandy invasion."

When landing assault tasks were assigned to the craft of the flotilla for the amphibious operation against Sicily, it was learned that LCI (L) 323 and another craft would not embark troops but would be assigned the unglamorous duty of being in reserve, a replacement for any of the craft that might break down. Frank said:

> As we proceeded toward the beach, the devastation and violence of the invasion became apparent. After a run to the beach to determine if we could be of assistance to the beach master, we rejoined our flotilla to assemble for a return to Bizerte in North Africa. Our mission in the assault on Sicily had been accomplished.
>
> However, LCI (L) 323 would remain in Italian waters. Our craft was ordered to take Italian prisoners aboard for delivery to Licata, a POW area. Although they had but recently been deadly enemies, we welcomed these bedraggled, war-weary soldiers with refreshing, saltwater outdoor baths using the fog spray nozzle of our fire-fighting equipment. We had an ulterior motive in providing the baths, however, since we suspected that the men were probably full of lice. The prisoners were never sullen, but rather, seemed grateful to be free of the war. I asked one of them how he felt about being shipped to an internment camp in the United States. In broken but pointed English, he said, "Me going to New York—you stay here." We both knew that he was getting the better deal. We got to go ashore in Licata. I met a couple of Italians who had lived in my hometown of Brooklyn. One of them asked me for a pair of shoes. I asked him what about the shoes Mussolini had supplied. He pointed to the rags on his feet and said, "Mussolini shoes? Here's your Mussolini shoes."

Fighting Flotilla Four returned to North Africa to train and stage for the Salerno invasion on the mainland of Italy in September 1943. The flotilla was to carry British troops, Indians, officered by English, to the beaches of Salerno. Frank described that scene:

> We hit the beach at Salerno facing heavy fire from the Axis defenders. Our troops rushed ashore for a dry landing since we were able to drive our craft high enough on the beach to drop the ramp on the sandy soil. But the troops couldn't advance more than a few yards because they were under heavy fire from the entrenched defenders. An American medical corpsman ran up the ramp of our craft to see if we had a doctor aboard or any morphine. We had neither, but we were able to provide him with stretchers, and I sent half the crew ashore as stretcher bearers. The wounded were in horrible condition. None of these British soldiers, lying out in the hot sun, had received any medical attention other than first aid for twelve hours.
>
> We evacuated about half the wounded off the beach, even while the enemy resistance grew more intense. We were shelled and were under machine-gun and small-arms fire, which made the moving of the wounded onto our landing craft extremely difficult while we carried the wounded up the steep ramp in the litters. The deck was soon packed with the wounded. So many of them were in great pain. We tried to make them comfortable, placing them on top of rubber boats and getting them out of the hot sun whenever possible.
>
> I was standing directly under the ship's bridge supervising the movement of the wounded into the number two troop compartment when an 88 mm shell passed through the bridge about five feet above my head. The shattered armor hit me and the crew who were carrying the wounded. One of the crew yelled, "They got me!" Upon inspection, we found that he had only been struck in the back with a piece of flying armor fragments that had not penetrated his clothing. The shell passed just inches over the left shoulder of another of the crew who was on the bridge. You can imagine the shock it gave him. The shell failed to explode on impact, as it passed through the bridge and out into the water. However, it did considerable damage to the craft as it tore up the bridge and knocked out the compass and the annunciator, our means of communication from the bridge to the engine room. An exact line of heading to the 88 mm gun could have been sighted as we were beached, immobile, and the shell left a line of sight with the two holes in the conning tower. We recovered twenty-one casualties from the beach and retracted as best we could with the disabled bridge controls.
>
> We sailed through the invasion flotilla in search of a doctor for our cargo of wounded, sending messages with our blinker lights, while trying to make the wounded as comfortable as possible. We finally found an LST (landing ship tank) that had a physician, pulled alongside, and evacuated our dead and wounded. It was a grim task.
>
> The following nights and days we were under constant aerial attack, but we escaped damage, even though we had some close calls including one near miss that shook the vessel so violently that many of the crew thought we were

surely hit. We did witness a sad sight as we passed several lifeboats from a hospital ship that had been sunk, despite being properly identified and lit in accordance with the Geneva Conventions. We subsequently delivered follow-on waves of American troops onto the beach in uneventful landings.

After the Salerno operation, some of the Coast Guard officers of the flotilla were ordered back to the States. Now an experienced combat veteran and master seaman, Frank Riley left LCI (L) 323 to command USS LCI (L) 319, also a veteran craft that had suffered four or five casualties during the aerial strafings at Salerno. The LCI flotilla sailed out of the Mediterranean to England. Half the flotilla anchored south of Falmouth where the flotilla commander set up his temporary headquarters. The remainder, including Frank's LCI 319, proceeded north of Plymouth to anchor at a small town, Saltash. The trip from the Mediterranean to England was uneventful for Frank and his craft, although one of the flotilla LCIs did lose its way in the English Channel and was challenged by a British destroyer.

USS Landing Craft Infantry (L) 319 commanded by Lt. j.g. Francis Riley,
USCG

Photo from USN archives

"Although the LCI gave the proper response to the destroyer, the destroyer's commanding officer found it hard to believe that a single, small landing craft was sailing alone in the channel without an escort," Frank said. "So he signaled the LCI asking where it had come from and where it was bound. The LCI skipper responded, 'From Gibraltar to England,' which really must have made the destroyer captain suspicious, as he responded, 'Alone?' The LCI captain having a rare sense of humor and seaman's sense of pride, answered, 'No, the other twenty-three ships are lost.'"

After North Africa and the Mediterranean landings, Saltash provided a respite for the crew of *LCI 319*. They were able to take advantage of Plymouth for training, rest, recuperation, and recreation while preparing for the Normandy invasion.

"Plymouth had been severely damaged by German bombings," Frank said. "Block upon block of houses had been destroyed. The streets were still recognizable, but only the shells of buildings and rubble remained where brick and stone houses had once been."

Frank was prophetic of the catastrophe of 9/11 and the destruction of the World Trade Center when, long before that event, he expressed this thought:

"If one wanted to see what could happen to American cities during the next war, one only needs to have seen Plymouth during the latter stages of World War II. But even though it may be more horrible in the next war, I am confident that survivors will still carry on under extremely trying circumstances, as did the stoic people of England."

The Plymouth-based flotilla trained with American Army troops for the amphibious assault on the continent for nearly a year. One of these landing exercises, code named TIGER, was conducted in April 1944 (LCI 319 did not participate). Eight LSTs were included in the exercise convoy, code named T-4. (The LST, no longer in the Navy's active inventory, was a fairly large amphibious ship capable of being beached to deliver mechanized vehicles and infantry. It was 522 feet in length and capable of carrying about three hundred troops. It was crewed by thirteen officers and 244 enlisted.) During the exercise, nine German high-speed torpedo E-boats, (capable of operating at speeds of thirty-four to thirty-six knots) from the Fifth Schnellboote Flotilla out of Cherbourg, slipped past the protective cordon of Navy ships and attacked the convoy. Three of the LSTs were torpedoed; two sank, and the third was able to limp back into port. The other LSTs and two British destroyers opened fire on the E-boats, which used smoke and speed to escape. The attack resulted in 198 Navy and 551 Army dead and missing. The majority of the troops were lost from the First Special Engineer Brigade. Frank speculates that more soldiers and sailors died in LSTs in Operation TIGER than were killed disembarking from the same ships during the actual invasion. The loss was considered a major setback in the preparations for the invasion of Europe. The casualty count was not released until after the invasion to deny the Germans information of the success of their Schnellboote raid.

It was during one of these exercises that Frank was stung by the remarks of a Navy admiral embarked on his craft who was wary of the seamanship of landing craft sailors when maneuvering alongside cruisers. Frank was more favorably impressed with another passenger who rode in his LCI during one of these exercises—Gen. Omar Bradley, who chatted freely with Frank and insisted on carrying his own luggage.

Frank and the other flotilla skippers were finally called to an inland military base to receive a copy of the plan for the amphibious operation "Overlord." The plan provided for LCI 319 to pick up assigned troops at a designated port. It gave the time to leave port; it assigned a convoy, a designated landing beach, an assault wave, and a time of landing. They would eventually embark and deliver 199 infantry from companies C and D, Twenty-second Infantry, Fourth Infantry Division, to depart from Salcombe Harbor, Devon, England, on June 5, 1944.

Mass aboard LCI 319 in the troop compartment the day before D-Day.
Official Coast Guard photo

The landing beach, code named "Utah," was about twenty miles south of Cherbourg and fifteen miles west of Omaha Beach. On June 6, 1944, D-Day, at 0725, the flotilla arrived in the amphibious transport area about eleven miles off the beach. At about 1017, they landed, and their infantry troops disembarked under heavy fire from about a thousand yards inland. While other LCIs left the beach area after offloading their troops, LCI 319 remained, performing salvage and firefighting duties in the beach area. Frank and his crew spent the remainder of June sixth, seventh, and eighth salvaging six landing craft and rendering assistance to ships beached in the area, removing dead from ships and craft, and fighting fires. At 0225 of 9 June, Frank received orders to retrieve and beach two ammunition barges that had drifted off their beach moorings:

> They were two hundred by fifty feet, full of ammunition, and had drifted into the minefield area. We were ordered to bring them back to the beach where they were urgently needed by the Army. We knew and were concerned that a Navy mine sweeper operating in this same minefield had been sunk. The barges were drifting through the minefield toward an island called San Marcouf, about five miles off the beachhead. At one point, they came within two hundred yards of striking the island. Two LCMs (landing craft mechanized) were assigned to help us with the task, and I ordered them to take one barge while we took the other. It was a chancy operation, and there were times when I thought the barge had us in tow rather than the other way around. By 0830, both barges had been secured and beached. There had been many parted lines and close calls, and the crews had worked all that early morning under extremely difficult and dangerous conditions. The following morning, after the barges were secured and I was recording the event in our log, I noted that the last four letters on the barges identification number were "AMEN." I thought, how appropriate—thank the Lord, amen.

Frank Riley earned the Bronze Star with a combat "V" for the retrieval of the barges and the salvage of numerous landing craft. Several members of his crew were cited for their courage and seamanship under those trying conditions. The worst damage suffered by LCI 319 during this period came during a storm when a Navy-manned LCI broke from its moorings and rammed into the craft, ripping several holes in the hull. The craft took on a lot of water and nearly capsized before the large holes were temporarily repaired with makeshift damage control materials. LCI 319 remained in the area, engaging in salvage and firefighting operations until June 22. By June 23, they were back in England, moored in Dart River, Dartmouth, Devon.

The rest of the story is hardly anticlimactic. Frank Riley continued his career in the Coast Guard, being assigned to four sea- and two shore-command billets as well as staff duties at the service headquarters. At one point, he was patrolling out of Eureka, California, when he received a report that a shrimp boat was missing during a storm. He searched the Pacific for long hours without finding a trace of the shrimper. On their way back to the station, Frank and his crew caught sight of a vessel aground in the surf, swaying rhythmically as the waves pounded against the hull. As they approached the vessel, they could see something suspended high in the riggings, swaying as the boat rocked in the waves. The pendulum was the lifeless body of a man, hung upside down. The shrimper had been caught in the topmast in one of the rolls of his boat as he struggled to survive in the violent surf.

"It was a macabre sight," Frank said. "It was like something out of an Alfred Hitchcock movie—and hard to forget."

The union of Frank and Rosemary produced five children, ten grandchildren, and four great-grandchildren. Capt. Frank Riley retired from the Coast Guard in 1972. Upon retirement, he and Rosemary traveled to every continent except Antarctica, visiting 227 countries. They moved to Falcons Landing in 1996 where they are active on the chapel committee and as the official greeters to new residents in their apartment building. They selected Falcons Landing for their retirement because they thought that it would meet their requirement for a first-class, continuing-care, living facility. They haven't been disappointed, and the community is better for their presence.

4

Alden P. Colvocoresses

As the crow flies, Falcons Landing is about a half mile from the Potomac
River. It's just a nice walk along a golf course and through a park populated with
deer. Downstream, about thirty miles, one mile south of the Woodrow Wilson
bridge, there is a small island, of about 3.7 acres (depending on the tide), which
bears the name Colvo Island.[2] When Dr. Alden P. Colvocoresses, known to all as
Colvo, discovered that the island had not been properly registered by any government agency, he claimed and named the island, which is in the Dyke Marsh Preserve. Since 1987, Colvo and the federal government have battled over who owns
the property, which is technically controlled (but not clearly owned) by the

---

1. This profile is based on a series of interviews started in October 2004 and from per-
    sonal papers of Colvocoresses.
2. The references for this account of Colvo Island were drawn from personal files of
    Colvocoresses's articles from the *Washington Post,* the *Arlington Journal,* and the
    Fairfax Journal.

National Park Service. In 1987 Colvo claimed the wooded island with a quit-claim deed and deeded the island to himself under a legal clause called adverse possession. When he appeared at the county tax assessor's office to pay property taxes on the island, they told him that they didn't have any islands in Fairfax County. "You've got one now," he replied. The county assessor set a value and began collecting taxes.

Colvo the hunter

The island was created by dredging operations in the Potomac in the late 1950s and early 1960s. Although wooded and sheltering bass, ducks, and geese, it is not scenic. The river carries trash onto its banks, and there is still debris from the dredging operations. Nevertheless, Colvo has been ardent in his claim on the island. He has paid for its survey, paid taxes to Fairfax County on the property, and posted it as off limits to other hunters. He has offered to turn over his rights to the property in return for hunting privileges. He is an accomplished duck hunter and fisherman, and the island was his duck-hunting preserve. He would row out from a nearby marina with his Labrador retriever, Molly, often with friends or his grandson. In 1990, park rangers arrested him for carrying a loaded shotgun on the island. On the day he was arrested, he was wearing his hunting gear and carrying a shotgun in one hand and a duck in the other. He was given a suspended sentence and fined $100.

Colvo is a battler, with a distinguished record as a combat soldier. The overwhelming odds against him in his fight with city hall are no deterrent. The legal implications of his claim are complex, involving county, federal, and individual property rights, but that doesn't stop him.

Colvo didn't just stumble across the island. He holds a Ph.D. in geodetic science from Ohio State University in 1965. He operated mapping programs as a research cartographer while employed by the National Mapping Division, U.S. Geological Survey, from which he retired in 1992.[3] He is a prominent member of

---

3.   An interesting aside is that Dr. Colvocoresses was a colleague of the late B. K. Meade of the Coast and Geodetic Survey Agency who lived at Falcons Landing until his death. (Meade's wife, Ruth, is still a member of the community.)

a number of professional societies and has earned many awards for his contributions to the science. In 1988, he was elected president of the American Society for Photogrammetry and Remote Sensing. In 1976, a reef in the Indian Ocean was named for him. He invented two systems for mapping from space. In 1980, he defined and patented a mapping satellite system named MAPSAT. In 2000, the French launched a satellite (SPOT) based on the concept. As this was being written, the French satellite was still in orbit. Following Colvo's retirement, he continued to contribute to the science of the spatial mapping field, doing seminal work in defining features of the earth's land areas—when it didn't interfere with his hunting and fishing.

Colvo's career was not limited to being a scientist in the U.S. Geological Survey. He was also a professional soldier, serving in the U.S. Army for over twenty years, retiring as a colonel in 1968. In World War II he participated in ten combat campaigns. He served through three wars and was decorated seven times to include two Silver Stars, two Bronze Stars, and two Purple Hearts.

Notwithstanding his mellifluous surname of Calvocoresses, Colvo is only one-sixteenth Greek. He was born in 1918, in Humboldt, Arizona. His father, an 1890 graduate of Yale, was a prosperous mining engineer. His father met his mother, Alice M. Hagen, in New Caledonia, which is in the Coral Sea and is one of the Pacific's larger islands. Alice was of English-German descent and was living on a French possession where about a third of the population was European and half were Micronesians and Polynesians. She was one of thirteen children. Five brothers served in the French army during World War I.

Wedding party of Colvo's parents, New Caledonia, 1903

Colvo's great-grandfather, George M. Colvocoresses, came to America as a seven-year-old refugee from Chios, a small, 842-square-kilometer island of the northeast Aegean. The history of this beautiful island is one of tranquility interspersed with episodes of violence. In Greek mythology, it is the site where the king of the island plucked out the eyes of Orion, the giant son of Poseidon. The Ottoman Empire occupied the island for 350 years, from 1566 to 1912. In 1821-1822, Greece and Chios revolted against Turkish rule. The Sultan ordered his army and navy to retake and punish Chios, which they did with vigor. The majority of the Chions were either slaughtered or taken as slaves. Of the one hundred thousand Greeks, only forty thousand escaped the slaughter. By the end of the Turkish onslaught, only three thousand Chions remained. Colvo's great-grandfather was one of those who escaped. He made his way to America in 1823 to serve in the U.S. Navy and retired as a captain. He wrote a popular book documenting the U.S. Wilkes Expedition. Four geographic features were named for him, among them Colvocoresses Bay in the Antarctica and Colvocoresses Strait in the Pacific Northwest. The Wilkes Expedition (1841-1842), besides charting much of the West Coast of the North American continent, confirmed that Antarctica is a continent and charted islands in the South and Central Pacific that became important in World War II naval operations. Colvo's grandfather, George P. Colvocoresses, also served in the Navy, in combat, and retired as a rear admiral.

Life in Humboldt, Arizona, was good for young Colvo. It was there that he began his lifelong dedication to hunting and fishing. His father ran the smelter that was the sole industry of the city. However, in 1929, the smelter was shut down, and the family moved to Phoenix, Arizona. Colvo enrolled in the University of Arizona at Tucson as a member of the Army Reserve Officer Training (ROTC) program. He played on the varsity tennis team and, following in his father's footsteps, earned a bachelor of science degree in mining engineering. Upon graduation, he was commissioned a second lieutenant in the Army Reserve as a cavalry officer. Colvo worked for a brief stint with a mining company before the general mobilization for World War II. He reported for active duty in the Army at Fort Bliss, Texas, in October 1941. There was little need for cavalry officers in a war that was to be fought by mechanized forces, so, as a matter of routine, the Army was reassigning cavalry officers into the armored force based at Fort Knox, Kentucky. With his engineering degree, Colvo secured an assignment to the Sixteenth Armored Engineer Battalion of the First Armored Division. By May 1942, he was en route to Northern Ireland as part of the first major U.S. armored unit to deploy to the European Theater of Operations.

"For seven months my unit was in Northern Ireland, where we trained hard and acquired some 'Bailey' bridging, which later proved most valuable," Colvo said. "It was during this time I met June Caldwell (supposedly 17, actually 15) and fell in love. We didn't get to see much of each other, but we became engaged before I took off for combat in October of 1942. We sailed from Glasgow with about two hundred men aboard a shallow-draft ship that was the forerunner to the LST (an amphibious landing ship tank). We were at sea for nearly a month under really wretched conditions. Everyone got seasick. The food was terrible. We slept on the deck or on mess tables, with some lucky ones getting hammocks. We landed in North Africa to help capture the port of Oran. My job (with about half of my platoon) was to establish a road and rail block to make sure the French Foreign Legion did not join in the fight for Oran. My task force saw little fighting and suffered no casualties."

By late November, Colvo's unit arrived in Tunisia, meeting Rommel's German Afrika Corps, which was pushing west out of Libya. During one of the engagements with the German forces, platoon leader Colvo was wounded, and he spent the last half of December 1942 in a British military hospital in Algiers.

Colvo was officer-in-charge of building this Bailey bridge in Tunisia in 1943. It was one of the first operational Bailey bridges built by U.S. Army engineers.

Photo courtesy of Colvocoresses

The Tunisian campaign ended in May 1943, and the First Armored Division turned west to rest and refit in Rabat, Morocco. But one of the most daring exploits of his African experience came on December 2, 1942, following one of the first tank battles between the German and U.S. armored forces. He described that day:

At nightfall, I was given the job of taking a party out, picking up the wounded, and directing a chaplain to the dead, directing maintenance units to tanks to be towed, and, finally, to destroy all enemy equipment on the field. This was to be accomplished under long-range, enemy machine-gun fire. We were successful in all the first phases of the mission, and toward morning I was ready to destroy any abandoned enemy tanks that we could find. We had to save this task to the last knowing that a burning tank would light up the whole scene, and we knew that there were German patrols in the area. I set out with two peeps (an armored force term for jeeps) with four men. We located two U.S. M3 tanks that had already burned when first hit.

Finally, when we had decided that we had gone far enough, I noticed a tank about two hundred yards away. We crept around to where we could view the silhouette. Sure enough, it bore the unmistakable outline of the German Mark IV. As we inched toward the tank, I was surprised to see a dim light shining out of the turret and to hear its small radio motor humming. We were convinced that the tank must be occupied. But, since we had come this far, I felt that we should attack it. So, covered by three men and armed with a couple of grenades and a machine gun, two of us stealthily crept up to the tank. Now, while the Mark IV tank was a big baby, it was built low to the ground and by climbing up on the boogies (wheels upon which the tank tracks run), I was able to peer into the turret, which opened on the side. Empty! I breathed a sigh of relief. But we knew that the tank had not been abandoned, and that the crew would return. We quickly went to work preparing it for demolition. We examined the tank from stem to stern and there was no evidence that it was damaged. We assumed that it must have suffered some engine failure.

Then we heard the clank of a German track vehicle. (Their tracks were metal, while ours were rubber.) That told us that we had no time to spare and would have to get out of there quickly. We hurriedly poured five gallons of gas into the interior of the tank, and I ignited it by throwing a hand grenade through the turret door. The tank burst into flames, and we went hell-bent for our own lines in our diminutive peep. We drew some machine-gun fire on our retreat, but I think the Germans heard rather than saw us. When we were about halfway back to our lines, the ammunition in the tank exploded, and a pillar of flame rose about one hundred feet into the air. It made quite a sight. On the whole, I was pleased with our night's work.

Colvo should have been pleased with the performance of the four engineers. The Mark IV tank was the new "Cadillac" of the Afrika Corps, and it may have been the first to be destroyed by U.S. forces in the Tunisian campaign. A few days later in the campaign, Colvo earned a Silver Star. The citation reads, in part, as follows: "He was a member of a group sent out to destroy the railroad bridge spanning the Oued, northeast of Sbeitla, which was receiving intense enemy and friendly artillery fires. Before he arrived at the bridge he came under observation and small arms fire from enemy troops who were occupying a position approximately one-quarter of a mile from the bridge....After destroying the bridge...While returning through Sbeitla he, on his own initiative and with complete disregard for the increasing fire on the town, proceeded to destroy all the stores and supplies that he could find."

This is the German Mark IV tank destroyed by Colvo and three soldiers in 1942 in Tunisia.

Photo courtesy of Colvocoresses

Colvo was wounded twice during this period of the campaign. In March 1943, he earned his second Silver Star.

The following is Colvo's account of the mission that led to that Silver Star:

On the evening of March 25 at Zannouch, the combat command to which I was attached was planning a push, which had Station Sened as its objective. At about ten PM, under a full moon, we moved out. There was one platoon of infantry loaded in peeps, an engineer reconnaissance section of four men, and myself with a mine detector for clearing mines in the road ahead. Our mission was to clear a route to Station Sened and, if the town behind it (also named

Sened) was not strongly held, to move in and hold the town until our armor could come up from behind. All went well for the first part of the mission, but as we approached the station, the leading peep hit a mine. From then on, I had to stay out in front of the convoy, and my crew removed close to fifty mines before we got through the enemy minefields.

After getting through the mines, we ran into abandoned gun positions which had been left only a few hours before, probably because of an artillery barrage which had been laid on their positions just before dark. We moved in. Just at dawn, our eleven peeps, with nothing more lethal than a light machine gun, occupied Station Sened. We could distinctly hear enemy vehicles moving through an olive grove only a few hundred yards away, but we hoped that the Italians were going the other way.

We radioed back that the town was secure, and it wasn't long before our tanks rolled into the village. In the meantime, I took my two peeps and drove over to the mountains in the north, where we contacted another combat team of ours that was about to blast Station Sened with artillery. They were disappointed to learn that there was no enemy left at the station, only our armor.

I was ordered to reconnoiter the town of Sened, behind the station, which our staff believed to be free of enemy forces. I was supposed to be accompanied by a regular reconnaissance section, but they never showed up. We took off with two peeps, and as we approached some hills, we topped a rise and saw two Italians jump on a motorcycle and take off. I grabbed my rifle, and after the second shot, which was too close for their comfort, they spilled off the bikes and threw up their hands. We sent them back to the station. We caught three more Italians who were trying to escape into the mountains. While one of my peeps was taking the prisoners back to the station, three of us inched forward, and, before we knew it, we found ourselves in the middle of a battery of Italian field artillery.

Before we could turn around, we were surrounded by about a hundred Italian troops to say nothing of the two seventy-fives which they had trained on us. I actually saw one of the Italian guns before we were surrounded, but I thought it had been abandoned. I had put too much confidence in our intelligence reports.

The Italians were delighted that they had captured three Americans. There were several of them who wanted to shoot us on the spot, but the majority was too curious to do us any harm. Once they discovered that I was an officer, they treated me with respect, and I talked for about an hour with their officers in broken English and fractured Spanish. I could tell that they were disgusted with the war.

Eventually, the three of us were brought before their commander, a lieutenant colonel, about thirty-five years old, who had his headquarters in the canyon. He seemed to be a capable officer. He informed us that we were prisoners of war, that we would be well-treated unless we tried to escape, and that we would soon be on our way to Italy.

At about two PM, we were marched across the rugged mountains, escorted by six guards, to the town of Sikket, about seven miles away. As we left the valley, I was able to view their defenses and get a good idea of their strength, which later proved to be quite useful.

The only way out of Sened was an old camel trail, and along our march we met several caravans carrying everything from food, to mortars and antitank guns. Apparently the Italians in Sened, who numbered about a thousand, were being resupplied with this primitive form of transport.

Since none of the guards could understand English, we American prisoners could discuss various ways of eluding or overpowering them, but we never had the chance. That night we spent at Sekket, where the Italians had a small detachment commanded by a lieutenant. He was a pleasant person who spoke Spanish, which gave us the opportunity to converse. We were fed brown bread, dog biscuits, canned corn beef, and some eggs that they had procured from the local Arabs. We were also given some of their liquor, anisette, which is really quite good and seemed to be in good supply. They gave us blankets, and that night we got a short but much-needed rest. The next morning, March 27, we started off again with six guards toward the town of Bou Hamran, one of their strong points, from where we could be further evacuated by truck.

It happened that American forces at El Guettar were shelling Bou Hamran that morning and, as soon as they saw the bursts of the guns, our guards turned us around and marched us back to Sikket. At about the same time, a German Stuka came overhead and dropped some bombs in a valley just to the east of us. The Italians were convinced that they were surrounded. I later learned that the Stuka pilot had made a mistake and had actually bombed an Italian position.

The lieutenant decided to send us back to Sened, so off we went again, this time with an escort of about thirty Italians. We had gone only about two miles when we stopped at an Arab mosque nestled in the mountains. While we were resting at the mosque, an Italian captain came down the trail from Sened with the information that the town was being shelled, and that we were to remain where we were until he reconnoitered a route out of the mountains. He said that he would return at dark and left the lieutenant in charge with orders to keep us strictly guarded. All that afternoon, we sat at the mosque talking with our captors, mostly through one of our party, Private Kulick, who could speak Italian.

The Italian soldiers gave us the impression that they thought America was a utopia where everyone was rich. Nearly all of them had relatives in the States, and they would have given a great deal to see New York or Hollywood—particularly the latter. They knew the names of all the popular movie stars.

Our impressions of our captors were that they were a homey people, and that they spent a great deal of their time brooding about their homes and families in Italy. They would frequently curse Hitler and Mussolini, but never when their officers were present. The more senior officers seemed proud and confident that the Axis would win the war. On the other hand, the men and junior officers seemed not so certain of the outcome, and the prospects of their becoming prisoners did not bother them at all. Nevertheless, they were deadly afraid of being captured by the French and of being mistreated by the Brits. They seemed confident that, if they were captured by the Americans, they would be well cared for.

Whenever I got the chance, I would tell them how powerful our forces were. I was trying to convince them that they were surrounded by American forces, which, of course, was not true. I figured that the more they worried about being attacked, the less attention they would pay to us prisoners.

Dusk came, the full moon of the night not yet visible. Private John Kerekes and I were standing just outside the door of the mosque. The third man in our party, Private Kulick, was inside where the Italians insisted on keeping him. There were four guards around Kerekes and me. One had his rifle shouldered, and the other three had theirs leaning against the building next to them. Kerekes and I agreed that this was the time to make a break. We felt certain that when the captain returned he would be moving us back out of the mountains. In as calm a voice as I could muster, I counted, "One—two—three—let's go!"

Before the guards could react, we were running around the building toward an olive grove that offered some cover. The Italians reacted quickly. Before we had covered no more than forty feet, they let us have it. We split in order to give two separate targets, but the bullets were coming awfully close. Kerekes got nicked in the arm, and a round glanced off his helmet, but they failed to touch me. For the next ten minutes, they kept firing in our direction and set off some flares. It was the first time I had really run since I had injured my ankle some two years earlier. However, I'm confident that at that point, I could have given any four-minute miler a close race. Before long, I was winded and collapsed, while congratulating myself that I had escaped.

Having been a prisoner for that short period was an interesting experience. I have never been more miserable. I think I would have gone crazy if I had been forced to spend the rest of the war in an Italian prisoner of war camp. I also felt obligated to look after the two men who were captive with me. I felt certain that Kerekes would find his way to safety, and he did. I was determined to do everything I could to free Kulick who was still in the hands of our captors.

I whistled for Kerekes, but I was not surprised that he failed to answer, for we had run a good distance in opposite directions. It was now a bright night as I headed north through the mountains toward our perimeter. I had no compass, and the steep terrain often hid Polaris, but from my father's and Boy Scout's training, I found north from Cassiopia on the Big Dipper. Kerekes was an amateur astronomer and had no trouble navigating by the stars. It was about an eight-mile trip to the lower end of the canyon that led up to Sened, but I found a trail that made it fairly easy going. I made it back to our lines shortly after midnight. I commandeered a peep and went straight to headquarters where I briefed them on everything I knew about the Italian dispositions in that sector. As a result, by dawn, I found myself once again facing the canyon that led up to Sened. This time, however, we had three 105 howitzers and a company of infantry instead of one peep and three combat engineers to attack the town.

As dawn broke, our infantry moved up the ridges to take the high ground on either side of the canyon, but they were soon met by heavy machine-gun fire. Then our 105s opened up, and I was able to spot the Italian positions for the artillery observer. The Italians soon located the observer and me and started lobbing mortar rounds at us. They had us bracketed when I heard the whistle of a mortar round coming in which landed not ten feet from us, but, thank heavens, it failed to explode. The whistle we heard was caused by the mortar round pin that the gunner had failed to extract to arm the weapon before dropping it into the mortar tube. Our howitzers put the mortar out of business.

It was not long before Italian soldiers started coming down out of the hills we had been shelling, permitting our infantry to advance up the ridge lines. The battle was soon over. Even though the Italians outnumbered us by at least five to one, the largest artillery they had was an 81 mm mortar. They raised a white flag and marched out of their positions to surrender. The MPs took over six hundred prisoners back to Station Sened, although a number escaped, to include the Italian colonel. We did capture a major and a number of junior officers.

I was concerned about Kulick, who was still in the hands of the Italians. As soon as the town fell, I asked for a platoon to take over the mountains to the mosque where I hoped he might still be. That afternoon, we climbed the tortuous trail back over the mountain and, by sundown, reached the mosque. There were still a number of Italian troops there, and they got a real start when we brought them under fire. It was all over in a few minutes, and we were soon marching a captain, a lieutenant, and forty Italian soldiers back over the mountain as prisoners. I was completely exhausted and asked the platoon leader to rope me between two of his men as we made our way back over the steep mountain trail. Even, so I repeatedly stumbled and fell down twice.

Colvo later learned that Kulick was evacuated as a POW and was liberated at the end of the war. Colvo was awarded his second Silver Star as a result of his escape and subsequent combat against his captors. He was later assigned to a staff job and on 13 June 1943 wrote home from Algiers: "As you can gather, my military life has been greatly altered. A week ago I commanded the finest combat engineer platoon in the American Army, and today I find myself at a desk as a staff officer with a high headquarters." Colvo was transferred to engineer intelligence where he studied aerial photographs and other sources to identify minefields, evaluate the condition of bridges and roads, among other things. He became an adept aerial photo interpreter, a talent that led to his distinguished career in cartography and photogrammetry. Colvo was serving in engineer intelligence as the Army landed in Sicily and worked its way up the Italian Peninsula. At the conclusion of the Italian campaign, he reported to another staff billet in England. Always in the thick of the fight, Colvo seemed to live a charmed existence as he survived hazard after hazard even in the most serene circumstances.

"My trip from Naples to England was not without incidents," Colvo said. "During my last night in Italy, I was on the Naples waterfront when the Germans bombed it. The next day I was flying in a C-47 (DC-3) across the Mediterranean when we ran into a series of violent thunderstorms. We got hit by lightening. The hit knocked out part of our electrical system and started a small fire in the back of the plane that we were able to extinguish. On my first night in London, I found myself witnessing a V-2 raid. I was spending the night with my cousin Pandia Calvocoresses overlooking Hyde Park. We were supposed to go to bomb shelters, but instead we went up on the roof to watch the fireworks. Before long, the falling shrapnel drove us back to shelter."

Colvo was given a week's leave to go to Ireland to marry June. Her grandfather, John Ross, performed the ceremony. He was the minister of Belfast's largest Protestant church. The minister asked Colvo if he knew June's age. Colvo told him that he understood she was nineteen. He was shocked to learn that she was not yet seventeen. But June's age did not prove any impediment, and they were married February 26, 1944. The marriage did not long survive the end of the war, although it did produce a daughter, Colette, who remains close to Colvo and became the Lady Mayoress of Canterbury.

Colvo met his second wife, Kay (Katherine Rose), in Arizona while he was working as a mining engineer after the war. Colvo and Kay had three children. His four children have produced nine grandchildren.

Colvo landed on Omaha Beach on "D plus five" with the advance staff of the First Army and stayed with the staff through the fall of Paris and the battle at the Ardennes. He directed the First Army Air Photo program throughout the European campaign. Colvo was in Europe when the war ended. On April 25 he wrote this in a letter home: "I spent the day going through a Nazi concentration camp (Buchenwald), and like thousands of other American soldiers, I shall never forget the sights I saw or the sounds I heard. This was one of the biggest camps overrun so far, and since congressmen and MPs have also been through it, I imagine that you have already heard a good deal about them. I hope that every soldier gets to see one of them, for they supply the real answer to why we came over here and what our men have fought and died for."

Before the end of the war, Colvo was offered a regular commission in the Army. He declined the offer but chose to remain in the reserves. Upon his return to the States he was mustered out and returned to his profession as a mining engineer. On February 11, 1949, he married Katherine Rose in Lordsburg, New Mexico. Colvo reported back to active duty for the Korean War and went to Korea in 1953, serving as a photo interpreter and intelligence analyst. This time when he was offered a regular commission in the Army with the promise of further schooling that led to his doctorate, he accepted. He served in Vietnam as a colonel, in charge of all U.S. mapping activity. In 1990, he was hired into the U.S. Geological Survey, Department of the Interior, by Rad Radlinski (now also a resident of Falcons Landing and a subject of one of these profiles). He retired from government service a second time in 1996. Kay Colvocoresses died in 1974, twenty-three years before Colvo moved to Falcons Landing. Colvo's two-bedroom duplex mirrors his love for hunting and fishing. The walls are adorned with mementos of the game that he has brought home. It has the distinct air of a bachelor's pad.

In 2004, the U.S. Library of Congress accepted Colvo's technical files of numerous publications and papers dealing principally with his post-World War II activities. The files focus on the technicalities of mapping from space. The Library of Congress assures Colvo that these files, which include two models of patented remote sensing systems, will soon be available for public viewing in Washington, D.C.

There are few men who have lived the full life of Col. Alden P. Colvocoresses, U.S. Army (Retired), holder of seven military decorations, veteran of fifteen combat campaigns, recipient of a doctorate in geodetic science, husband, father, and grandfather. As this is written, Colvo is eighty-six years old. He continues to hunt and fish. He also plays water volleyball in the Falcons Landing pool and is a popular figure in the community. When he ambles into one of the public spaces, he always has a smile. He lights up the room!

5

Elmer F. Smith

1965 photo courtesy of McDonnell Aircraft Corp.

On the front page of the 26 December 26, 1945, edition of the *New York Times* there appeared an article headlined, "Truman Flies Home Amid Ice and Sleet Grounding Airlines." The lead paragraphs read:

---

1.   This profile is based on a series of interviews with Elmer Smith commencing in July 2004, and upon records in his files.

President Truman was home for Christmas tonight after one of the most hazardous "sentimental journeys" ever undertaken by an American Chief of State.

After its take-off from Washington National Airport had been postponed for more than four hours in the hope of clearing weather, his plane, 'The Sacred Cow,' zoomed down the runway in a driving sleet storm with slush above the rims of the landing gear. Throughout the flight of almost six hours de-icing equipment threw large hunks of ice from the ship's propellers back against the fuselage.

The President was determined that nothing short of an outright refusal by the Army Transport Command should prevent his getting back to Independence for the annual family Christmas get-together. Veteran ATC pilots in Washington said that they had seen worse weather in their time, but never such weather in which a non-military flight was ventured.

The *Times* editorialized in the same edition:

The President landed at the municipal airport in Kansas City yesterday....The trip was described as his twenty-seven-year-old custom. It was also called hazardous. Certainly it troubles many American citizens.... This is no time to be careless. It is a time for considered judgment of essential values in a precarious moment of history. No one could possibly begrudge Harry S. Truman his holiday at home.... But there is a point at which Harry Truman becomes President and shoulders a responsibility that he ought not to set aside.

Ouch! Ouch for the pilots who had made the decision to fly the chief executive and commander in chief of the United States on this Christmas Eve. Ouch, whether or not the circumstances related in the newspaper accounts were so. The public perception would be shaped by what the *Times* and other national papers were reporting on those last days of 1945, only five months after the end of World War II. But the crew of the *Sacred Cow*, which included its copilot Maj. Elmer F. Smith of the U.S. Army Air Corps, was adamant that at no time was Mr. Truman's life or safety endangered. The flight was not delayed. It was not sleeting when they took off. When they encountered icing conditions, they were given permission to climb to a higher altitude into the clear. According to the crew, the flight was never in danger. In fact, it was a safe, comfortable flight for the president. The reporters who were covering the trip were describing the flight they had taken in a different aircraft, with different capabilities, flown at different altitudes, four hours later, which had not had the benefit of being in a hangar during the storms preceding the flight.

Nevertheless, it took some explaining by the pilot, Lt. Col. Henry T. "Hank" Myers to Gen. Hap Arnold, chief of the Army Air Corps, that he and his copilot, Maj. Elmer F. Smith, had operated well within the stringent margins of safety that were prescribed for the security of the president. While there were no serious consequences from the trip, such apocryphal tales endure. In his 1992 biography of Truman, historian David McCullough quoted from the *New York Times*[2] article and cited Mrs. Bess Truman's disapproval of the president's flight.

The unfavorable press received in this incident was one of the very few bumps in the otherwise smooth, exciting, and privileged thirty-year Air Force career of Elmer Smith, who retired in 1970 with the rank of colonel. Nine and a half years of that career were spent flying presidents, kings, ambassadors, generals, members of the cabinet, and other dignitaries around the world in the president's aircraft.

Douglas VC-54C "Sacred Cow"   USAF Museum

Currently the president's plane is known as *Air Force One*. In 1943, three C87s were modified to provide airline interiors for use by the White House and important persons. The C87 was selected because the bomb bay was close to the ground, which facilitated lifting the president into the aircraft. The aircraft was assigned to presidential duty in June 1943 and named *The Guess Where II*. It was retired from that duty in the summer of 1944.

2.   McCullough, David, *Truman*, New York: Simon & Shuster,1992, p 477

The second purpose-built aircraft for the president was a Douglas VC-54C, known as the *Sacred Cow*, which was pressed into presidential service in June 1944. It was unlike any other VC-54, because it had undergone significant modification to its flight characteristics and capabilities as well as to its comfortable, work-friendly interior. A special feature was the elevator that was installed behind the passenger cabin to lift President Franklin Roosevelt, in his wheelchair, in and out of the plane. Roosevelt used the *Sacred Cow* only once, in February 1945, when Hank Myers and Elmer Smith flew him to the USSR for the Yalta Conference. The ailing Roosevelt died shortly thereafter, in April 1945. He had been the first president of the United States to fly while in office when he attended the Casablanca Conference in 1943, traveling aboard a commercial Boeing 314 Clipper ship. President Theodore Roosevelt had been the first president to leave the country while in office. He, too, had flown but not while serving in the White House.

The senior pilots of these first presidential aircraft were selected from the ranks of commercial airlines, because they were the only multiengine pilots who had the necessary time in the cockpits to satisfy the requirements established for flying the country's president. (The required time was 12,000 hours. To put this in perspective, Elmer had accumulated only 5,000 hours after nine and a half years flying the presidential aircraft. He had 8,300 hours in the cockpit by the time he retired from the Air Force.)

On June 2, 1942, Japanese carrier-based aircraft bombed American installations at Dutch Harbor, Unalaska, Alaska. On the sixth of June, Japanese marines captured Kiska, while their army forces overran Attu, both undefended but strategically significant islands in the Aleutians. On the twelfth of June, the U.S. Army Air Corps' Eleventh Air Force heavy bombers struck the Japanese fleet at Kiska, hitting two Japanese cruisers and one destroyer while losing one B-24. Elmer recalled:

> After Dutch Harbor, Alaska was attacked by Japanese aircraft in June of 1942. I was part of a group of pilots who flew to Alaska for six weeks. We were tasked to check out pilots and fly support missions in the Alaska Theater. Shortly after my return to our home field in Long Beach, I was sent back to Alaska to fly as copilot and navigator with Hank Myers, who was flying a Senate committee that was checking on the progress of the war in Alaska. At the end of the trip, Hank asked me if I would like to come to Washington and fly as his copilot. The answer was an unqualified yes.
>
> I had no idea that I was volunteering to fly the president's plane. I didn't learn what my flight duties were going to be until after I got to Washington. That started nine and a half years of duty that gave me the opportunity to fly

around the world carrying presidents, cabinet members, kings, ambassadors, generals, and other dignitaries.

Elmer was born in Bishop, California, in 1917. His father was a miner, and his great-great-grandfather was a Mormon bishop. He graduated from San Jose State College (now University) in 1941, getting civilian pilot training from the Army while he was at the college. He was commissioned in the Army Air Corps as a pilot in 1942. Upon commissioning, he was assigned to the Air Transport Command, flying unarmed, single-engine aircraft from the aircraft plants on the West Coast inland to where they were more secure from potential Japanese shelling. In May 1941, the U.S. Army created the Air Corps Ferrying Command, which subsequently became the U.S. Air Transport Command (ATC) under the command of Maj. Gen. Harold L. George. The ATC was responsible for the delivery of planes and air transportable materials. Elmer said:

> Ten members of my class were assigned to deliver ten VulteeBT-13 Valiants to Gunter Field in Alabama. These were dual-seat, single-engine, training aircraft with a range of about 880 miles and a cruising speed of about 130 miles per hour. At that time, there were shortages of equipment for these airplanes. For example, we had radios, but they had no turning cranks, so all the radios were set on a frequency of 4495. We could talk to each other and ground stations but could not tune into navigation aids. There was also a shortage of maps, so they divided us into two flights and gave each flight leader a single map.
>
> The first leg of our flight was to Phoenix. No problem. The next morning we took off for El Paso. My flight leader regurgitated in our flight's sole map, opened the canopy, and threw the map out, leaving us without a navigation aid. Our flight joined the other for aid in navigating, since none of us had ever flown more than a hundred miles from our home base. We all followed the one pilot with the map who passed over Tucson and kept on the same heading, when we should have turned east to go to Rodeo and Cochise and then on to El Paso.
>
> The time had passed when I figured we should have been in El Paso. We hadn't seen any railroads or highways, and we became concerned that we were lost. We were entering mountainous territory and being the last plane in the flight, I flew down and buzzed a ranch. By the time I got back to altitude, six of the planes were landing on a dry lake bed, because they were getting low on fuel. The pilot with the map and two other pilots spotted a railroad beyond the dry lake and flew on, following the railroad north.
>
> At this point, I had plenty of fuel and didn't feel a need to land on the lake bed. I flew back to the railroad tracks, turned east, and after fifteen or twenty minutes, I saw smoke stacks on the horizon and flew over a town but saw no

airport. I figured there would be Americans there, so I landed in the sagebrush beside the smelter. I hadn't anymore than got the engine stopped before I was soon surrounded by all these little Mexican kids coming out of the sagebrush. They wanted to know how come I didn't land at the airport. I found that the airport was a nearby grass field with an old barn used for a hangar. I flew into the airport, where the Mexican army met me. They took me to a phone, where I was able to contact the American consul, and I asked him to send a message to Biggs Field in El Paso and gave them the names of the pilots on the dry lake bed. I told them that I didn't have any information on the other three pilots, and I signed off as Lieutenant Smith.

There was more than one dry bed lake between where I was in Chihuahua, which is over two hundred miles south of El Paso, and the one where the six pilots were. To make certain of the exact lake they were on so as to direct trucks to deliver fuel to them, I took a Mexican pilot with me and flew back to the other planes. I talked to the pilots from the air and told them that fuel was on the way. I returned to the airport, dropped off the Mexican pilot, refueled, and flew on to Biggs Field. When I landed, I was met by the base commander who asked, "Where in the hell have you been? We know about the six on the dry lake and the other three, but, where have you been?" I had to defend myself and told him that I was the one who had sent him all the information as to our flight's disposition. It was not an auspicious flight for any of us.

Vultee BT-13B "Valiant"   USAF Museum

Hank Myers, Elmer, and their crew flew their first overseas flight with the *Guess Where II* in July 1943, when they completed an around-the-world flight with a delegation of five U.S. senators charged with observing and reporting on the progress of the war. The stretch from India to China took them over the famous route known as "The Hump." During World War II, the ATC flew 1,118 round trips carrying 5,327 tons of precious payload to supply Chinese and

American troops fighting in that area of operations. All overland routes were held by the Japanese. Occasionally, Japanese aircraft would challenge the unarmed Americans. Flying conditions could be horrendous, and the landing fields were primitive. The Hump operation was the first test of the ATC's capability to move vast quantities of cargo over long, difficult routes. It was the birth of mass strategic airlift.

Elmer described a harrowing overwater flight:

> In late August of '43 we flew from Chabua, India, to Kunming, China, over "The Hump." We flew the route at twenty thousand feet, somewhat higher than the usual route taken by the pilots of the Air Transport Command. It was viewed as one of the more hazardous legs of our trip, and some of the senators requested side arms for use in the event that we went down. We didn't accommodate them. After stops in Kunming and Chungking, we returned to India. In early September, we left Colombo, Ceylon. The next leg of the trip was a historic flight between Ceylon and Australia. It was the first time a land-based aircraft had made an overwater flight of 3,200 nautical miles. We had nothing but islands held by the Japanese on our left, and water on our right. The flight time was well over sixteen hours. After we made the flight, the Army Air Corps installed extra fuel tanks in C54s to give them the range to fly such routes more safely. Many top military and government officials were against our flying this long, overwater route, because if we got into trouble, there were no nice options. When we arrived in Carnavron, Australia, we had about seven hundred gallons of fuel left, which gave us about two plus hours of flying time or another five hundred nautical miles distance.

Elmer gives presentations to civic groups about his experiences. He tells of the routine they had established with the pilot and copilot alternating flying times on long trips by one pilot taking the controls for a two-hour period while the other rested. He tells of being struck by lightening twice. One time, the jolt knocked him out of a bunk. The aircraft lost its antennas and compasses. He tells how Bess Truman's mother also used the elevator fashioned for Franklin Roosevelt on the *Sacred Cow* to embark on the aircraft. A favorite tale relates the flying of President Truman to the historic Potsdam conference attended by Stalin and initially Winston Churchill, and after the retirement of Churchill, by Clement Atlee of Great Britain. It was the conference that had the unintended consequence of solidifying the "Iron Curtain" and initiating the Russian-American Cold War.

Elmer learned about protocol, including the maxim that you never delivered a dignitary to an airfield reception early. There was at least one prominent passenger who spent so much time with a bottle of spirits that Elmer feared that he would fall into the controls when he visited the cockpit.

These audiences often ask him, "Who, among those important people you flew, did you like most?" and, "Who did you like least?" Smith always identifies President Truman as the person who was most friendly and considerate of the crew. Mrs. Roosevelt comes in a very close second. There were none that he disliked, but some, such as Gen. George Marshall and Madame Chiang Kai-shek, were less friendly. He described some of those meetings:

Mrs. Roosevelt was especially considerate. At the end of a flight around the Caribbean and South America, she came up to the cockpit and thanked us for a nice trip. She said, "You are busy and so am I, but I want you to come to the White House tonight for cocktails and dinner." My wife, Joyce, was at the airport to greet me. I had been away for an extended period, and she was looking forward to an evening together. When I told her that I had to rush home, take a shower, and leave for the White House for dinner with the first lady, she was understandably disappointed. This was not how she had planned our evening.

Mrs. Roosevelt had the enlisted crew in for cocktails early, and the officers later for cocktails and dinner. The president didn't join us because he was not feeling well. Once dinner was over, Mrs. Roosevelt sent me home to Joyce with an apology for taking me away on my first evening home. A few days later, she invited Joyce to the White House for tea. She gave me a cherry wood salad bowl with mixing tools. The bowl had a silver inscription—"In memory of our Caribbean and South Atlantic Trip"—and her signature.

President Truman was probably our favorite. Once we would be airborne, he would leave his compartment and come to the cabin to sit in either the pilot or copilot seat to visit and talk about the flight for sometimes as long as an hour. When traveling from Washington to his home in Independence, Missouri, he would ride in the cabin until we got to Cincinnati and would say, "Well, I got you boys past all the breweries, I guess you can handle it the rest of the way on your own." He would then return to his compartment.

In a flight from Washington to Key West, via Jacksonville, Florida, he decided he would "put one over on the press" who were following in a Constellation that had departed twelve minutes after we had taken off. The routine was to have the press plane overtake us and land at Key West to meet the president's plane. The president came forward into the cabin to check our position vis-à-vis that of the press. He expressed the desire to land before the press aircraft so that he would be on the ground to greet them rather than the other way around. We complied and landed at Boca Chica, Key West, five minutes before the media's Constellation. The president quickly disembarked and met the press with a note pad and pencil to interview them as they were leaving their aircraft.

While still flying the *Sacred Cow*, Elmer flew to such diverse spots as the USSR, Rio de Janeiro, Quebec, Berlin, and Mexico. (The *Sacred Cow* was replaced by a modified DC-6, which was named the *Independence* in honor of President Truman's home town in Missouri. It was retired in October 1961 to the Air Force Museum, where it was restored as an exhibition piece.) In the *Independence*, Elmer flew to thirty countries including Newfoundland, Switzerland, Venezuela, Iran, Ecuador, and many points in between.

The *Sacred Cow* was actually the "birthplace" of the U.S. Air Force. President Truman signed the "National Security Act of 1947" while on board the aircraft. President Eisenhower increased the presidential fleet to three aircraft, updating the new planes with sophisticated electronic equipment. In 1958, there was a major step forward with the Air Force introducing two Boeing 707 jets into the fleet, with the call sign *Air Force One*, which became the official name after President Kennedy took office.

In February 1945, the Big Three allied leaders—Stalin, Churchill, and Roosevelt—met at Yalta in the Crimea to discuss the reorganization of Europe in the postwar period. The secret Yalta agreement provided protocols for the occupation and governing of Germany, the independence of Poland, the creation of Yugoslavia as a state, the reaffirmation of the Russian intention to fight Japan, and significant agreements on the reordering of the post-war world.

Elmer recalled highlights of that trip:

> Our Yalta trip was full of surprises. We left Washington for the Yalta Conference on 2 February 1945, flying to Bermuda, the Azores, Casablanca, Tunis, and into Malta. From Malta we made a survey flight to Saki, the airport in Russia that we would use when we flew the president to the Yalta Conference. From the airport at Saki, we were taken by bus to a Russian resort that had not been damaged during the war, although it had changed hands several times between the Russians and Germans. We were billeted in a sanitarium which had comfortable accommodations. Our first experience with Russian customs came when we asked where we could take a shower. We were escorted to a building that had a shower room. The shower was much like we see in men's locker rooms—a large open area with multiple shower heads that afford no privacy. We noticed that there was a pass-through partition that separated us from a group of Russian women clothed in white smocks and big rubber boots. The women stoked the pot-bellied stove that provided hot water. Once we were in the shower, the women, still fully clothed, joined us, adjusting the water temperature and scrubbing our backs. It was a unique experience for us, and once you got over the shock of it, not so bad. We were later treated to a Russian lunch with rather basic fare but accompanied with a welcome glass of vodka.

We returned to Malta to await the arrival of the president, who was scheduled to travel there by ship. On February the second of forty-five, we departed with the president for Saki. From Saki, the president traveled to Yalta by auto, a seventy-mile trip. We had a fighter escort of six P-38s for this leg of our flight. It was the only time we had ever had such an escort.

We took the aircraft for a test flight on the eleventh and a push rod broke on one of the engines. We had a spare engine at Saki but discovered that it had been sent back to Cairo. We had a problem. The president was due the next morning for an 0700 takeoff. So we pulled another C-54 in front of ours, and we exchanged engines. The Russians brought up two big searchlights which provided us with both light and much-needed heat. By 0600, we could make a test flight and found that the new engine was fine, and that everything checked out for flight. The president and his party arrived shortly after 0700, and we were airborne by 0755 on the twelfth, for a flight to Deversoir, an airport along the Suez Canal. Our fighter escort missed takeoff and didn't catch up with us until we were over Turkey.

The Independence
Photo by Boeing

In October 1950, Frenchy Williams, Elmer Smith, and the crew of the *Independence* flew President Truman from Washington, D.C., to Wake Island, a small coral station in the middle of the Pacific, to meet with General MacArthur who was serving as Supreme Commander of the Allied Powers, commanding the forces waging war in Korea. MacArthur had other responsibilities overseeing the reconstruction of Japan following World War II which made him, effectively, the dictator of Japan. There had been little admiration or respect between the president and MacArthur before this, their first meeting. Mr. Truman had characterized MacArthur as "a play actor and bunco man."[3] MacArthur, reportedly, was no more enthusiastic about Truman. The press was eager to play up the differences between the two, and there were stories of how MacArthur had tried to embarrass the president by circling the airport in his aircraft before landing so as to put Truman in the position of having to wait on him. But it didn't happen that way.

Elmer recalled, "As the *Independence* taxied up to the parking area, officials, press, and personnel on Wake Island gathered to witness the meeting of the president of the United States and the general. History has shown that the meeting between the two was cordial and productive."

Elmer Smith left the "best flying job in the Air Force" in October 1951 to pursue a more conventional career in the Air Force from the Pentagon, to squadron commander, to weapons system management and procurement. His career took him many places where speaking before large groups was required. He continues to make public-service presentations on his experiences now that he is retired and living at Falcons Landing. He retired from the Air Force in 1970 and worked in government for the Department of Energy before retiring a second time. He and his wife, the former Joyce Robinson of Milwaukee, moved to Falcons Landing on November 8, 1996. Tragically and unexpectedly, Joyce died two days later. She was an exceptional lady. Although she did not have a college degree, she studied the law in night school and passed the bar examination while holding a secretarial job. There are three daughters and five grandchildren.

When Elmer looks back on his career, he can recall the faces, the courtesies, and the idiosyncrasies of the dozens of prominent figures who made the history of the twentieth century. There were Harry S. Truman, Eleanor Roosevelt, Bernard Baruch, Dwight D. Eisenhower, Douglas MacArthur, Madame Chiang Kaishek, Dean Acheson, foreign presidents, prime ministers, kings, shahs, members of the United States Cabinet, and congressmen. Not a bad life, and what memories! They are memories he often shares when prompted by an eager and worldly audience of friends at Falcons Landing.

---

3.   McCullough, p703.

6

Mollie Van Harlingen

There are many prominent entertainers who have served the public well into their eighties. Bob Hope made his last overseas tour to entertain the troops in 1991 during the first Gulf War at the age of eighty-eight. George Burns appeared in the movie *Oh, God!* in 1977 at the age of eighty-one and was on the stage in Las Vegas in 1994 at the age of ninety-eight. The hilarious Senor Wences, a frequent performer on the *Ed Sullivan Show*, was still performing at the age of eighty-four, appearing on the stage of New York's Chateau Madrid in 1980. Leopold Stokowski was directing symphony orchestras at the age of ninety, as was Igor Stravinsky when he was well into his eighties. Arthur Rubinstein didn't retire from piano concerts until he was eighty-nine. Irving Berlin didn't quite make the list—he was only seventy-four when he wrote his last musical.

---

1. This profile is based on a series of interviews starting in February, 2005 and from written inputs from Mrs. Van Harlingen.

Mollie Van Harlingen of Falcons Landing isn't alone in being a creative, productive octogenarian. Over the past nine years, she has written, produced, and directed twenty-four musical shows at Falcons Landing and has directed a chorus in which more than fifty people have sung to her piano accompaniment. The productions have included: annual Christmas galas; an opera review; *The World According to Cole Porter*; *All God's Children Got Music*, exploring the spectrum of religious song; *Accentuate the Positive*, remembering World War II; *In Spring a Young Man's Fancy...*, a musical paean to the emotion of love; *Guys and Dolls*; and *Scrooge*, to name but a few. Mollie announced the December 17, 2002, Christmas gala in the *Falcons Landing News* as follows:

'Tis a week before Christmas and all
through our house
We all should be stirring, every
dog, cat and mouse.
We should not be nestled quite
snug in our bed
But should sit on the edge of our
bedstead instead
For at 8 o'clock sharp, there'll arise
such a clatter
We should dash to the auditorium
to see what's the matter—
And there to our wondering eyes
will appear
Our chorus—our friends—and
beaucoup Christmas cheer!
Ukrainian bells, and some
jingle bells, too—
Four snow-bound lovers with
much whoop-de-doo
A waltz that is nutty, a cat
that is high—
A king and a queen and
a homesick GI!
The music's calypso, the music
is grand
We'll be so delightful, we'll give

us a hand!
And when it's all over—it's over
we fear
Our gala will not come again
'til next year!

While the talent she directs at Falcons Landing may, for the most part, be amateur, Mollie is not. For more than five years during the 1950s, she was a director of religious broadcasting and a producer in the Department of Public Affairs at CBS in New York City. She also has performed for many years as a concert pianist, an example of the stretch of her creativity. There are those who propose that there is a continuum of creativity that extends across a spectrum with "interpretation" at one end and "innovation" at the other, each having equal but different artistic or productive values. At one end of the continuum are performers, who for the most part, are interpreters. Original thinkers, such as composers or producers, are at the innovative end of the continuum. Mollie has demonstrated skills across this spectrum from artistic creator with productions at CBS, Falcons Landing, and other venues to artistic performer as a concert pianist. During the decades of the 1960s and 1970s, Mollie played and traveled extensively with a group of sixty duo-pianists—extraordinary, Julliard-trained women who gave many formal concerts throughout Connecticut. They frequently played Bach's three-piano concerti, and in the early 1970s they presented *The Twelve-Piano Symphony*, a concert with twelve pianists sharing the stage, six on grand pianos, and Mollie playing the lead.

During the eighties, she played many two-piano concerts in South Carolina with talented colleague Peggy Peyton, who studied music in Paris as a beneficiary of a Fulbright Scholarship. Recently Mollie was invited to play a concert with Peyton in the South Carolina governor's mansion, but time and distance precluded her from making the commitment.

Mollie has had a colorful life filled with both privilege and adversity. Born in Australia, Mollie McCall moved to the United States as a child and has enjoyed the luxury of being raised in a secure, caring family that valued and encouraged scholarship and a dedication to the arts. However, she also has been tested. She lost three husbands; she had her postgraduate legal schooling truncated to care for an ailing parent; and she experienced being at the financial edge, struggling to help support the family. But she has been more than a survivor. She has succeeded where others may have surrendered. She is a lady of great talent, energy, vitality, substance, and grit who can still elicit an appreciative male whistle. Here's her story in her words:

> I was born in 1920 in Melbourne, Australia, on the rather tactless date, for a British citizen, of July Fourth. I lived there only two years before being brought to America.
>
> My mother was Florence May Beresford-Jones, English-Welsh, a delightful, fun-loving lady of four feet eleven inches, who played tournament tennis, loved to dance, and taught mathematics at the University of Melbourne.
>
> My father was Oswald Walter Samuel McCall, Scotch-Irish, a dynamic and handsome man of six feet one inch, who also was possessed of a robust sense of humor—and great charisma. He was a bit of a scalawag in his youth, avoiding school until, forced upon him, he finished university with distinction. His career as a clergyman ran the gamut of racing his horse, Bob, before Australian bush fires in order to preach at isolated villages, to later, earning the degrees of doctor of divinity and doctor of literature.
>
> Reportedly, my dad's parents met in Ireland, went separately to Australia, met again, and married. There were eleven in the McCall family when his father moved them into a larger Melbourne house that had been infected with tuberculosis. The sad consequences of such a choice were not appreciated in those days. First, Dad's father died. Then Tom, the eldest died. Then the sisters, Lizzie and then Lilly, who was engaged to be married. Then Bert, of the golden singing voice. As the youngest, my dad's memories were filled with admonitions: "Now Ossie, you must be brave." One of the five survivors, his brother Bill, became town clerk of Melbourne—equivalent to our mayor. Dad's mother lived into her nineties.
>
> Just why my dad decided to move us to America is not so hard to understand, given his lively temperament. He had already served with the Aussies in World War I. He was a keen student of history and found Australia provincial and isolated. England was the "home" country. He felt shackled by the conservative Methodist views of the time that, for instance, frowned on his young wife's dancing. He was an adventurous romantic. I think he sailed to America, albeit with two young daughters and a wife pregnant with twins, with an overwhelming need to conquer new worlds! We lost little twin Patsy as a baby, so that I grew up with an older sister, Betty and a younger sister, Peggy.
>
> We arrived in San Francisco and found California to be a pleasure. We daughters often teased Dad that, on arrival, he had not the least idea whether he would: (1) investigate Hollywood for an acting job; or (2) investigate the Indians just so he could be part of American history. It became evident, however, that his heart remained wedded to the idealism and faith of the church.
>
> The year was 1922. The First Congregational Church of Berkeley was looking for an interim, short-term pastor while it investigated a minister from Boston. My father agreed to fill that temporary role. Smitten with his minis-

try, the congregation withdrew inquiries about the Bostonian, and Dad stayed with the church for seventeen years.

Mollie describes her father's theological bent as being an independent thinker and a liberal. A devout Christian, his theological focus was on "biblical criticism," an all inclusive term for various approaches to study the meanings of biblical passages. It relies more on reason and the study of history, than on faith, inspiration, or revelation. His association with the Congregationalists was fortuitous, given their devotion to liberal theology and the precept that each church organization should be autonomous. She recalled:

> From the outset, his Berkeley ministry was a splendid, going concern. A new church was built, the congregation rapidly doubled, the students and faculty from the University of California campus flocked to hear him.
>
> You can imagine the rich, academic atmosphere of Berkeley that complemented my father's imbuing in my sisters and me a respect for scholarship. He relished the challenging intellectual association with the university faculty. The children I played with were, for the most part, children of these professors. As a result, I have always had a great affection for academic communities and, as I look back on my life, I realize much of it has been spent in one academic environment or another.
>
> My father wrote under the name of O. W. S. McCall. He preached and lectured in a wide variety of pulpits, both religious and sectarian, as his reputation spread, frequently disappearing to Chicago, New York, or London. Although he was particularly noted for the eloquence of his preaching—a dramatic figure, in and out of the pulpit—the scholarship and poetry of his seven books were also recognized.
>
> Meanwhile, up in the Berkeley hills, my mother was coping with three active daughters and a lively church. Always the romantic, my dad had built us a Spanish-style home on the hilltop behind the campus—complete with a logia, a patio, tile floors, and several balconies. From that vantage, we would watch the fog roll in through the Golden Gate every evening—cover the Bay and devour Berkeley.
>
> As a warm, loving mother, Mum was faultless, always resourceful, always cheerful. Though scared to death, she would push a pillow behind her small frame and, with much clashing of gears, would taxi her young up and down the steep Berkeley hills. She was the hostess of our regular monthly Friday night "Open House" gatherings—delightful, crowded affairs—all those cucumber sandwiches.
>
> Besides the de rigueur assortment of cats, kittens, and dogs, we had exotic pets: Cinny, the marmoset monkey, Paddy the loquacious parrot, Peter Pan and Wendy, marmosets who had their own high chairs at meal hours.

The family contributed to the opening of Lake Tahoe in the twenties. I recall the narrow, dirt roads and the excitement of a forest fire. For seventeen years we spent a part of our summers there. One year, we lost a school chum aquaplaning on the icy water. Another year we were lost in the mountains while on horseback.

In 1928, a Chinese lady fleeing an abusive American husband came to Dad for help. Characteristic of our parents, we took her two children, Lydia and Peter, into our home for more than a year, walking them to school using hidden routes to protect them from their father.

To the surprise of our friends, we girls fenced, played lacrosse and chess. We spoke with English accents and lived in a tight little English island in the middle of Berkeley. Across the years, we frequently exchanged letters and packages with our Australian relatives, listened to such records as "Bird Calls of the Australian Bush," and, of course, awoke without fail at four AM every Christmas morning to hear the king's greetings from Buckingham Palace. So it is no surprise that my sisters subsequently married Englishmen.

I was given a great education at Bentley, a private college preparatory school for girls in Berkeley, grades seven through twelve. There, I wore a uniform, acted in Shakespearean dramas, sang in the glee club, played on the tennis team, was an uneasy cheerleader, and became student body president.

There was always a love of theater in our home. We girls memorized Shakespearean soliloquies from recordings of John Barrymore, Maurice Evans, and others. We would declaim them freely about the house, much like Jo in *Little Women*. At school, I frequently played men's roles and was a stirring Marc Anthony, Richard the Third, and Shylock. Our church, unusual for those days, owned a radio station, and station KRE gave us still another venue in which to perform.

However, mostly I was addicted to music. From age six, I took two private piano lessons a week, played in many recitals and for school and church events. In the ten years I was studying with that studio, I progressed from easy scales to Gershwin's "Rhapsody" and Beethoven's "Appasionata." It was an exciting journey.

In 1936–1937, Daddy took a year's sabbatical leave, and we all went to England, postponing my senior year and contributing greatly to my education. We lived in a charming cottage near London with a thatched roof and the enchanting address: The Bridal Path Cottage, Loudwater Lane, Rickmansworth, Hertfordshire, England. We loved it! When sightseeing was difficult, we attacked the local library. That winter, I read practically all of Dickens, Scott, Thackery, and the Brontes. The rest of the year we discovered Ireland, Scotland, and Wales. We wrung our hands over Edward, the Prince of Wales—I was 16 and in love with him, waited overnight on the curb of the mall to see George and Elizabeth's coronation parade, went to a garden party at Buckingham Palace where Princesses Elizabeth and Margaret Rose, ages eight and six, wore little white gloves and were delightful.

When we returned to the States, my father was called to the First Congregational Church of Chicago, and we moved in January to Evanston, Illinois. Andrew Dole of the pineapple family, and a parishioner, generously bought us a house near the shore of Lake Michigan. It was beautiful and large—so large that we dubbed two of the fifteen-by-twenty-two-foot rooms 'The Embarrassment' and "The Superfluity." I finished my senior year at the Evanston Township High School but still got my diploma from Bentley. Evanston High School was very competitive—very big. Except for me, our large, advanced physics class consisted of all boys, all building cars in their backyards—and here I was, a refugee from a girls' school. How they cheered when I raised my test scores from the initial zeroes I had collected.

I enrolled at Northwestern upon graduation. By now, my older sister had left home, but Peggy and I were still living with our parents—indeed, we did so all through our college years.

This was the 1940s, and during the raging of World War II, I was stuck in isolationist Evanston, Illinois. I changed my major from political science to journalism, because I was impressed with the work of Helen Kirkpatrick, the *Chicago Daily News* war correspondent operating with the troops in Europe. I was certain that was what I wanted to do. However, while earning my degree in journalism and taking frequent reporting assignments in Chicago, I became disenchanted with the discipline and with the lifestyle and began to consider the law.

Now, the plot thickens. At this point, in 1943, Dad decided to accept a call from the United Church of Canada, to a beautiful cathedral church in Vancouver, British Columbia. He bought a house in that lovely city, and he, my mother, Peg, and I moved to Canada.

But I was far from content. At the age of twenty-three, what I really wanted was to live in the United States, not Canada, to study law, and to stop living at home. I was becoming an adult. So, with great reluctance, my parents let me go and put me on a train bound for Chicago. This was at the height of the war, and the only money I was allowed to take across the border was five dollars. So for four days, all I had to eat was an orange in the morning and a doughnut at night. My train, the Empire Builder, was full of soldiers—I was very popular.

On arrival in Chicago, Mollie enrolled in the Northwestern School of Law with an academic scholarship and led a busy life. Weekdays she attended classes from eight to twelve, then boarded a trolley for Chicago's West Side to start work at 12:30 at the Illinois Lock Company. She described those early days:

In the office, I was such a neophyte and easy target of veteran workers who, for instance, sent me to the supply closet for a paper stretcher. At five o'clock, I would take the elevated to my rented room in Evanston, wait on tables at the local restaurant, and then study for the next day's classes. Weekends were devoted to library research.

My favorite subjects were torts and contracts. My bête noir was criminal law, largely because the exam questions were invariably based on our casebook's footnotes, and I didn't have the time to research them.

In 1945 (I had just completed two years of my three-year law course), I learned that all was not well in Vancouver. In 1943 my older sister had married an Englishman in the Foreign Service and moved to London. And in 1944 Peg had completed her college degree at the University of British Columbia and moved to London to study at the Royal Academy of Dramatic Art, where she met and married her husband. The distressing news was that Mum and Dad were ill; particularly my father, who was in a grave condition. Since I was the daughter closest at hand, I took the year off from school to go to Vancouver to provide care for my parents.

By the time Mollie was no longer needed as a caregiver at home and free to return to law school, too much time had passed for her to continue and she would have had to start all over again.

"I was not willing to do that," she said. "However, back in my undergraduate days, I had met and grown fond of Ken Mansfield, a Phi Beta Kappa, a member of the debate team, a musical scholar—he was quite an impressive guy. We used to have discussions on the merits of German versus Russian literature and music. When I entered law school, he had been drafted and sent overseas. When he returned, we decided that we would marry."

It was a good marriage. The young couple moved to New Haven, Connecticut, where Ken entered Yale on the GI Bill and earned a Ph.D. in international relations.

"That was an interesting time to be at school," Mollie recalled. "Most of the students were veterans, also on the GI Bill, so the student housing was full of returned military. Many of the men were still recovering from the shock of war. Tales from the South Pacific flowed freely during meal and cocktail hours, many of them graphic and distressing. I supported Ken during this period with a series of interesting jobs. I worked for Russell Davenport. Davenport had been a contributor to the team of the 1940 presidential candidate Wendell Willkie, and he also worked with Edward R. Murrow. My job with Russell was to read the country's leading newspapers and, once a week, to compile a three-page condensed list of the major stories and most important news events for use on Murrow's CBS news broadcasts."

Mollie then secured a job at the Yale Law School as director of faculty services which she considered "great sport."

"I was in charge of the clerical staff, edited and did ghost writing for professors who were writing books, and I oversaw the publishing process," she said. "There were a number of prominent academicians with whom I worked, for instance: Myers McDougal who wrote on city planning; Eugene Rostow, subsequently dean of the school, who wrote *A National Policy for the Oil Industry*; Fred Rodell who introduced me to his friends Supreme Court Justice Willliam O. Douglas and Secretary of State Dean Acheson—and especially, David Reisman. I worked with Reisman closely on his best seller, *The Lonely Crowd*."

Those were wonderful years for Mollie and Ken. She found her work intellectually stimulating. The faculty was not at all "ivory tower academic," but very much involved in the real world, she said. Ken had always been a brilliant student, and he was in nirvana. And then, just as he finished schooling, she lost him. Mollie said:

> I pulled myself together, as one must, and continued at my job there at Yale. I brought my parents down from Vancouver to New Haven, a relief for all of us. Dad took over the ministry of the First Congregational Church in Milford, Connecticut, and I moved in with them for a year to take care of Mum.
>
> Life returned to an active, interesting pace. I took part in the law school's production of *Trial by Jury* and joined Dad in a weekly radio program during which we provided a clergyman and his daughter's views in replies to written questions of listeners. And, the pièce de résistance, I served on a TV game show panel, distinguishing myself by asking Jose Greco, the best-known Spanish dancer and choreographer of the period, "And what do you do?" "I dance," he said laconically. Debby Reynolds was also on the panel, a remarkably well-informed woman.

Mollie met Joe O'Connor at the Yale Drama School. He was a talented and brainy guy, recognized as a "Student of the House" for academic achievement and was doing graduate work in playwriting. They had so much in common, including a love of the arts reinforced by Joe's robust sense of the ridiculous. At Yale, Joe had taken some classes with the French composer, Darius Milhaud, a member of 'Les Six,' who had been a teacher of Dave Brubeck and Burt Bacharach. A Jew, he had fled Germany in 1939 to become one of the most prolific composers of the twentieth century. Notwithstanding their commitment to one another, Joe and Mollie decided to wait on marriage until Joe had a chance to hone his skills, write at length, and, hopefully, publish.

Mollie's favorite play written by Joe was based on the life of Ezra Pound, the American poet who, in the late 1930s, was active in defending fascism and attempting to avert war. Pound had made a series of addresses to American troops from Rome attempting to dissuade them from their mission. At the end of the war, he stood trial in the United States, was found unfit to plead on the grounds of insanity, and was committed to Saint Elizabeth's Hospital in Washington, D.C. Strangely, his imprisonment led to an artistic renewal.

Joe's writing, with its orientation to Greek drama and classical themes, wasn't popular and didn't sell. The couple did not want to postpone their nuptials any further, so they married and moved to New York City.

Some members of the law faculty who knew Richard Salant, then president of CBS, wrote a letter of introduction to him on Mollie's behalf. They all signed, asking that CBS look after this "promising young woman."

"On arrival in New York, and with scant cash, I again attacked a television game show and won $75, the first month's rent for our Greenwich Village one-room apartment," Mollie said. "The apartment had seduced us with its garden, complete with classic Roman statues, its balcony, and its fireplace. So what if it didn't have a kitchen?"

"Then I heard from CBS, and they started me on the radio program *Gangbusters*. And before long, I was transferred to the Department of Public Affairs and became a producer. My first assignment was to write and produce a show on, 'Which makes the better pet—a cat or a dog?' The research was fun and extended all the way from the Egyptian worship of cats to Samuel Johnson's soliloquy to his dog—'Oh, I'm not so great. Stop fawning on me....'"

In the meantime, Joe took a job as a typist at an ad agency to bolster the family resources. Within weeks he was creating clever ads. Though he disliked the advertising business, he was a natural in that creative medium and rapidly climbed the ladder to copy chief. By 1958, he was a vice president of Geyer Advertising at 666 Fifth Avenue. Mollie said:

> We enjoyed Greenwich Village, the benign fifties in New York City, and we had a stimulating life together. I became a director of religious broadcasting and had a board of directors of the major denominations and faiths work-

ing with me, from Christian Science and Mormon to Jesuit Catholic and American Baptist; there were eighteen in all. I recall my fascination when the Russian Orthodox priest would sweep into our building with his robe and high crown to sit in on our meetings and discuss broadcasting policy and religious themes. The job was challenging, because not only was I in charge of arranging regular religious broadcasting, such as 'Church of the Air,' with clergy all around the country, but I also traveled to various cities, such as Salt Lake City, to establish remote broadcasts. And there was more: I was responsible for such seasonal broadcasts as Christmas and Easter, frequently with celebrities, and for specials such as the Jewish Tri-Centennial celebration and the National Day of Prayer programs with, I remember, the lovely Deborah Kerr as narrator. My work included auditioning choral groups, selecting music, directing dramatic presentations, and, once a week, meeting with other producers to discuss program ideas. CBS was exciting because I worked with very interesting, prominent personalities.

Mollie knew Edward R. Murrow, who is probably the most renowned figure in the history of American broadcast journalism. David Halberstam once wrote that Murrow was "one of those rare, legendary figures who was as good as his myth." There is a plaque at CBS that reads, "He set standards of excellence that remain unsurpassed." She worked on the phone with Daniel Shorr, the last of Murrow's legendary team, when he was in Russia. Walter Cronkite occasionally conferred with her about some program impasse. Then Mollie took a break in her career:

> From 1953 to 1957, I was in and out of miscarriages—three to be exact. So on a fourth pregnancy, I knew I must take better care of myself. I resigned from CBS, and we moved to Connecticut. I lost that child too, at about six months.
>
> Searching for a less demanding position, I joined the National Council on Alcoholism, a national medical organization, not a rehabilitation program, located on Fifth Avenue. I was in charge of public relations and coined the phrase, "Alcoholism is a disease not a disgrace." I held that job less than a year when I got pregnant again. So I resigned, went home, and literally lay down for nine months. For those months, Joe would make and leave my breakfast and lunch by my bedside before he would leave for work. In the fullness of time, and with great joy, we welcomed our daughter, Collin.

A Silvermine 12 Piano Concert with Mollie playing lead piano at the left front.

Photo courtesy of Mollie Van Harlingen

In 1963, our long quest for a son was fulfilled when, with equal joy, we adopted laughing little ten-month-old Jonathan. When we met, he toddled straight up to Joe and presented him with a toy truck. It was love at first sight.

Mollie settled in to the full-time rearing of her children. Soon, however, she was seduced by her long-standing love of music, and she joined the Silverman School of Music, playing concerts with the Silverman Duo-Pianists, a group made up of sixty superb women pianists. She began teaching daughter Collin the piano and before long was teaching about thirty students. She talked about her music:

> In the late sixties I was invited to head the piano department of the New Caanan Country School, considered one of the finest day schools in the country. I moved into a four-room studio on the top floor of their main building where I had eight pianos, including two Steinway grands—and a large number of students.
>
> The school encouraged the conduct of a full music program throughout the school year. Before long, I was presenting ambitious "Happenings" in our auditorium, writing material for both faculty and students. What delighted me most about the regimen was that the boys, often little reluctant dragons who avoided piano lessons and tolerated, at best, saxophones, gradually became converts and as enthusiastic as their sisters.
>
> Meanwhile, at home, Collin was playing up a storm and, at the young age of thirteen, won a Connecticut music competition and played Rubenstein's Piano Concerto in D Minor with the Norwalk Symphony Orchestra. Such excitement!
>
> Joe was enjoying a successful career in the advertising business in New York City when, in 1978, Geyer Advertising went bankrupt, and abruptly he

was out of a job. He tried for several years to find another position, both in New York and in Connecticut, but advertising is a young man's game and, in his late fifties, he had but sporadic luck. He eventually did what he did best; he went back to graduate school, received two more degrees, one in education and a second in library science, and became the head reference librarian at the University of Bridgeport in Connecticut.

By now, I had started teaching full time. I had ninety-three private students each week, some faculty, some kids, some university students. My day was from seven to seven, propelled by interest in each student. I was also adjudicating the annual Connecticut state piano competitions and entered my own students in solo, concerto, and duo events with at least forty teams entered in the latter.

Joe and Mollie's sojourn through Fairfield County, Connecticut, included living in the towns of Stamford, Darien, Norwalk, Wilton, and Westport. But, in 1982, they decided to retire and moved to the historic and beautiful city of Beaufort, South Carolina, where Joe's sister and brother had relocated. There in Beaufort, Mollie joined Century 21 and sold commercial real estate, which she found more challenging and more remunerative than residential sales. She likened discovering properties in town and out on the barrier islands to a treasure hunt. But again, Mollie's love of music prevailed, and she quickly returned to the world of the concert pianist:

> I found a duo-pianist of great merit, Peggy Peyton, who had fine training and owned a large plantation west of Beaufort. The two of us gave frequent concerts locally and at the University of South Carolina.
>
> In April of 1988, Joe died after a long, miserable siege of leukemia. Pretty much all of Beaufort turned out to honor him at the National Cemetery.
>
> It was late 1989 when Bill Van Harlingen and I married and moved to Southbury, Connecticut. "Van" as he was known, was a retired Army brigadier general, a quiet, brilliant, powerful man with encyclopedic knowledge and courtly demeanor. Joe and I had known him for years.
>
> I recall that just before Van and I were married, he surprised me with an ultimatum. He was scheduled to go to West Point to celebrate his fiftieth anniversary of graduating from the military academy, and I was eager to go with him to meet his friends and classmates. However, because we weren't to be married until the following week, he wouldn't let me go—it wouldn't be seemly. He was such a delightfully considerate fellow!
>
> Van and I nested in a community called Heritage Village and traveled extensively, until suddenly, in 1991, he died of a fibrillation heart attack. We had just returned from an afternoon walk when he collapsed.
>
> Following Van's death, trying to recover and decide how to proceed with life, I studied for a Connecticut real estate license, took the exam, and worked

in real estate in Southbury for about six months. However, the lure of Beaufort friends brought me back there, and I returned to giving concerts with Peggy Peyton and selling property in and around the city. Life returned to a stable rhythm.

Mollie moved to Falcons Landing in 1996, having read about it in the military magazine *TROAA* (now *MOAA*). Because of her longtime association with academic communities, she also considered moving to the Forest at Duke, which has a relationship with Duke University. She said:

Visiting the Forest at Duke, I recall two professorial types walking the halls after dinner when I caught a bit of their conversation: "But if there is such a being, need we call it God...?" And I thought, "Ah, yes, the ivy halls of academia!" I was tempted by the North Carolina retirement community, but I realized that I had no academic credentials for teaching at the university level while I did have military affiliation by virtue of my marriage to Van. And also, while in Beaufort, not only did I play piano for the Marine Corps Parris Island recruit graduations and for associated events at the Marine Air Station, but also there were a great number of retired Army officers and their families in the area. For eight years I had played tennis with, gone to church, and socialized with the military.

When I moved to Falcons Landing, it had just opened. I recall that in the dining room, there almost seemed to be more staff than residents, and our paramount concern was getting to know one another. Plus, we were a relatively small group, finding our way among the myriad details and decisions a new place requires. We formed committees, wrote council bylaws, chose dining room linens and flatware, arbitrated the garage squeeze caused by two cars, formed assorted clubs and tennis and bowling teams, selected a stained-glass window for the "chapel" the name we voted to give the multipurpose room.

Not only were we smaller than we are now, we were more diverse, because, initially we welcomed residents from all branches of the government, not just military. Many of the residents were still much involved in their former careers and, at dinner, many spoke freely on the state of their health. It seems to me today's residents, on the other hand, check each other for the latest health of our friends but then move on to activities, trips, views on the White House and on world events. Politics and religion are discussed freely and with animus only among those who have learned each others' bent and respect it.

From the outset, I've been most impressed by the quality of the residents. I have a sister-in-law who has moved into another retirement community in Fort Myers, Florida, and I'm distressed by how uninteresting the people are. They have no "intellectual soul," are provincial, have scant curiosity and limited interests. They are a boring group.

> Trying to avoid pretension, but still being honest, the folks here at Falcons Landing have lived all over the world, are well educated, saturated with wide-ranging interests and great autobiographical tales. Of course, they might be a bit too predictably conservative for my politics, but, never mind politics.

Mollie's observations might be amplified by Clem Irons, who makes an annual study and report on the census. As reported by Clem in the May 2005 edition of the *Falcons Landing News*, in that year, of the total of 452 residents, the U.S. Air Force represented 43 percent of the retired population, while the Navy represented 21 percent, and the Army 19 percent. There were 8 percent who were senior executives from the Department of Defense, the Marine Corps and the Coast Guard. The remaining 9 percent were from other government departments and agencies such as the Department of State and the Central Intelligence Agency. There were two undersecretaries of defense, twenty-three officers of flag rank (i.e. generals and admirals), one ambassador, and 127 field grade officers (major/lieutenant commander through colonel/captain). There were 135 couples, forty single men, and 142 single women. The average age was eighty-two with twenty-seven residents age ninety or older, and fourteen under the age of seventy. The youngest person at Falcons Landing was sixty-two. There were several residents who were still working at full- or part-time jobs.

Mollie's observation about the subjects of conversation in social groups was addressed in the same issue of the *Falcons Landing News* by an anonymous, caricaturist wag who reported on the nature of the discussions that took place over the tables in the dining and lunch rooms. He found that food and the quality of service were always safe subjects; that children and grandchildren were also favorites, but that they were subjects that could be overdone. Discussion of the weather was always safe among those who were not on familiar terms. The state of one's health and the medications taken could become obsessive if not curbed by a self-appointed table monitor. Mollie's reference to the health of conservatism at Falcons Landing, the hint of her philosophical bent and her reluctance to pursue the subject, is typical of the tendency to avoid the discussion of politics and religion. The danger of expounding on one's career and accomplishments was addressed in the article, because one could be embarrassed to learn that one or more of the group had a career or accomplishment that may have been many times more illustrious. Good humor, the titillating pun or joke, always seemed acceptable. However, ethnic, seamy, and cruel stories are simply not told. Finally, during nearly every mealtime discussion, the researcher found that there was a predilection to congratulate oneself for making the good decision to live at Falcons Landing.

Reflecting on her family and her career, Mollie said:

> I have been asked, "Who is the most interesting person you have known?" I have to say my Dad. He was always free with such pithy aphorisms as "You can't be eccentric until you have a center." He was a fascinating fellow, and I say that even though 'to fascinate' is defined as the ability to attract or repel. His rejection of the materialistic side of life—his frequent criticism of what he considered to be American excessive pursuit of "The almighty dollar"—has probably skewed my understanding of what makes the world tick.
>
> However, I believe that my sisters and I have lived in lively cultural venues precisely because my father embraced the aesthetic, the literate values in life. Look at my sister Peg. After leaving the Royal Academy of Dramatic Art in London, she became a BBC-TV arts producer and has spent her life traveling the world with assorted members of the literati, making documentaries on their lives, opinions, and values. She was with Laurence Durrell (novelist, poet, dramatist and travel writer) both in Greece and Australia; she filmed Dave Brubeck (legendary jazz pianist) in Connecticut and Henry Miller (American novelist) in Los Angeles. It's been quite a life for her, and it was a life shaped in her early years by our father.
>
> I have been asked who was the most interesting person I have worked with, and that is a much tougher question to answer. I found that nearly all the people on the faculty of the Yale Law School were dedicated to ideas, and intriguing because of that. Dave Reisman, on loan from the University of Chicago, probably heads the list. To converse with him was to sense a pioneer in progress. At CBS my choice would be the Jesuit priest from next door at Saint Patrick's Cathedral. A handsome man, his intellect, training, and personality often dominated my board of directors meetings.

The adage of the limb not falling far from the tree seems to be confirmed as Mollie talks about her daughter:

> In 1998, Collin set aside her devotion to music, at least temporarily, to earn a J.D., summa cum laude, at the University of Connecticut, graduating first in her class, while she earned ten scholastic achievement awards, was editor-in-chief of the Connecticut Law Review, authored six law review articles—and then earned an LL.M. degree at Yale. After a three-year, time-consuming legal practice at Goodwin Proctor in Boston, she recently moved to Connecticut to serve as permanent career law clerk to the chief judge of the U.S. District Court, District of Connecticut, and thus secure more time with her family. Talk of schizophrenia, she's already started to teach her son piano!
>
> My son, Jonathan, who is an attractive, articulate lad with a truly wicked sense of humor, joined the Army when he was about twenty-two. He paints

well, reads widely, and is presently a staff sergeant serving in Iraq as a flight engineer—flying in Chinook helicopters. I cannot but worry.

When Mollie was asked how she started producing shows at Falcons Landing, she said that in 1996 there was a meeting of the Recreation and Activities Committee which concluded that something had to be done along the lines of a gala or a show. She volunteered.

> We had our first show December 1996. We opened up the auditorium in the morning, and residents brought all manner of things to put on display, from clothes they had made to furniture they had built. From two in the afternoon until 4:45, we had exhibits and competitions. From 4:45 to 5:30 it was musical entertainment. From 5:30 until 7:00 there was a holiday buffet, and from 7 to 8:30 we put on a full show with "Dueling Easels," skits, a fashion parade, duo-piano, line dancing, etcetera. We were off and running.
>
> We started with several shows a year and now, in our ninth year, have settled for two big ones, in May and December. But there is much more, for the chorus sings every Sunday for the Protestant service and performs for many special functions, which means that they are in practice or performing for much of the year.

The shows are demanding events. There are so many details that soon after the curtain falls on one show, Mollie must start preparing for the next. She is ably assisted by some regulars, particularly by a retired Air Force officer, Craig McKee. Craig started as a "go-fer" (although he protested being called a rodent), but he almost immediately became indispensable providing "technical support" for stage lights, sound, and the cameras that record each show. Because of his experience in community theater, his suggestions have been invaluable.

Mollie's inspiration for the next show does not descend in complete epiphanies. It takes some zigzagging and back and forthing as music is explored and resident talents ebb and flow. When a theme is determined, however, the chorus rehearsals commence immediately. Some thirty chorus members, all well over sixty, and most with a mature wanderlust, do not necessarily turn up for every rehearsal, which means that an hour's program can take up to four months of rehearsal.

As time passes and enthusiasm builds, the need to rewrite some music, to revise some words, to concoct alternate skits, compose here, cut there, all contribute to the intensity of the effort. And yet, without a doubt, every participant feels that the exhilaration of working toward a completed product is worth the effort. The performers treasure the rush they get following each performance when they are rewarded for their efforts by the enthusiasm of their fellow residents who have packed the auditorium an hour before the performance to ensure they get a premier seat. For many, it is one of the highlights of their year.

Mollie is a warm, endearing personality, but when she leads her chorus or puts her cast through a rehearsal, she is more the sergeant major, and that seems to be the way she has led her life, leading the pack, using her many talents and opportunities to the fullest, and fighting through adversity.

"My children have told me that I have a Machiavellian capability to shape events when I am in trouble," she said. "They say that I have a lot of grit in my makeup, and that no matter what happens, I keep moving and going, and that I am a born leader. Basically, all they are saying is that I am a survivor. I think that life is very challenging, exciting, and profound, and I love to be involved in it. And, like the Roman lady Cornelia and her two adored children, I have 'Cornelia's jewels.' Who could ask for anything more?"

So, in her mid-eighties, Mollie continues with her life, unmindful of age, always eager for the next challenge, and deriving great satisfaction through the expression of the tremendous creative urges she embodies. She has found a welcome venue in this retirement community. The residents recently presented her with a handsome plaque:

> To Mollie Van Harlingen
> with love and appreciation
> for bringing so much joy
> to the residents of
> Falcons Landing

Mollie might well quote Cicero's essay on "Old Age" ("De Senectute") about her contribution to the entertainment of her community: "This work is so delightful that it has not only obliterated the annoyance of age, but has rendered existence more charming than it is possible for life to be in youth."

7

Kenneth E. BeLieu

The Army-McCarthy hearings dominated the national media during the spring of 1954. A formerly obscure senator from Wisconsin, Joseph R. McCarthy had gained national attention by charging that Communists had infiltrated the Department of State. To some, the term McCarthyism has become an eponym for career-shattering false accusations and sensational tactics in investigation. To others, "McCarthy was not tilting at windmills. He was tilting at an authentic Communist conspiracy that had been laughed off."[2]

---

1.   Ken BeLieu died before the writing of this book. The profile is based on the book he authored: Kenneth E. BeLieu, *The Captains and the Kings* (Gateway Press, Inc., 1999) and comments by his widow, Markie BeLieu.

2.   Ann Coulter, *Treason: Liberal Treachery from the Cold War to the War on Terrorism* (New York: Crown Forum, 2003), 11.

In April 1954, the senator accused the secretary of the Army, Robert T. Stevens, of attempting to hide evidence of Communist espionage his staff had uncovered at Fort Monmouth, New Jersey. The Army, on the other hand, had charged that McCarthy and his staff had used improper influence in an attempt to obtain preferential treatment for draftee Priv. G. David Shine, a former consultant to the subcommittee. McCarthy's chief counsel Roy Cohn wanted Shine to be commissioned and assigned to duty with the subcommittee. Cohn had become a *cause celebre* in his subcommittee role. In a 1954 article, columnist Mary McGrory wrote, "Mr. Cohn has something of an air of the Quiz Kid. He has a powerful memory, he gives ready, rapid-fire answers. He has many decided opinions.[3]"

McCarthy contended that the investigation of Shine's alleged preferential treatment was aimed at diverting his investigation of the failings of Army security procedures. A sideshow to the Private Shine issue was the conduct of Roy Cohn, during a visit to Fort Monmouth. Ken BeLieu, later to become a resident of Falcons Landing, was one of the witnesses called for that part of the hearings that dealt with the Fort Monmouth incident. Following is a partial transcript of those proceedings as reported in the Congressional Record:

The United States Senate
Committee on Government Operations
The Permanent Subcommittee on Investigations
(Army-McCarthy Hearings, 25 May 1954)

SENATOR MUNDT (presiding member of the subcommittee): Do you solemnly swear the testimony you are about to give will be the truth, the whole truth and nothing but the truth, so help you God?
COLONEL BeLIEU: I do.
MR. MANER (a counsel for the Subcommittee on Investigations on a staff that also included the young lawyer Robert F. Kennedy): Will you please, sir, state your full name, your rank and your present assignment?
COLONEL BeLIEU: Kenneth E. BeLieu, Colonel, United States Army, and Executive Officer in the Office of the Secretary of the Army (Robert T. Stevens).
MR. MANER: For how long, Colonel BeLieu, have you been Executive Officer in the Secretary's office?
COLONEL BeLIEU: I first joined the Secretary's office in 1951, after I came back from Korea.

---

3.   Mary McGrory, April 28, 1954, as cited in the *Washington Post*, April 23, 2004.

MR. MANER: For the benefit of the record, Colonel BeLieu, when did you first enter the United States Army?

COLONEL BeLIEU: I enlisted in the enlisted reserve in 1937. I was commissioned a second lieutenant of infantry in 1937, about six months later. I entered active duty in 1940, and commissioned a regular Army officer in 1946. I have been on duty since.

MR. MANER: In your capacity, Colonel BeLieu, as the Executive Officer, did you have anything to do with the matters between the committee or the staff of the McCarthy Committee and Mr. Adams (John Adams, the Army General Counsel) and the Secretary himself?

COLONEL BeLIEU: Yes. My job is an administrative job mostly and a personal assistant to Mr. Stevens. I, of course, arrange many administrative details for various meetings that Senator McCarthy or Mr. Cohn or the Secretary had. I had only one personal experience or opportunity to watch the committee in action. That was the Fort Monmouth trip, about October 21st.

MR. MANER: Did you have anything to do with arranging that trip, making the physical arrangements?

COLONEL BeLIEU: Yes sir.

MR. MANER: Now, if you will, tell what the purposes of the trip were.

COLONEL BeLIEU: Mr. Stevens had never been to Fort Monmouth since he was Secretary of the Army…as long as Senator McCarthy was having investigations of the Monmouth area, or activities thereabouts, that it would seem like a good idea to the Secretary that they might discuss those activities on the spot.

MR. MANER: Now getting to the meat of that trip was there an untoward incident which happened on that trip on the 20th of October?

COLONEL BeLIEU: Yes, I think so.…The incident of the denial of entrance of Mr. Cohn and others of the party to the secret or classified laboratory.

MR. MANER: Were you present, sir, when that happened?

COLONEL BeLIEU: Yes.

MR. MANER: Tell, if you will, who was present when you arrived at the building.

COLONEL BeLIEU: All right. Of course, the Secretary of the Army was present, Senator McCarthy, Senator Smith of New Jersey, Representative Auchincloss, General Lawton was there—he commands the Post—General George Back, Chief Signal Officer. Mr. John Adams (Army general counsel), myself, certain of General Lawton's staff, of course, who would normally be there. I do not know all of them. Mr. Jones of Senator Potter's office, and Mr. Harold Rainville, from Senator Dirksen's office, and Mr. Cohn.

MR. MANER: What was this building you were to go into at that time?

COLONEL BeLIEU: It was a building that contained classified or radar apparatus.

MR. MANER: Were there certain people who entered that building and certain people who did not enter?

COLONEL BeLIEU: Yes, sir.

MR. MANER: What was the reason for that, Colonel BeLieu?

COLONEL BeLIEU: The security officer...challenged the right of entrance to this building, then was overruled by the Secretary as it pertained to the elected representatives of the Senate and Congress who were there. I started to stay out, and one of the officers recognized me and said, "Come on in, you are entitled to come in." I started in the door and got, I suppose, maybe ten or fifteen feet into the inner sanctum of the building. I heard someone building up a storm outside, and I turned around and went out. Mr. Cohn and Mr. Adams were there, and Mr. Cohn was quite irate at not being allowed entrance to the building....Mr. Rainville and Mr. Jones were in the vicinity. I think they were across the road, however.

MR. MANER: So far as your memory would permit you to do so, Colonel, would you relate what was said by Mr. Cohn there in your presence?

COLONEL BeLIEU: Yes, sir. In effect, he said, "This is it. This is war with the Army. I don't understand why you let Communists work in here, and you won't let me in. I have been cleared for classified information. I have access to FBI files when I want them. You are doing this just to embarrass me. We will investigate [the] heck out of you."

Then he went on to say there was no need for him to stay there the remainder of that day, but would take the investigation to New York. He wanted a car to get out of there and go back to New York.

I made some remark about, "Well, this wasn't done to embarrass you. You know we have to have security regulations."

He said, "Well, these people here just don't know how to do anything. They are doing it to embarrass me." He repeated that he was going to investigate the heck out of the Army, again.

This conversation went on for, I would say, about fifteen or twenty minutes, maybe more....

MR. MANER: What was the condition of Mr. Cohn at that time as to being angry and disturbed on the one hand, or being calm on the other hand?

COLONEL BeLIEU: I thought he was very angry...I thought he was blowing his top, in fact.

MR. MANER: What was the effect of his conduct there on you, Colonel BeLieu, whether it disturbed you or not?

COLONEL BeLIEU: I was embarrassed first because he was a guest on a military post, and I never had any experience with congressional committees before....

MR. MANER: Was there a second building inspected to which Mr. Cohn was not admitted?

COLONEL BeLIEU: Yes, I think there was, but I don't believe that created anything, because when they left the first building they went over to the next place, and everybody knew who could and who couldn't go in, so there was a good bit of griping, and that is all. I think Mr. Cohn was taken to another building to be shown some nonclassified data or information, but about that time I was getting concerned about getting the motorcade back and making sure everybody got in the proper cars, and my memory is a little hazy on that.

MR. MANER: What was the effect on Mr. Adams of Mr. Cohn's outburst?

COLONEL BeLIEU: I can't tell you what was in his mind. His expression indicated that he didn't like it; that he felt uncomfortable...Just generally an uncomfortable situation. He tried to placate Mr. Cohn or to ease his hurt feelings, I believe, as you would do to any guest in your house or at an installation where something unpleasant might have happened.

MR. MANER: Were you likewise present, Colonel BeLieu, at the luncheon on that date?

COLONEL BeLIEU: Yes, sir.

MR. MANER: Were you there when the Secretary made some statement in the nature of an apology?

COLONEL BeLIEU: Yes, sir....

MR. MANER: As a member of this great Army of which you say you are proud and of which we are all proud, its proud tradition that the secretary has talked about, did you feel it was becoming to the highest officer of that Army to make an apology to Mr. Cohn under the circumstances?

COLONEL BeLIEU: It is never unbecoming to be polite if that is your nature, and that is Mr. Steven's nature, I think. (Implicit in this exchange is the concern by many that Mr. Stevens was something of a milquetoast and that an apology was not warranted.)

MR. MANER: You thought it was entirely proper on that occasion?

COLONEL BeLIEU: I think it was. I say I would not have done it that way, but then I am not Mr. Stevens, nor is he me.

MR. MANER: I believe that is all, Mr. Chairman.

SENATOR MUNDT: Did you stay with Mr. Cohn throughout the entourage of these security quarters?

COLONEL BeLIEU: Yes sir, most of the time....

SENATOR MUNDT: Did he remain irate and hostile throughout the period of the inspection or did your efforts to explain placate him somewhat?

COLONEL BeLIEU: Well, it was sort of a slow simmer, I think, sir.

SENATOR MUNDT: He came down from a hot boil to a slow simmer?

COLONEL BeLIEU: Yes sir.

SENATOR MUNDT: You made some progress....Have you a point of order? (This question was in response to an interruption by Senator McCarthy. His repeated "Point of Order!" broadcast over the television networks became a popular national idiom.)

SENATOR MUNDT: Have you a point of order?

SENATOR MCCARTHY: No, I would be the last man to object to questioning by the Chair. I am not sure that it would get me anywhere. But may I say that there is no question but what Mr. Cohn was irritated, that he was invited to Fort Monmouth and was denied entrance to this building. This has nothing to do with the Army's charge to get special consideration. I am willing to concede that Cohn was irritated, that Rainville was irritated, that Jones was irritated. Why we waste time on something that has nothing to do with the charges, I don't know.

SENATOR MUNDT: The point of order is overruled. I am leading up to this point. At some place in this conversation, you heard Mr. Cohn say something to the effect that, "This is war, we are going to investigate the heck out of the Army," et cetera. Was this at the stage that he was at what you call a hot boil or by the time he had gotten down to a slow simmer?

COLONEL BeLIEU: I would say reasonably up to the top of the notch, sir.

SENATOR MUNDT: At the beginning or shortly after you went out there?

COLONEL BeLIEU: As I say, this conversation lasted maybe fifteen or twenty minutes. Again, I do not know Mr. Cohn well. That is the first time. So it will remain for somebody else to judge how his temper operates.

SENATOR MUNDT: What was your reaction? As an important officer in the Army, did you have a trepidation that something serious and dire was going to happen to the Army now?

COLONEL BeLIEU: I have always been of the opinion that the American Army can take care of itself, but I don't like to see somebody take ahold of it and try to do something to it.

SENATOR MUNDT: You are not afraid, then, you simply were concerned over the alleged threat?

COLONEL BeLIEU: That is right.

SENATOR MUNDT: Senator Dirksen?

SENATOR DIRKSON: Colonel BeLieu, I am inclined to agree with Senator McCarthy that this has no great or world-shaking bearing upon the issue that is before us, but certainly these explosive matters of minds have been testified to and ventilated pretty freely in this hearing. I suppose there is nothing lost by taking it just a little step further. Did you all leave Washington on the same plane with the exception of Senator Smith and Representative Auchincloss?

COLONEL BeLIEU: That is right, sir.

SENATOR DIRKSEN: And what time did you leave Washington?

COLONEL BeLIEU: About 10:15, sir.

SENATOR DIRKSEN: And what was the plan about coming back to Washington?

COLONEL BeLIEU: We were to fly back on the same plane when we finished our inspection up there.

SENATOR DIRKSEN: And when did you actually leave Fort Dix and come back?

COLONEL BeLIEU: This is Fort Monmouth, sir.

SENATOR DIRKSEN: I mean Fort Monmouth.

COLONEL BeLIEU: I think we must have left the fort...we got in Washington, I believe, about 4:15 in the afternoon. I would have to check that to be accurate. It is about an hour or hour and ten minute flight, and about a twenty-minute drive from Fort Monmouth.

SENATOR DIRKSEN: That means you landed there roughly about 11 or 11:30 and you left there probably about three o'clock.

COLONEL BeLIEU: That is about right.

SENATOR DIRKSEN: So you had substantially about three and a half hours?

COLONEL BeLIEU: About two and a half hours....

SENATOR DIRKSEN: Well, now Colonel, I am not a very hard taskmaster in so far as my office is concerned, but I certainly am reluctant to let a staff man go and spend the day on a social jaunt unless I think he goes away on the public business and does something worthwhile and constructive. That was the reason for my asking whether there was a plan. He had to leave my office early at nine o'clock to get down to the airport and get back perhaps at half-past five in the afternoon, so he was gone a whole day. That would be true of the rest of the members of the committee staff. And that leads up to this question: If you took a whole day and took a crowd of people up there who are busy, off of Capitol Hill, and suddenly you got up to a laboratory that harbored secret things and they could not get in, wouldn't you be irate too? Wouldn't you be mad? Wouldn't you raise the devil?

COLONEL BeLIEU: Respectfully, sir, not if it weren't any of my business.

SENATOR DIRKSEN: They make a lot of Roy Cohn losing his temper and getting a little explosive and aggressive. I don't know what attitude one of my assistants (Harold Rainville) expressed up there. He has never told me about it except to say that he spent the day. I said, "What did you do?" and he said, "Well, we have accomplished exactly nothing, because when we got to the place where there were some things that probably would be interesting, we couldn't get in, and the Army had not even made provision for the necessary clearances before we left Washington." Wouldn't you be mad under those circumstances? Frankly the Junior Senator from Illinois would have been as mad as the devil about it.

COLONEL BeLIEU: Frankly sir, I didn't get the impression that Harold Rainville was very mad. He spent quite a bit of time with me....

SENATOR DIRKSEN: Colonel, the only point I make about it is this, and it is in the spirit of the answer you made a little while ago to Mr. Maner's question about whether you would have made the apology that the Secretary made at the luncheon. It is, after all, a matter of personal viewpoint, and the Lord hasn't treated us all the same. Some people's temperament is a little more equable than others. Some tempers are a little shorter than others. But the point I make is this: that there was a whole day devoted to the trip to Monmouth. There was a lovely luncheon, I suppose, and a motorcade. Then to come to a building and not to be admitted, the question is, what does it do to a temperament that might be normally regarded as a little on the explosive side; and my answer is simply that if I had been in that predicament I am not so sure that perhaps my otherwise even temper—and I say that modestly—might have slipped its tether a little bit, and I might have used something besides mellifluous [sic] language. Maybe I would have become aggressive and used language that was tart and vigorous. Isn't that about the most you could have said about Mr. Cohn's language?

COLONEL BeLIEU: On the language subject, sir, when I entered the Army they had mule skinners. He wasn't quite up to that standard. I know you would not want to create the impression that this was a social gathering, sir. The lunch consisted of sandwiches and coffee brought in around a conference table, even as this is. So it was business all the time we were there. If people were interested in what the laboratories did and how they handled their security procedures, then I would assume that they would get something out of it, unless they already knew....

SENATOR DIRKSEN: Colonel, this is a wholly speculative question. If it had occurred to you at the time you were making these time and space arrangements, would you have gotten clearance for everybody in the party to enter that laboratory?

COLONEL BeLIEU: Not unless I was certain that they had a need to know that information, sir....

SENATOR DIRKSEN: There has been a good deal of speculation as to whether Mr. Cohn was entitled to enter that structure or not. Do you know whether he had a high clearance on other occasions before this Monmouth trip?

COLONEL BeLIEU: No, I do not know, sir.

SENATOR DIRKSEN: My understanding is that he did have; that there was made available to him a great many details concerning confidential matters because he did, you know, as a matter of fact, prosecute the Rosenberg case, and that required that he come into possession of secretive and confidential data.

COLONEL BeLIEU: I don't doubt your description of that, sir. However, a military person who is in charge of classified information or equipment cannot afford to take a chance, and I think, in the interest of the country, you always must make the choice against the person seeking entrance unless you specifically and precisely know....

SENATOR DIRKSEN: Let me finish one question, and then I shall have concluded with Colonel BeLieu. I am fully sensible of what you say, but I still make the point, Colonel, that a whole day was devoted to this, and suddenly when there comes that one piece of information they might have gotten or the satisfaction of going into a room that had answers.

SENATOR DIRKSEN: Colonel, if you were a guest in my house and I wouldn't let you go into a room—wouldn't you be put out?

COLONEL BeLIEU: Respectfully, sir, not if it were none of my business....

SENATOR SYMINGTON: Colonel, I was listening to one of my distinguished colleagues. You were in no dilemma with respect to Fort Monmouth, were you?

COLONEL BeLIEU: Not that I know of, sir.

SENATOR SYMINGTON: You were simply doing your duty as you saw it, is that right?

COLONEL BeLIEU: That is right, sir.

SENATOR SYMINGTON: I have been looking at...How many battle records have you got there?

COLONEL BeLIEU: Well, all through the European campaign, sir, all the campaigns from Normandy to Czechoslovakia.

SENATOR SYMINGTON: Did you ever count them up, just for fun?

COLONEL BeLIEU: I think there were five campaigns in Europe and three in Korea, sir.

SENATOR SYMINGTON: You say you enlisted in 1936?

COLONEL BeLIEU: Seven, sir.

SENATOR SYMINGTON: How old were you?

COLONEL BeLIEU: I must have been about twenty-two or three, sir.

SENATOR SYMINGTON: I see you were wounded twice, is that right?

COLONEL BeLIEU: Yes sir, once in Normandy and once in Korea.

SENATOR SYMINGTON: And in Korea, you could have had permanent disability, is that right?

COLONEL BeLIEU: Yes sir. I lost my left leg below the knee.

SENATOR SYMINGTON: I see you have the Silver Star, is that correct, for gallantry in action?

COLONEL BeLIEU: Yes, sir....

SENATOR SYMINGTON: Will you agree with me that one of the most important things in the world is to prevent the growth of Communism all over the world, Communist aggression, is the morale of the United States Army?

COLONEL BeLIEU: Yes, sir.

SENATOR SYMINGTON: Have you, in every action that you have ever taken, always had that in mind?

COLONEL BeLIEU: I hope so, sir.

SENATOR SYMINGTON: I have said before, and I say again, as long as so many people in this country have relatives in the Army, that in my opinion along with that of other witnesses here, you are a great credit to the country. No further comments or questions, Mr. Chairman.

SENATOR McCLELLAN: I will not ask you to repeat them, but I will ask you this: You saw the expression of the author of the statements at the time he made them?

COLONEL BeLIEU: Yes, sir.

SENATOR McCLELLAN: You were able to evaluate and analyze his attitude at that time, his demeanor as well as the verbal expressions that you heard?

COLONEL BeLIEU: Right, sir.

SENATOR McCLELLAN: Did you immediately or soon afterward report them to the Secretary of the Army?

COLONEL BeLIEU: Yes sir, I did.

SENATOR McCLELLAN: Did you report them to him there on that occasion before he left the post?

COLONEL BeLIEU: Yes, sir.

SENATOR McCLELLAN: You were the one who heard them. You are the one who had the best opportunity to evaluate them. Did you regard those statements as a threat against the Secretary and the Army?

COLONEL BeLIEU: Yes, sir.

SENATOR McCLELLAN: Did you regard them as an effort to intimidate the Secretary of the Army?

COLONEL BeLIEU: I don't think I did then, sir, particularly, because I don't see how a man can intimidate the Secretary of the United States Army.

SENATOR McCLELLAN: Well, an attempt to do so?

COLONEL BeLIEU: Yes, sir.

SENATOR McCLELLAN: You did regard them as an attempt to do so?

COLONEL BeLIEU: I think I do, yes, sir.

SENATOR McCLELLAN: May I inquire now if you so took them at the time? Did you realize at that time—were you evaluating them at the time as a threat or an attempt to influence the action, the decision of the Secretary of the Army?

COLONEL BeLIEU: I think at the time they actually occurred, I took them as evidence of distemper....

SENATOR McCLELLAN: Did he state to you then on that occasion that he did have access to FBI files?

COLONEL BeLIEU: Yes, sir.

SENATOR McCLELLAN: Who else heard those statements? In whose presence were they made?

COLONEL BeLIEU: Mr. John Adams was there....

SENATOR McCLELLAN: That is all, Mr. Chairman.

SENATOR MUNDT: Senator Jackson?

SENATOR JACKSON: Colonel BeLieu, who else was denied access to the laboratory on that day?

COLONEL BeLIEU: The three principal individuals who were denied access were Mr. Cohn, Mr. Harold Rainville, and Mr. Jones of Senator Potter's office. I would assume there would be other people on the Monmouth post who had no need to know that information, but I paid no attention.

SENATOR JACKSON: I mean of the immediate group.

COLONEL BeLIEU: Of our group, those I think are the only three who were denied entrance. Mr. Rainville and Mr. Jones—they expressed displeasure that they weren't, but they didn't complain vocally—or loudly, rather. I went over and talked to them to see what their attitude was.

SENATOR JACKSON: Did they use any comparable language to that which you have testified as an outburst?

COLONEL BeLIEU: No, sir.

SENATOR JACKSON: How long did this incident last?

COLONEL BeLIEU: I would say fifteen to twenty minutes, the best of my judgment, sir.

SENATOR JACKSON: Were the statements repetitive?

COLONEL BeLIEU: Somewhat, yes, sir.

SENATOR JACKSON: That is all.

SENATOR MUNDT: Senator McCarthy or Mr. Cohn?

SENATOR McCARTHY: Mr. Chairman, if this were in my opinion an issue in this case, I would have questions. Apparently there is nothing here which has to do with any improper influence or anything of the kind. This witness has testified that Mr. Cohn was angry because he was invited to Fort Monmouth to inspect the facilities. Facilities that were security risks and where Communists were working, and when he got to the door he was denied the right of going in. I can also testify that Mr. Cohn was angry. Mr. Rainville was, Mr. Jones was. I would be also. I think this is a vast waste of time. Therefore, I am not going to spend any more time on that question with this witness. No questions.

SENATOR MUNDT: No questions from you, Mr. Cohn?

MR. COHN: No, sir.

SENATOR MUNDT: Anybody else? Colonel, you are dismissed, and thank you very much.

These committee meetings climaxed two weeks later, on June 9, 1954. The Army had hired, as counsel for the hearings, the avuncular Joseph N. Welch of the prestigious Boston law firm of Hale and Dorr. While questioning Roy Cohn, Welch facetiously asked him to make certain he had exposed all Communists in the government. Columnist Mary McGrory described Welch's approach as follows: "As things progressed, (Welch) seemed to adopt toward Mr. Cohn the kindly attitude one might take to a frisky puppy. 'Down boy, down,' sums it up."[4] Senator McCarthy interrupted Welch with what Mundt interpreted as a point of order.

SENATOR McCARTHY: Mr. Chairman, in view of that question...

SENATOR MUNDT: Have you a point of order?

SENATOR McCARTHY: Not exactly, Mr. Chairman, but in view of Mr. Welch's request that the information be given once we know of anyone who might be performing any work for the Communist Party, I think we should tell him that he has in his law firm a young man named Fisher...who has been for a

---

4.   McGrory, Ibid

number of years a member of an organization which was named, oh, years and years ago, as the legal bulwark of the Communist Party....

Knowing that, Mr. Welch, I just felt that I had a duty to respond to your urgent request that before sundown, when we know of anyone serving the cause, we let the agency know...I have hesitated about bringing that up, but I have been rather bored with your phony requests to Mr. Cohn here that he personally get every Communist out of government before sundown. Therefore, we will give you the information about the young man in your own organization.

MR. WELCH: Mr. Chairman, under these circumstances, I must have something approaching a personal privilege. (Welch had been given to believe that he had a pre-hearing agreement with Cohn that the issue over Fred Fisher, a counsel in the firm of Hale and Dorr, would not be brought before the subcommittee.)

You won't need anything in the record when I have finished telling you this. Until this moment, Senator, I think I never really gauged your cruelty or recklessness. Fred Fisher is a young man who went to the Harvard Law School and came into my firm and is starting what looks to be a brilliant career with us.

When I decided to work for this committee, I asked Jim St. Clair...to be my first assistant. I said to Jim, "Pick somebody in the firm who works under you that you would like." He chose Fred Fisher, and they came down on an afternoon plane. That night, when we had taken a little stab at trying to see what the case was about, Fred Fisher and Jim St. Clair and I went to dinner together. I then said to these two young men, "Boys, I don't know anything about you except that I have always liked you, but if there is anything funny in the life of either one of you that would hurt anyone in this case you should speak up quick."

Fred Fisher said, "Mr. Welch, when I was in law school and for a period of months thereafter, I belonged to the Lawyer's Guild...."

I said, "Fred, I just don't think I am going to ask you to work on the case. If I do, one of these days that will come out and go over national television, and it will just hurt like the dickens."

So, Senator, I asked him to go back to Boston. Little did I dream you would be so reckless and so cruel as to do an injury to that lad. It is true that he is still with Hale and Dorr. It is true that he will continue to be at Hale and Dorr. It is, I regret to say, equally true that I fear he shall always bear a scar needlessly inflicted by you. If it were in my power to forgive you for your reckless cruelty, I would do so. I like to think that I am a gentle man, but your forgiveness will have to come from someone other than me.

Senator, may we not drop this? We know he belonged to the Lawyer's Guild, and Mr. Cohn nods his head at me.

Let us not assassinate this lad further, Senator. You have done enough. Have you no sense of decency, sir, at long last? Have you left no sense of decency?

Mr. McCarthy, I will not discuss this with you further. You have sat within six feet of me and could have asked me about Fred Fisher. You have brought it out. If there is a God in heaven it will do neither you nor your cause any good. I will not discuss it further. I will not ask Mr. Cohn any more questions. You, Mr. Chairman, may, if you will, call the next witness."

When Welch finished, the gallery, which had been stunned by his audacity, burst into applause. A befuddled McCarthy turned to Cohn and stuttered, "What happened?"

This June 9, 1954, session of the thirty-six days of hearings was the capstone of the fall of Senator McCarthy from public favor. A senate investigating committee chaired by Milliard Tidings found the McCarthy charges that the Department of State was harboring Communists a fraud and a hoax. The 188 hours of televised hearings revealed the tactics of Joseph McCarthy, and the term "McCarthyism" became synonymous with duplicity in the publication of accusations of treason without supporting evidence. The proceedings led to McCarthy's censure by the Senate on December 2, 1954.

The following are excerpts from an article titled "The Outsider" by Murray Kempton, which appeared in the *New York Post* on May 26, 1954:

> Yesterday, Col. Kenneth E. BeLieu, a member of the combat infantry club in the best standing, testified against Joe McCarthy in the Senate caucus room. Col. BeLieu is neither as young nor untouched as he looks; he was wounded in Normandy nearly ten years ago, and he has been wounded since in Korea. He won the Silver Star for walking his troops out of a hot corner on a shattered leg.
>
> After that, they brought him to the Pentagon and made him executive officer to the secretary of the Army. He worked one month for a Democrat Army secretary; we may thus presume that he is a Fair Deal holdover and, by Joe McCarthy's definition, a participant in four weeks of those twenty years of treason.
>
> He has no politics. Yesterday, he said very simply that he was proud of the U.S. Army; it is a pride of blood. He was a piece of fresh air among the sewer pipes. Joe McCarthy looked at him the way a bug disturbed under a flat rock looks at the sun and fled for cover. McCarthy forbore to question BeLieu. He said that his story was not important....
>
> The combat infantry badge is a test of character; and Kenneth BeLieu had Joe McCarthy and Roy Cohn tabbed as no civilian could. Against him, they had no weapons. They shuffled him off, and went back to blowing smoke. The history of America has not before been written with the likes of Kenneth

BeLieu losing to the likes of Joe McCarthy; and seeing yesterday's tableau, you had to assume against all odds that history will not be written that way this time....

Ken did not play a key role in these 1954 proceedings, but he was a player. During one of the pre-hearing interrogations, he was asked if he had ever knowingly associated with a Communist. He answered, "Yes."

The interrogator pressed on. "When and where?"

He replied, "Either October twenty-first or twenty-second in North Korea. There were about three thousand behind us and several divisions in front of us, and we were shooting like hell at the SOBs."

His participation in the hearings was far from being the high point of his career. Nevertheless, his testimony reveals much of his character and achievements in a life of public service. The boy who had a passion for the Army rose from private to colonel, distinguishing himself in combat. After fifteen years of active duty, Ken retired from the Army and served first in the legislative and then the executive branches of the government. The soldier retired to a series of governmental positions on the Hill as a professional staff member in the Senate (1950–1960). He then joined the executive branch to assume the second-most senior slot in the Department of the Navy, serving as undersecretary of the Navy in 1965. He took leave from government later in 1965 and, for about three and a half years, he prospered in the private sector as executive vice president, president, and member of the board of Leisure World Foundation, and as a member of the boards of advisors for RCA, the Ryan Aeronautical Corporation and Continental Motors. During this stint in private industry, he still found time to provide service as a member of the Defense Science Board. He returned to the government in 1971 when he was appointed undersecretary of the Army.

Ken BeLieu was born in Portland, Oregon, on February 10, 1914. He graduated from the University of Oregon in 1937. In 1955, he finished his formal education, graduating from the Harvard Business School Advanced Management Program. His first job after graduation from Oregon in 1937 was with I.J. Newberry, a five-and-dime store, earning $17.50 a week. The early days in the Depression era were tough. He moved up from the five-and-dime store to working for the Mail Wells Envelope Company, where he discovered he had a talent for sales and earned an impressive $125 per month. He liked to tell of his experience selling to a "Nob Hill" grocery store in one of Portland's upscale neighborhoods. The owner, Arnold Strohecker, had a glass eye that he would take out and roll back and forth in the pencil trough of his desk. The rolling eye was meant to challenge the composure of salesmen who were presenting their wares to the grocer. BeLieu passed the Strohecker eye test and was able to sell him his goods.

He claimed that his training as a salesman stood him in good stead in later years as he pursued Margaret "Markie" Catherine Waldhoff of Naoka, Minnesota. They married in 1951 and celebrated their forty-ninth wedding anniversary at Falcons Landing.

As BeLieu tells it, he was once vectored to the side of the road by an elderly policeman in rural Virginia. When the police officer looked at BeLieu's license it read, "Authorized to drive if fitted with a proper prosthetic device." The officer asked Ken why he wasn't wearing his glasses.

Ken responded, "I don't wear glasses, officer."

The officer replied that prosthetic devices meant glasses.

Ken parried, "I have an artificial leg."

The officer asked if BeLieu was a "soldier boy."

"Yes, sir," answered Ken.

And the officer said, in disgust, "Why didn't you tell me before I started writing this here ticket?"

In 1996, after living in Alexandria, Virginia, for forty years, Ken and Markie moved the thirty miles to Falcons Landing. As with so many of the residents, one attraction was that they had many friends who were or would be sharing the hospitality of the community. A phenomenon of military life is highlighted in Falcons Landing in that so many of the residents have been brought back together after sometimes decades of separation. Quite by chance, the second half of the BeLieu duplex would house Tyler and Aline Port, whom they had known for over fifty years. Ken and Tyler had served together in the Pentagon in the offices of three secretaries of the Army. Tyler later joined the International Staff of NATO in Brussels, Belgium, where he held the position of assistant secretary general for defense support. They also became Falcons Landing neighbors of Vernon and Sarah Coffey (with whom BeLieu had served in the White House), Georgia and Frank Ball (a comrade in the Second Infantry Division), Paddy and Penny Paddock, (a Navy couple who had been neighbors in Alexandria, Virginia), and Richard and Marjorie Blair (BeLieu and Richard had served together when Ken was the undersecretary of the Department of the Navy).

Ken BeLieu died of prostate cancer in 2001. As of the drafting of these lines, Markie is still making Falcons Landing more convivial by her presence.

Ken once wrote: "I've said we rejoined our own generation at Falcons. We residents speak the same language. As fine as the physical plant is, the inhabitants are Falcons' greatest assets."

8

James McCullough

He wouldn't call it genius. But how else to describe the exceptional creative talent of Col. James McCullough, United States Air Force (Retired), that is found in his dioramas?

What is a diorama? One dictionary defines a diorama as "a scene in miniature, reproduced in three dimensions by placing objects, figures, etc. in front of a painted background." We have all seen such impressive displays in museums and galleries, most often displaying animals in their natural habitats or historical scenes.

So, what makes Jim's dioramas so special? To the best of Jim's knowledge, no one else produces dioramas that are so devoted to the principles of perspective that they will create a shadowbox scene only six inches deep that gives one an extraordinary sense of depth and reality. Jim's story and the wonders of his work

---

1.   This profile is based on a series of interviews commencing in May 2005 and from written inputs from Col. James McCullough.

are best illustrated in the photographs of several dioramas printed on these pages. Still, the photos do not do justice to the craft. It is necessary when looking at the picture to be aware that what you are viewing is a twenty-by-thirty-one-inch shadowbox only the length of a hand in depth. The written discussions that appear beneath the dioramas are by Jim, as edited for this publication.

Jim calls them "American Heritage Dioramas in Perspective." They reflect his interest in early American history. They are exercises in plane geometry. He explained:

> It is trickery, trickery that your eyes and brain play on your senses. When I decided to make a diorama, I didn't know where to start. I had never seen work that I thought would satisfy my concept of what one should look like. I knew of no books that described the process. A box scene we had purchased in Juarez, Mexico, some twenty years earlier was my challenge. Because the craftsman had not properly applied the principles of perspective, the scene bothered me. It didn't look right. It made me uncomfortable. I wanted to build one that obeyed the physical laws of perspective.
>
> In January of 1974, three months after I retired from the Air Force, I started to craft my first diorama. I was fascinated by the challenge of the laws of perspective and the demands of experimenting with a variety of materials, tools, and techniques. I was so obsessed that I fabricated fifteen dioramas in that first year. I never again achieved that level of intense production.

Jim continues to look for works by other artists that approach his dedication to the laws of perspective. A few have been found that show a fundamental appreciation for the art, but none achieve the standards Jim has set for compliance down to the smallest detail.

Jim is a master craftsman using both hand and power tools working with wood, cast lead, plastic, molded clay, fabric, and rubber. The scenes are augmented with paintings to achieve illumination of varying intensities, glowing fires, gleaming candles, and sunlight. Each diorama takes about 150 hours of production, from the planning and sketching stages to completion. Jim has made over a hundred dioramas and has sold ninety-three, some of which were crafted to order for clients. Such attention to detail doesn't come cheaply; his prices start at $3,500.

Jim has retained eleven dioramas that he displays in a gallery he has created in his Falcons Landing home that is open to residents on a daily basis. He has created historical scenes of the Wright Brothers' machine shop, a one-room school house, a post office, a hardware store, a general store, a music shop, an apothecary, a sawmill, and other sites in exquisite detail. The dioramas are in private collections across the United States and abroad.

In November of 2003, Jim and Louise McCullough moved to Falcons Landing from their home in Lake of the Woods, Orange County, Virginia, where they had retired following Jim's thirty years traveling the globe as an Air Force pilot. Jim retired in October 1973 and was confronted with a decision. Should he apply the many skills he acquired in the Air Force to industry or should he devote his energies to his passion for solving the complex problems of the perfect diorama. He chose the latter and was a happy man, satisfying his creative, artistic urges.

He talked about his early years:

> I graduated from high school in Chicago in 1942, working at various jobs before taking the Air Corps Flying Cadet examinations. Having passed the written examinations, I was rejected physically for bowed legs. The following day I took the Navy V-12 examinations. I passed both the written and physical portions, but the Navy would not accept me because they had a regulation that they could not accept an applicant who had previously failed another service examination. It was a real Catch 22. So I bided my time. I secured a deferment to attend a local junior college, where I majored in interpersonal relationships. I had a great extracurricular schedule, serving as class president and learning all the dances of the period with the resident sorority ladies, while incidentally taking a couple of academic classes.
>
> During that period, I met a lovely pianist, Louise Soper, and within a few months we were engaged. When Louise graduated in June of 1943, I again applied to the Army Aviation Cadet Examining Board. This time I passed both the written and the physical examinations. I was on my way to doing what I had wanted to do ever since I was a youngster. I was going to fly.
>
> The year 1945 was a big one for me. In March, I was awarded my wings, my commission as a second lieutenant in the Army Air Corps, and Louise and I were married. The Air Force gave me the opportunity to serve in some interesting assignments, in some interesting places. It gave me the opportunity to secure a bachelor of science degree in mechanical engineering from the University of New Mexico and a master's degree in engineering management from the University of Southern California. It was probably my background in engineering that prompted me to attack the riddles of scaling models in perfect perspective.

In moving to Falcons Landing, it was not easy for Jim to close his shop and parcel out the majority of his treasure trove of woodworking tools. However, it had to be done before they moved into their duplex home in the Air Force retirement community. There was some indemnity in that he knew that the community had a well-equipped woodworking shop and that he would be working with friends who had similar interests. Louise and Jim have proven to be welcome additions to Falcons Landing. Louise has been most generous with her time and talents as a pianist and vocalist. Jim is an active, valuable member of the wood-workers group. Jim's gallery of dioramas is one of the favorite attractions of the community. They are a gregarious couple and quickly cultivated a wide circle of friends.

1870 HARDWARE STORE

This scene is representative of the period of the Industrial Revolution. Iron and steel products were being mass-produced, and stores began to specialize in the wide line of goods afforded by factory production. By 1870, the hardware store was well established. Multiple tools, spare parts, and fasteners required a well-organized arrangement of storage to make for easy stock retrieval. For decades, hardware stores were characterized by the small drawers and pigeon holes needed to store their wares. The ceiling provided useful, visible storage space. Kegs were useful for the bulk shipment of nails and became racks for tools.

The name on the window of this diorama comes from a hardware store in Carlisle, Pennsylvania, which claims to be the second-oldest establishment of its kind that is still in business.

This diorama was bought by Mr. Richard England, former chairman of the board of the Hechinger company, a large hardware chain that at one time dominated the hardware market in the Washington, D.C., metropolitan area.

THE WRIGHT BROTHERS' MACHINE SHOP

This diorama is modeled on the birthplace of aviation. It is the shop where Wilbur and Orville Wright fabricated their devices for a heavier than air machine in the early 1900s. The shop was moved from its original site in Dayton, Ohio, to Henry Ford's Greenfield Village in Dearborn, Michigan, where Jim studied and photographed the exhibit.

In the left background is a one-cylinder engine. It ran on a fuel of illuminating gas to power the system belts, pulleys, and shafts that drove the machinery, a drill press, lathe, band saw, and grinder. On the rear wall is a representation of the wind tunnel built by the Wright brothers. It was the first one to be built in the United States and gave the brothers insights into flight that made their flight tests a success where others had failed. In the left foreground, is a representation of the first engine that was used in 1903, made in this shop, because they could find no machine shop that would undertake the project. The Wright brothers were bicycle repairmen, and this was the shop where they conducted that business.

This diorama is the property of Christel and Doug Eilers of Albuquerque, New Mexico.

THE POST OFFICE/GENERAL STORE

This was the first diorama of several to depict a post office. No two McCullough dioramas are the same, but different dioramas have been crafted that treat the same subject.

The "small box" units for each of the vertical dividers are non-parallel, which was necessary to maintain perspective. Each divider required a separate mathematical calculation. It is also interesting that the checker players' chairs stand entirely alone. They touch neither the wall, nor the covering glass, nor the cracker barrel which supports the checker board. They are affixed only to the floor of the scene. Since all of these items are placed in a space only 3.75 inches between the glass and the back wall, it is obvious that they are highly compressed. (Actually, they are in a space of about one inch.)

The basket of apples is "woven" of electrical bell wire, and the oaken buckets hanging from the ceiling are carved of oak. The tools have honed metal blades, but the hams aren't really ham—they are crafted of wood. In the general store, much of the stock was traded, the storekeeper accepting the surplus of the farms and products of the craftsmen in the community in exchange for the wide variety of goods offered in the store.

THE GUNSMITH'S SHOP

The gunsmith dioramas were inspired by Jim's appreciation for the highly skilled artisans who developed the Pennsylvania Rifle in the shops that were centered about Lancaster, Pennsylvania. These Swiss and German immigrants painstakingly crafted a rifle with an accuracy rarely found in that time period (about 1750 to 1850).

Making the barrel was the most difficult process in the fabrication of the rifle. The bars of iron and the tools that were available at this time handicapped the gunsmith. It was necessary for a smith to form a flat sheet of iron about a mandrel and forge weld it to make a tube. Following the forming and welding, the tubes were buried in a bed of hickory coals and allowed to cool overnight to anneal or soften the material for further treatment and to relieve the stresses in the metal. The barrel was then hand-filed into an octagonal shape, reamed to remove gross internal imperfections, and rifled on the bench shown in the left foreground. Rifling of the barrel was done by pushing a tiny tool known as a broach in and out of the barrel while revolving the tool so that it made a single revolution of a cut the length of the barrel. A minute amount of metal was cut out by the broach each time it was drawn through the barrel. After many trips, a single groove was created. The tool was then "indexed" to the next pair of slots and a second groove was cut. When all the groves were cut, a very accurate gun barrel had been fabricated. In this diorama, all of these steps of manufacture are shown.

THE ONE-ROOM SCHOOLHOUSE

The map that is displayed over the cloakroom door reveals the time period of this schoolhouse, because it displays the Oregon territory as part of the United States and shows West Virginia as part of Virginia. On the sides of the cloakroom are revealed the stock of books, a precious commodity in those days, and one sees the forgotten scarf that hangs on a peg. Benches for the seating of children of different ages and sizes were generally made by the community. The teacher's table has a dictionary, a quill pen, an apple, and a pointer. (Or is it a hickory stick?)

The walls have copies of the Declaration of Independence, the Constitution, samples of student penmanship, the pendulum clock, a picture of President George Washington, as well as student papers and the "duty rosters" for keeping the water bucket and coal scuttle filled. On the bench, along with McGuffey's readers is the schoolmarm's hand bell and the right rear window holds the high stool with the conical "dunce cap." Out of the right window are two small buildings labeled "Boys" and "Girls."

HECHINGER'S HARDWARE STORE

This scene was created from a photograph of the Hechinger hardware store of 1927. The diorama is a part of the corporate art collection of the chairman of the board of the now-inactive Hechinger Corporation. Every detail that could be identified in the photograph of the store was included here, and where the details were not obvious, Jim was licensed to innovate. There are hundreds of details in the diorama all completed in an exacting perspective.

Jim McCullough recalled, "I was told that Hechinger's history involved the founder purchasing surplus buildings at the end of World War I, and that the Georgia Avenue store in Washington, D.C., was the first outlet for materials that were recovered when the buildings were razed. The store was still in business when I designed this diorama in 1983. The floor tiles and the lighting fixtures in the diorama are examples of the use of recovered materials. The sign over the window that reads, 'BIG TREES MAKE GOOD LUMBER' was done on a thin slice of a large tree trunk. The diorama sign was also a slab cross-cut from a tree trunk. In the right foreground is a stairway to the lower level, and in the background is a stairway to the second floor. Seen out of the window on the right is the lumber yard."

THE DONNELLY PRESS, 1868

This scene represents Jim's impression of what an 1868 press room might have looked like when R. R. Donnelly started the largest printing operation in the world. Every aspect of the printing operation is covered: composing, layout, lockup, proofing, and the press run. The press shown is in the Smithsonian museum in Washington, D.C.

This diorama was commissioned by the late Gaylord Donnelly of Libertyville, Illinois. Mr. Donnelly, grandson of the founder, was chairman emeritus and honorary director of the R. R. Donnelly Printing Company. The diorama hangs in the firm's corporate offices in Chicago. This subject, in addition to a subsequent diorama made to illustrate the "hot type" printing process, displayed the linotype and monotype casting machines that revolutionized printing and that hadn't much changed since Guttenberg invented movable type.

THE VIENNA CLOCK SHOP

This diorama depicts the clockmaker's shop as it would appear in 1850. In this scene, we have the clockmaker's workbench with a jeweler's lathe on the left side showing multiple hand tools and the tiny drawers that hold the spare parts. In the center foreground is a gear generator, a device that was used to divide a circle into various numbers of equal parts and that then indexed a blank into a fixed number of equally spaced gear teeth. In the right foreground is a table with a bushing press and jeweler's stake for sheet metal fabrication. In the scene are representations of antique clocks such as the "banjo," "beehive," "acorn," "mirror," "spire," and "ogee," as well as two "tall clocks," often misnamed grandfather clocks.

This diorama is owned by Mr. and Mrs. Eugene J. Sobel of Potomac, Maryland.

BOB KISTLER'S WORKSHOP

This diorama could serve as the example of how to organize and maintain the perfect woodworker shop. It is modeled on the workshop of Bob Kistler of Wayne, Pennsylvania. He kept the diorama in his office so that he might see it from his desk and reflect on where he would like to be. The diorama represents the artist's first attempt at constructing models of a lathe, a radial arm saw, band saw, and jigsaw as well as a number of hand tools. Enough shavings and saw dust have been left around the feet of the power tools to indicate a shop that is often used.

"Mr. Kistler commissioned two additional dioramas," Jim said. "One was his grandfather's grocery store in Reading, Pennsylvania, that was designed from a cherished family photo. The other was a representation of the family living room at Christmas. The workshop and grocery store dioramas were made as an inheritance for Bob's two sons. The Christmas scene will go to his daughter."

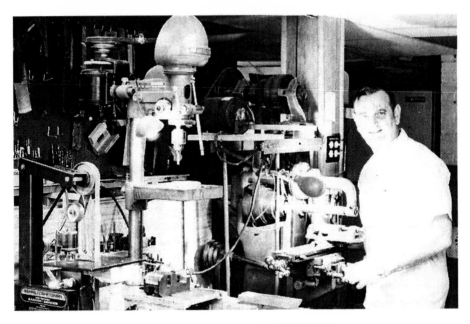

JIM McCULLOUGH AT HIS WORKBENCH

This photograph was taken of Jim with his beloved machinery in the basement of his home in Camp Springs, Maryland, in the early years of his diorama labors. Shown are a belt and disc sander and a drill press. He is operating a horizontal milling machine. A metal working lathe is around the corner, behind him and to the left. All available wall space was covered in pegboard, which held the many tools and jigs used to speed up repetitive processes. He had a large inventory of hand and power tools and dozens of dental drills, burrs, and abrasives of carbon and diamonds. Jim normally sat at his workbench on a raised stool with caster feet that allowed him to roll about the workshop. He claims that he much preferred his labors here to "working for a living."

9

John J. Pesch

Photo courtesy of John Pesch

In Italy, you would call him *un uomo di buon umore*; in France, *un bon type*; in Spain, *un senor muy bueno*. However, in American English, he is just a good guy. Maj. Gen. John J. Pesch, U.S. Air Force (Retired), is a friend to all at Falcons Landing. As a widower, he is special to the ladies, upon whom he showers attention and gallantry without favoritism or blandishment.

The following poem attributed anonymously to "The Ladies of Falcons Landing" appeared in the Falcons Landing monthly newsletter:

---

1.   This account is based on an interview with John Pesch as related to Darwin Beauchamp that appeared in *Falcons Landing News,* March 2000, 14-15, a letter from John Pesch to author/historian Ivo M. de Jong of the Netherlands, dated June 19, 1999 (in the archives of John Pesch and J.C. Scharfen), and a series of interviews of Pesch by Scharfen on April 14, 2004.

Ode to John Pesch[2]

If you only knew
When you smile at me
That my heart is happy
My spirit free.
There's music in my heart
And a twinkle in my eye
So when we meet again
Please don't pass me by.
For when I see you coming
I don't ask much, you see
The only thing I want
Is that you should smile at me.

Pesch is a raconteur, a magician, and a generous volunteer. He has also been a warrior. John flew thirty-one combat missions in the European Theater of Operations during World War II. The majority of the missions were deep penetrations in which he, a captain at the time, was flying as lead (pathfinder) pilot. His plane was badly damaged from enemy fire on several occasions. Once, he brought the ship back on two of four engines with just himself and his copilot. The other eight members of the crew had bailed out of the aircraft. But the story of Captain Pesch's flight and survival is better told in his words.[3] The setting is March 21, 1944, with the 731st Bombardment Squadron, 452nd Bombardment Group, Eighth Air Force, Deopham Green, England. He wrote:

> Our target that day was an aircraft assembly plant at Brunswick, Germany. We would be flying the Four Freedoms, a B-17, heavy bomber (Flying Fortress). The day began with the usual 3 AM wakeup call with no fire in our little pot-bellied stove. We quickly donned our flight gear and jumped into the back of an open truck for the half-mile ride to the mess hall before reporting to the briefing room. After the flight crews were identified on the security list, the door was closed and locked, and the briefing began. A curtain covered one side of the room. When the curtain was removed, we could see that the mission

---

2. *Falcons Landing News*, January 2001, 9.
3. This account was derived, in part, from *Air Power History*, Volume 38, Number 1, spring 1991, pp 23-25.

target was deep inside Germany. Audible groans filled the room. This would be a tough day.

We had a short ride to the flight line. We made our preflight checks. When we saw the green flare from the tower, we knew the mission was a "go." *Four Freedoms* was the number two aircraft, flying the right wing of the mission leader. As we taxied down the runway, I opened the four throttles. With engines revving up to 2,600 rpm, we soared into the black night.

We formed our group formation as we climbed to 18,000 feet and set course over the North Sea. Soon, the enemy coast was in view, and the usual greeting of scattered puffs of flak smoke greeted us. We test-fired our thirteen 50-caliber machine guns. By this time were at 25,000 feet. P-38 and P-47 fighters would escort us as long as their fuel permitted.

Our lead navigator put the group on course, and soon the target was in view. Before reaching the target, about thirty F-109 and FW-190 German fighters attacked the formation, and the skies were dense with flak. We all dropped chaff as we vectored onto the IP (Initial Point). We dropped our bombs and turned off target, closing the bomb bay doors as we headed for the rallying point. *Four Freedoms* had sustained major, crippling damage. Both left engines had been knocked out. The ailerons, elevators, and parts of the fuselage were heavily damaged. The communications system, to include our intercom, was useless.

We lost altitude and speed, and we were soon alone. We couldn't tell if the crew had suffered casualties.

We limped out of Germany and into Holland, hoping that the number three and four engines could keep us aloft. We were successfully nursing maximum engine power against a gradual descent. But two German F-109s spotted our crippled aircraft and attacked. They made a single pass from six o'clock, inflicting more damage. I spotted a solid undercast beneath us and did a wing over in hopes that we could escape the German fighters. Since we had lost all communications, I could not tell the crew of my intentions.

The navigator assumed that both the copilot and I were dead, and that *Four Freedoms* was in a diving, death spiral as the aircraft passed through 11,000 feet, almost upside down, at an air-speed of 325 mph. Our navigator opened the nose hatch, and he and the bombardier bailed out. When the engineer saw the chutes open, he and the remainder of the crew bailed out through the bomb door. The right waist gunner had been wounded but they rigged him with a chute and dropped him from the aircraft. The eight landed safely but spent the remainder of the war in a prison camp. At one point, I ordered my second lieutenant copilot to bail out, but he refused—he told me that it would take two people to bring the plane home, and that he would take the gamble with me.

The German pilots must have thought they had shot us down. However, we were still flying, if even with great difficulty, since major portions of the control surfaces were inoperative. I became convinced that ground fire would shoot us out of the skies, when a providential, lone P-51 appeared as our savior. The pilot came alongside and gave us a thumbs-up. He then escorted us to the channel while strafing the sites from which the ground fire was coming. I still wish we could have learned the name of the fighter pilot who saved us.

When we made landfall, we searched for the first available airfield. We had little difficulty finding one of the British fighter bases along the coast. We took a straight-line approach, and I called for landing flaps and the gear. Luckily they both responded. As we crossed the runway, I throttled back on number three and four engines and carefully released the pressure on my knees which I was using to control the elevators. The fatally damaged *Four Freedoms* performed well and came to rest without breaking up. We quickly examined the fuselage and tail section for the crew and found the plane empty. We had seen our crew's parachutes and were relieved that we had suffered no fatalities.

Our crash landing drew a crowd. The following day, we returned to our base at Deopham Green where we underwent debriefings. We and our comrades were grateful for our survival but mourned the loss of our crew of eight courageous airmen. The stout *Four Freedoms*, having suffered over one hundred hits, never flew again.

But John flew again. He continued to fly deep missions into Germany, including the first shuttle mission out of England to Poltava, Russia.

Almost sixty years after the last flight of *Four Freedoms*, a Russian television crew filming a documentary on one of those shuttle missions contacted Pesch requesting an interview. The Russians came to Falcons Landing in February 2004, turned John's apartment into a TV studio, and filmed his recounting of the story of the Poltava incident. On May 28, a different interviewer and cameraman, from Russia's Channel Two, called on him to do a special report for the sixtieth anniversary of the World War II incident. There are few American historians who know the World War II story of Poltava, but many Russians do. The name "Poltava" has great historic significance to the Russians. It was here that Peter the Great smashed the Swedes in 1709 to defeat Swedish aims for the conquest of the Ukraine. Pesch's reporting in the two interviews followed this story line:

Up until 1944, military cooperation between the United States and the Soviet Union had been mostly limited to lend-lease. Americans wanted to use Soviet bases for staging flights against Germany and initiated such a proposal at the Teheran conference in November 1943. The flights would originate in Italy or England, strike their targets in Germany, rearm, refit, and refuel at a Soviet base and attack German targets on their return to their home bases. It was a concept of economy of force that had a political facet. It was also hoped that a successful program might encourage the Russians to permit the American use of bases in

Siberia for raids on Japan. The program was dubbed FRANTIC. The negotiations with the Russians to establish the shuttle program did not go well. Approval was finally given only after the personal intercession of Josef Stalin, and then only three airfields were to be made available, all in the Ukraine: Piratyn for the accompanying P-51s and Mitrogod and Poltava for the B-17s. Fuel, armament, spare parts, and a minimum number of Army Air Force personnel were shipped and flown into Soviet bases by way of the Murmansk convoys and the Persian Gulf Command. For their part, the Soviets insisted on maintaining, controlling, and defending the Russian bases. (Such Soviet insistence on providing security at the Poltava base would be critical, as we shall see later in this account.) At the outset, the Americans questioned the air defenses at all three of the Soviet air bases.

Two previous shuttle flights had been flown into Russian bases with varying degrees of success. A successful mission of June 2, 1944, flown from Italy, was heralded as the "high tide of our military relations with the Soviet Union." On 21 June, the Eighth Air Force, out of England, scheduled its first FRANTIC mission. Two full-combat wings of the Eighth Air Force would be committed. To put the mission into perspective, on the day of the operation, there were nearly 2,500 American aircraft in the air pounding targets in Germany. John's squadron, the 452nd of the Forty-fifth Combat Wing, was briefed for this mission that would take them to Russia, then North Africa, and back across France to their home base in England. It didn't happen that way. What did happen was that a task force of 114 B-17s and seventy P-51s of the Eighth Air Force, flying out of England, bombed a synthetic oil plant at Ruhland in Eastern Germany and made for Poltava. However, a German HE-177 long-range reconnaissance bomber shadowed them as they flew into the Soviet base after an eleven-hour flight. The Heinkel circled the field taking photographs. The Americans pressured the Soviets to permit them to send up Mustangs to intercept and down the Heinkel. However, the Soviet commander refused their request, and the German aircraft returned to its base in Minsk with the report of its find of a lucrative target. There, the German commander, Wilhelm Anthrup, assembled a strike force of 150 HE-111s and JU88s and launched them against Poltava. The German air armada had planned a twenty-minute raid, but the attack was such a success that they continued the destruction for over an hour and a half. The Russians' defenses were ineffectual against the German aircraft flying at about twelve thousand to thirteen thousand feet. The Germans' air armada dropped about 110 tons of bombs on the B-17s and Mustangs aligned along the runways.

"We had arrived at Poltava with seventy-two aircraft," John said. "Of that number, forty-three B-17s, two C-47s, and one F-5 were destroyed. There were nineteen B-17s and two F-5s that were damaged but repairable. Only one of our 452nd squadron survived the attack. There was extensive damage done to the American transportation and communications systems, and 200,000 gallons of gasoline were lost. Ordnance caches were also destroyed. We lost 465 of our 250-pound (high explosive) bombs and 1,400 incendiary bombs as well as thousands of rounds of ammunition and other supplies. Watching all that ordnance explode has ruined Fourth of July celebrations for me ever after because you can't imagine the fireworks that much ordnance fired off at one time can produce."

All German aircraft were able to return to Minsk. Fortunately, there were few Army Air Force crews at the base during the attack, because they had been billeted some distance away. As a result, only one American was killed. The Russians had twenty-five killed as they tried to save the aircraft and base facilities. The fact that the Germans had dropped a number of anti-personnel mines complicated the salvage effort. A number of Russian aircraft were destroyed. It was one of the most successful German attacks on the Army Air Force during the war. The American crews were stranded for about a week at Poltava until transport aircraft were flown from England to return them to their bases. The crews used that time to make friends with the hospitable Russians.

John was not the only member of the Falcons Landing community who was at the Poltava disaster. The late Col. William M. "Bill" Jones, USAF, was on the operation as well. Bill is survived by his wife, Alice Jones, who still is an active part of the community. Bill and Alice attended a reunion of Air Force veterans of the Poltava operation in May 1988 in the Ukraine. The group had been promised that they would visit the old airfield where the Eighth Air Force had suffered so much damage. However, due to what must be assumed was Soviet secrecy and paranoia about revealing the site of an active air base, they did not get to visit the airfield.

This is what Bill wrote of the 1944 Poltava operation:

> There were only three major shuttle bombing operations (FRANTIC) conducted. One was from Italy (and back) in May 1944. The second was from England (with a planned return via a shuttle bombing from Russia to Italy and from Italy to England) on June 21, and the third from Italy in September. I was the lead navigator for the Eighth Bomber Command's force of some 150 B-17s and some fifty escorting P-51s on the June 21 operation. Poltava was the designated landing base for some seventy-five bombers; Mirograd for the remainder, and Piriytan for the P-51s.... German bombers attacked the Pol-

tava base that night destroying some sixty of the seventy-plus B-17s that landed there. (The following two nights the Germans bombed Mirograd and attempted to bomb Pirityn. Only five or six B-17s were lost at Mirograd, the force having used the intervening twenty-four hours to refuel and disperse to deeper bases. The Germans failed to find Piriytn at all and bombed the wrong 'cow pasture.')...Soviet casualties were some 150 fatalities and an unknown number of wounded (the Soviets having rushed troops onto the field in an attempt to save the burning B-17s and they—in the dark—ran into numerous butterfly bombs [anti-personnel, air-dropped mines] sowed by the Germans). German losses were one bomber lost to navigation error and its crew captured.[4]

John Pesch returned home for leave in New York following his thirty-first combat mission on July 19th, 1944.

John was born on Long Island into a family of five boys and five girls. He attended parochial grammar and high schools, won a scholarship to Brooklyn Polytechnic and attended the University of Maine. His father died when John was thirteen. A brother, Christopher, eighteen years older than John, took over the reins of the family. John still speaks of Chris in reverential terms as being the best example a young man could have. Christopher, a lineman with a telephone company, would send John to the store with fifteen cents to buy a ten-cent cigar. They both knew, but neither would acknowledge, that John was to keep the extra nickel. John learned that he could buy the cigars at three for a quarter. Prudently, in buying by threes, he increased his profits and savings. As the two grew older, John would try to thank Chris for his kindness and generosity not only to John but to the family at large, but his brother would never let him do so. Therefore, John composed a letter expressing his gratitude and that of his brothers and sisters. It was a letter that was saved and obviously treasured. Surprisingly to John, it was read as Christopher's eulogy at his funeral.

John continues to enjoy the company of his extraordinary family. Another older brother, George, and his wife cared for John's mother for many years. George is now ninety-three, and his longevity gives hope that John will be a fixture at Falcons Landing for many more years.

When John returned from the European Theater of Operations in 1944, he was transferred to Maine. John decided to leave the active Army Air Force in 1946 to return to college at the University of Maine. He joined the Maine Air

---

4.   Jones, William M. unpublished manuscript held by Alice Jones at Falcons Landing. The careful reader will note that there are discrepancies between the accounts of losses at Poltava that are not resolved in a search of official archives.

Guard as a major and flew with that squadron until it was mobilized for the Korean War in 1951. He remained in the Air Force until his retirement. He met his life's helpmate, Gloria, at Dow Air Force Base, Maine, in 1944. They married in 1945. Their marriage produced three daughters and two sons. They lost one of the sons, John Junior, a fighter pilot, in 1978 at the age of twenty-eight. The other son, a lawyer and professor yet unmarried, lives on Guam. The daughters are married and living in Virginia and Colorado. Gloria suffered a disease that took her from John in 1992 after a long illness during which John was the principal caregiver.

John had a successful career in the Air National Guard and was the director of the Guard at the time of his retirement in 1977. Gen. David Jones, United States Air Force, former chairman of the Joint Chiefs of Staff, and now a resident at Falcons Landing, was the official who retired him after his thirty-five years of distinguished service. John was one of the first to commit to Falcons Landing and made the move in July 1996. He participates in a number of group activities, volunteers to provide community services, and shares an interest in ballooning with another resident, Gen. Lew Allen, former Chief of Staff of the Air Force.

Actually and metaphorically, Maj. Gen. John J. Pesch, USAF, brings magic to Falcons Landing.

10

Denise Munchmeyer

Photo courtesy of Mrs. Munchmeyer[2]

Denise Munchmeyer recalled where she was when World War II began:

> I was twelve years old when France and England declared war on Germany. It was the third of September in 1939. My mother, father, and I were vacationing at my grandfather's home near the historic city of La Rochelle in France, on the Atlantic coast. With the proclamation of war, my parents left La Rochelle and returned to Paris. Notwithstanding the recommendations of

---

1. This profile is based on interviews commencing in May 2004 and written inputs from Mrs. Munchmeyer.
2. All photos in this profile are courtesy of Mrs. Munchmeyer.

my father's employer that we should return to the States, my parents had decided to wait out the war in our Paris apartment. They were confident that the war would be short, and that it would pose no physical threat to us. Nevertheless, in their concern for my safety, they left me at a boarding school in La Rochelle as they returned to Paris.

I was born in San Antonio, Texas. My father, Casey Hirshfield, was born in 1898, a Texan. My mother was French, born in La Rochelle. My father had been stricken with polio as a child and suffered a physical handicap as a result. Nonetheless, he served overseas in the Army Adjutant General Corps during World War I. In 1917, while in France with the American Expeditionary Force, he was stationed in La Rochelle where he met my mother, Madeleine Laidet. (Laidet is pronounced "lady." My mother was wont to entertain people by telling them that she was a "lady" before she married my father.) My father returned to the States in 1918. My mother had no expectation that their friendship would continue after the war. However, in 1926, my father returned to France to win the hand of my mother, and they were married that year.

Denise with father and mother in Houlgate, France, 1935

Denise's mother and father returned to the States and settled in San Antonio. After a few years, her father took a position as a newspaper representative providing the business office overseas for several well-known newspapers such as: the *New York Times*, the *London Times*, and Argentina's *La Prensa*. They moved back to Paris in 1933 when Denise was five and a half:

French became my first language. Father, a dedicated Francophile, spoke fluent French. We were a French family. All our friends were French. We lived in French quarters, ate French foods, and I attended a French school just across from our apartment. My grandfather's home in La Rochelle was our vacation hideaway. My grandmother died before I knew her, while fairly young, but my grandfather lived to be ninety-three. He fascinated me. He had been a sailor in the Merchant Marine and would delight me with tales of his adventures at sea and port visits. Perhaps these stories were the genesis of my lifelong attraction to travel.

Denise and mother at Fouras, France in 1934

The year 1939 was the beginning of the "phony war." The fall and winter were uneventful, except for the occasional air raids that intensified in the spring of 1940. We were not totally removed from the aerial bombings, since a suburb of La Rochelle, La Pallice, was a submarine base and a target for German bombers. But La Rochelle was virtually untouched.

On the tenth of May 1940, the German armies invaded Holland, Belgium, and France. Five weeks later, the Germans entered Paris. Retreating to La Rochelle, my mother and father caught the last train out of Paris before the Germans entered the city.

Denise recalled how efficiently the Germans extended their conquest and occupation of France. They would parachute a pair of uniformed motorcyclists with small bikes into a region. Once on the ground, the soldiers would assemble their bikes and ride into a town or village, ride up to the town hall to call the town officials together to inform them that they were now occupied and subject to German jurisdiction.

Denise recounted her family's difficult departure from France:

> France was thoroughly defeated and split into two sectors. There was occupied France, the Nord/Pas-de-Calais area, that came under the German command, which was headquartered in Brussels. Germany occupied three-fifths of France. Both La Rochelle and Paris were in the occupied sector. Occupied France included all the coastal areas of the country, both Atlantic and Mediterranean. In the center, was Vichy France, headed by the aged (eighty-four years old) Marshal Henri Philippe Petain, who had been an illustrious general during World War I. The senior leaders of the French, in the hopes of preserving some small degree of sovereignty, agreed to the plunder of French

resources and to sending French forced labor to Nazi Germany. (My uncle, an able-bodied man, was sent to Germany for a period under that program.) These were hard, humiliating times for the French.

Each day the situation became more intolerable for us. My mother and father knew that we had to leave France for America as quickly as possible. But you couldn't leave Occupied France without the permission of the Germans, regardless of your nationality. Initially, there were three bureaus that issued exit visas. One was in Paris. Another was in Bordeaux, and a third in Strasbourg. Since we were closest to Bordeaux, my parents elected to go there to apply for an exit visa. However, on our way to Bordeaux, we learned that they had closed that office and the one in Strasbourg as well. So, in June, we sent our requests to Paris by mail.

My mother had a problem. Her passport was French, and it was due to expire on the sixth of August. She couldn't get a new one because passports were issued only in Vichy, and there were no communications between the two sectors of France. She wasn't going to be able to get her passport renewed by the sixth of August. Therefore, it was imperative that she leave France before then. I, being a minor and an American citizen, had no passport of my own. I was carried on my father's American passport as well as my mother's French issue. I would travel on my mother's passport.

By late July, there was no answer to my parent's written request to the Paris office for a visa. Desperate, Mother appealed to the local German commandant. He granted her the required documentation but refused my father who still hadn't received his papers authorizing him to leave. So it was finally agreed that my mother and I would leave by train for Spain and wait for my father at the railroad hotel in Irun, Spain, the town immediately over the border. Dad would meet us as soon as he had his permit.

Mother went to the bank to get money to augment the paltry funds the Germans authorized us to take out of the country. Since I was a minor, they had not provided for any of my expenses. That meant that our authorized money was ridiculously inadequate. My mother concealed in her clothing the unauthorized funds she had drawn from the bank.

On August 5, we boarded the train from Bordeaux. When we disembarked in the small town of Irun, Mother was immediately placed under arrest for bringing more money out of France than the Germans authorized. We didn't have any idea how they knew about the money. Perhaps they assumed that such was always going to be the case with people leaving the country. Perhaps they knew because there was a routine exchange of such information between the Franco-led Spanish and the Germans. Perhaps they assumed, that we looked as if we would have such funds at our disposal, so of course we would try to take more out of France than we were authorized.

We were taken to the police station where my mother dissolved into tears. The Spanish police officer in charge appreciated her plight and recognized that she was no criminal. He did not confiscate our funds. Nevertheless, he told us that we must get out of the country on the next train. He was adamant that we would not be permitted to wait for my father in Irun as we had planned. There was a train that left that afternoon for Portugal.

We went to the hotel and left a message for my father to tell him what had happened. My mother wrote that he could reach us in Lisbon by going to the American Express where he would find a note from us. Since it was impossible to telephone or to send a wire into Occupied France, that was the best we could do.

We boarded the train for Lisbon. We shared a compartment with two well-dressed, middle-aged Americans, a husband and wife. We didn't have much conversation with them. At the border between Spain and Portugal, possibly Spanish officials came through the cars and selected people for interrogation and inspection. Again, my mother and I were the ones selected from our car. As we left to be searched, my mother asked our American companions if they would hold her wallet that held the extra money. They agreed to do so.

An elderly, obviously poor, lady searched my mother. She found some recently minted "gold" coins in my mother's purse that were actually of little value. Mother offered the woman the coins, and that delighted her. She passed us through the inspection without difficulty.

We were permitted to return to our compartment on the train. Immediately, the man told us that he had hidden the wallet in an overhead air vent because he was afraid that he would be found with it. He claimed that through some bad luck, the wallet had dropped into the vent and could not be retrieved. We were destitute. We had practically no money, were in an alien country, and were separated from my father. My mother could hardly ask for assistance to recover the wallet that held funds we were not authorized to carry. The American couple made no offer to help by lending us money or assistance. My mother couldn't bring herself to suspect that the couple had stolen our reserves but assumed that they panicked in fear that they would be caught with it. She did fault the couple for not offering us assistance or even a modicum of sympathy.

Our train to Lisbon stopped far short of the city. Officials told us that we would not go into Lisbon but would be delivered to various villages around the capital. Lisbon was too congested with refugees to accept any more travelers. There was a car that would proceed on to Lisbon, but we wouldn't be on it. Now, my mother really broke down. We had so little money. How would my father ever find us? There was no way we could contact him in Occupied France. She found the senior conductor and, through her sobs, told him of our plight. My mother was a pretty, petite, very feminine woman. The exercise of those qualities won us a transfer to the section of the train that was going to Lisbon.

Once in Lisbon, we checked into a comfortable but not elegant hotel. Thank God, there was a check from my father's company waiting for us. However, when my mother attempted to cash the check, she found that it was made out to him and could not be cashed on her signature. We remained penniless.

The only thing for us to do was to wait for my father to arrive. In the meantime, we would have to pay hotel bills. Mother explained the situation to the hotel manager. She attempted to assure him that payments would be no problem once my father arrived. We never forgot his response. He told us that the city was full of refugees with stories of terrible loss. Ours was far from being the worst. There were, for example, refugees from Eastern Europe with heartrending stories that made ours seem petty. Nevertheless, the kind man told us, 'If you can pay me, fine. If you can't, so be it.'

We ate all our meals in the hotel where we could charge them to our room. Since we didn't have enough money to pay for public transportation, we walked all over hilly Lisbon. We tried to book passage to America on an American ship due to sail in but a few days. However, my mother was told we could not make a booking for my father without his being present. There was nothing we could do until Dad arrived.

Every evening for a week, we would walk to the railway station to meet the train from Irun hoping my father would be aboard. Every night we would walk home alone and dejected. On the seventh evening, we spotted him hurrying down the platform. What a joyful reunion it was!

The reason my father was so delayed was that, failing to get his exit visa in Bordeaux, he had gone to Paris to see what was holding up his permit. Once there he found that there was no record of his having made an application to leave. It had evidently been lost somewhere en route. He had no problem getting the necessary papers in Paris and took the next train to Irun. Our note was delivered to him in Irun, and he immediately left for Lisbon. The family was back together, we had enough money to pay our hotel bill and cover our expenses, and we began to negotiate our passage to America. The American ship had already sailed. There was a Portuguese freighter with a cargo of cork that was destined for Armstrong Cork Company in Pennsylvania. We secured passage and boarded the freighter within a week of our reunion with my father.

You can imagine our surprise when we discovered that the two Americans who had lost my mother's wallet were on board the same ship. We never spoke to them, and they avoided us.

Our crossing of the Atlantic went without incident. We were not reassured, however, when the captain briefed us that, should we be torpedoed, we should grab a bale of the cork and await rescue. Fortunately, we didn't need to use the cork cargo as life preservers. However, the next time the ship made the trip it was torpedoed, sunk, and all hands and passengers were lost.

This was a poor ship with a poorly paid Portuguese crew. There were only about a dozen passengers aboard. Rations were spartan, and the diet was heavy with potatoes. We started from Lisbon with a cow and some chickens on the stern. By the time we reached landfall at Wilmington, Delaware, there was neither a cow nor a chicken left. We had eaten everything. I do remember the wonderful olive oil served on the ship that we poured in great quantities on everything we ate.

At Wilmington, my father's younger brother, my uncle, Jimmy Hirshfield, who was in the Coast Guard, and my Aunt Marjorie met the ship in a Coast Guard cutter. We left the ship for the cutter and were on our way to my father's sister in Philadelphia. This would be another world for a young girl who had been brought up in France, who spoke little English.

Denise was enrolled in a Catholic boarding school outside of Philadelphia under the wing of her Aunt Dorothy Loder. She had lost much of the English she had learned before moving to France. She was homesick for her parents. The family was reintegrated at the close of the school year when Denise's father bought a house in Pelham Manor, close to New Rochelle. (Remarkably, they had ventured from La Rochelle, France, to New Rochelle, New York.)

Denise slowly made the conversion from her French life to being an American schoolgirl. She attended parochial schools for her first two years of high school and the last two years in Pelham's public school. She attended the University of Rochester and went to graduate school at Columbia University where she earned a master's degree. Denise's passion for traveling led her to a career working for the airlines. Her longest stint was with BOAC, which subsequently became British Airways.

Denise's uncle, Jimmy Hirshfield, became Admiral Hirshfield, assistant commandant of the United States Coast Guard. In one of the many coincidences that are found at Falcons Landing, his widow, Marjorie Hirshfield, now lives in this same community in the building adjacent to Denise's.

From an early age, Denise had a close association with the Coast Guard, and it was through that organization that she met Comdr. Fred Munchmeyer while on a flight to Europe. Fred, understandably impressed with Denise, was most solicitous of her well-being on the trip. His attention led to their romance and marriage in 1963. Fred retired early from the Coast Guard on a medical disability. He subsequently earned a master's degree from Massachusetts Institute of Technology and a Ph.D. from the University of Michigan in naval architecture. Denise and Fred lived in Hawaii for twenty-five years where he taught mechanical engineering at the University of Hawaii. In another of the many coincidences Falcons Landing residents share, part of Fred's term at the university was served during the tenure of Falcons Landing's Harlan Cleveland when Harlan was president of that institution. Fred and Denise subsequently moved to New Orleans where Fred became the first director of the school of naval architecture at the University of New Orleans.

The move to Falcons Landing was Fred's idea. The change in tax laws liberalizing the estate tax provisions on the sale of a home was the clincher for them, and they moved in 1996. They have been active and supportive members of the community as volunteers in a broad range of activities. There are only seven representatives of the Coast Guard at Falcons Landing—two widows, a widower, and two couples. That represents a mere 1 percent of the residents. But the Coast Guard group, which includes the Munchmeyers, Capt. Frank and Rosemary Riley, Bob Park, and the two widows, Marjorie Hirshfield and Bertha Putnam, are special citizens of the community and make up for their lack of numbers with their wonderful energy as volunteers and contributors to the social agenda of Falcons Landing.

11

William "Rad" Radlinski

By his account, William Anthony "Rad" Radlinski did not join the U.S. Army as a private in 1940 out of a sense of patriotism. He certainly did not enlist for the money, and, at the age of nineteen, he was not looking for a career. Rad just wanted to get out of Salamanca, New York. He wanted to be free of the small-town cycle—the cycle of working in one of the local factories on the Allegheny River, marrying a local girl, and raising a family where his children could start the cycle all over again.

After graduating from high school in June 1938, Rad had spent two years working in temporary jobs including six months with the Civilian Conservation

---

1. This profile is based on a series of interviews in late 2004 and early 2005, from written input from Mr. Radlinksi and also from Radlinski, William Anthony, "My Military Service" December 2000 (Unpublished, in libraries of author and W. A. Radlinski family).

Corps (CCC) near Franklinville, New York. Rad's odyssey took him from a most fortunate marriage to Terry Harmuth on through the perils of World War II in Europe. When the war ended, he went to Hofstra College, using the GI Bill to earn a bachelor of arts degree in three years. His thirty-year civilian career was with the U.S. Geological Survey. Throughout his civilian life, he maintained his affiliation with the U.S. Army Reserve. He retired from the Army Reserve at age sixty, with twenty-one years and nine months of creditable service. (At age sixty, Army reservists with twenty years of service earned by actively participating in the Reserve programs, plus any active duty, may retire with the same benefits as the retired veteran of the regular Army.) One might say that from the age of nineteen, Rad has always been a soldier. He has held the enlisted ranks of private through staff sergeant and the commissioned ranks of second lieutenant through lieutenant colonel.

Rad underwent basic training at Mitchel Field on Long Island, New York, in 1940. After basic training, one of his early assignments was to a secret "War Room" that kept track of German U-boats and attacks on shipping in the Atlantic. He was soon assigned to a variety of other duties, from packing parachutes to working in a photo laboratory to working as a draftsman. By 1942, he had been promoted to staff sergeant, advancing to that rank from private in only two months. His journey through this wonderful life to Falcons Landing is best told in his own words. Following are extracts of the military history he wrote as a legacy to his children "…of a tall skinny, naïve, Polish kid from a small town in western New York State, who, in 1940, at age nineteen, went out into the world by joining the Army."[2]

The B-18 used to drop-test parachutes. Rad rode in lower bubble

2.   Radlinski, op. cit.

Rad wrote:

> I took my first ride in an airplane during my parachute-packing days. We spot-checked the parachutes we packed by attaching them to 180-pound dummies and dropping them out of the bomb bays of available planes. My first time up was in a B-18 bomber. I sat with an old sergeant in the bombardier's bubble, which was located under the cockpit in the belly of the plane. As we were landing, I noticed the sergeant craning his neck to look backwards under the plane. I asked what he was doing and he replied that he was looking to see if the wheels were down. Naively I said, "Doesn't the pilot know?" He responded, "Kid, it doesn't hurt to look!"

Rad responded to a notice on a bulletin board soliciting applications for a warrant officer program but was told that, at age twenty-one, he was too young. His direct supervisor, a Colonel Glenn, told him, "You don't know enough to be a warrant officer." He then applied for and was accepted for the engineer's Officer Candidate School at Fort Belvoir, Virginia.

Rad continues in his memoirs:

> You have no rank in Officer Candidate School and are addressed simply as "mister." The initial enrollment in our class was nearly two hundred. About half were weeded out after the first month and about twenty in the next two months. Only eighty of us graduated. The training was grueling, both physically and mentally. Because I was tall and stood out, I got "picked on" at the very first formation and told to come front and center and explain to the class how a soldier marches. I, of course, flubbed it, whereupon the "Tack" officers, who were our mentors, proceeded to belittle me mercilessly and told me to spend the next hour 'double-timing' around a nearby building. For the rest of that week, they harassed me continuously, but when I didn't break down, they let up and didn't bother me much thereafter. We had some very unkind names for our tack officers whose job it was to see if they could make us fold under pressure.
>
> Most of my OCS graduating class of eighty was, upon graduation, assigned to either Combat Engineers or the Amphibious Engineers, both high-risk duty. (See profile of Alden Colvocoresses for confirmation of the hazards of combat engineering.) There was an opening however, for a topographic engineer for which I was selected, because my record showed that I had once been a "map-maker."

Staff Sergeant officer candidate Radlinski had never been a map-maker. His identification as such was derived from the fact that he had worked for four months following graduation from high school for the Farm Bureau. Here, he appraised property for tillable land from aerial photos. When such information is entered into Army personnel files, classifiers refer to the *Dictionary of Occupational Titles*. They find the nearest professional classification number, which often has a more impressive title than the jobs performed warrant. Thus, Rad was classified as a 'map-maker.'

Rad was commissioned a second lieutenant in the Corps of Engineers in early 1943. Terry, a bride of five months, was now expecting their first child. She joined Rad before his departure for the European Theater of Operations.

Rad continued:

> Terry went with me on my first assignment as a commissioned officer to Blackstone, Virginia. We arrived by train on a cold and snowy Sunday afternoon in February. We thought we would certainly be able to find a hotel where she could stay. Wrong. There was only one hotel in Blackstone, and it had been booked for months. So we went from door to door in the residential area looking for a room to rent. Finally, after trying for about an hour with no luck, a seemingly sweet old lady said that she did have a room. When I immediately responded that we would take it, she said, 'Don't you want to see it?' I said I would take it sight unseen. We were cold and desperate, it was snowing and blowing and Terry was pregnant. The woman insisted that we come in to inspect the room and asked, 'Where ya'll from?' Not thinking too clearly, I said, 'New York,' whereupon she pointed to the door and said, 'Get out. I will not have a Yankee staying in my house!' We finally found a room in a farmhouse on the outskirts of town which was rented to us on a night-to-night basis because the owner said her father was dying in an adjoining room. We never did see the father and often wondered if the reference to his presence wasn't a ploy.

Rad's assignments took him from an Engineer Topographic Battalion at Camp Pickett, Virginia, to Camp Sutton, in Monroe, North Carolina. There he joined the 672nd Engineer Topographic Company, an organization he stayed with until the end of the war. He was designated a topographic engineer officer.

While still in the United States, the company moved from camp to fort to camp with Rad being assigned the varied extra duties that fall to second lieutenants. Some of his additional duties included being a mess officer, supply officer, operations officer, special services officer, and war bond officer. This being the period preceding the Uniform Code of Military Justice, before the requirement that staff judge advocates (lawyers) prosecute and defend accused in courts martial, junior officers such as Rad were the point men in the administration of military justice. He took his turn, to include duty as an assistant trial judge advocate for a general court martial and, in the absence of the trial judge advocate, prosecuted and convicted several accused in desertion and other cases.

Once in Germany, the 672nd Company was assigned to the Ninth Army. After they crossed the Rhine River, the unit was transferred to the Third Army. Their mission was to provide topographic maps, photo maps, and ground-survey-control data. They interpreted and updated captured German maps using aerial photographs and other supporting data. The company of 120 men and five officers was organized into four platoons: a headquarters platoon, a photomapping platoon (commanded by Rad), a survey platoon, and a reproduction platoon. The company had a wide range of reconnaissance and technical capabilities designed to put accurate, current maps into the hands of the troops.

It was October 7, 1944, when Lieutenant Radlinski boarded the SS *West Point* and sailed for Europe.

Rad recalled:

> My record as an officer was almost seriously damaged on the Atlantic Ocean crossing. I was appointed the troop officer of the deck for the deck where the MPs were quartered. Because their assignment required them to keep odd hours, they would spend some of their off-duty time playing poker for small change. Gambling aboard ship was forbidden. The troop officer of the ship, an Army captain, walked in on one of their games, confiscated the pot, and dressed me down for allowing this to happen. He said he was going to have the men court-martialed. I argued with him against taking such action, and when he became adamant, I called him a "son-of-a-bitch." He then said he would report me to the captain of the ship and recommend I be court-martialed for insubordination. Nothing happened, however (someone up the line had better judgment), but I spent a few days worrying about my future and the future of the men in my charge. It did my heart good when weeks later, in Belgium, two GIs came up to me and said, "Lieutenant, we remember you. You stood up for us when were about to be court-martialed on the ship coming over. We want to thank you."

Rad and his crew disembarked in England, and immediately entrained for Southampton to sail across the English Channel in a Landing Ship Infantry (LSI), to land on Utah Beach, Normandy, France. They set up operations in Valognes, France, while searching for their trucks, map-making equipment, generators, stoves, and tents which had been lost on one of the beaches. Once they located their equipment, the unit moved to Totes, France. Somewhere during their migration, they confiscated a German bus as they moved across Germany. They named it 'Rad's Rascals' and used it for troop transport in lieu of two-and-a-half-ton trucks. The bus was taken from them by the MPs when they were assigned to the Third Army.

"We were in Totes on Christmas Eve, 1944," Rad said. "The Catholics in our unit wanted to go to a Christmas Eve Mass as well as take communion. There was a Catholic church nearby, but the French pastor could not speak English. He could read it, however, and he had an English copy of the Ten Commandments. So we came up with an arrangement that in the confessional he would read the commandments one by one, and we would respond with a 'yes' or 'no' as to whether or not we broke it! Midnight Mass in the old church was a delight, except that it was very cold in the unheated stone building. After the French congregation sang carols in French, we soldiers sang in English, with gusto. We also gave the French whatever goodies (chocolate, cigarettes, soap) we could scrape together."

Radlinski kneeling under the letters AS in front of the commandeered German bus.

Photo courtesy of Radlinski

The unit's interlude in Totes was short-lived. They were soon in the middle of the Battle of the Bulge. The attack began on the morning of 16 December 1944. The Germans intended it to be a massive, coordinated operation by creating a second attack in Holland and a third in Northern France. The military goal was to capture Antwerp and cut off the Allied troops to the north. The political goal was to cause a schism among the Allied forces. It was the largest battle ever fought by the U.S. Army with the commitment of over 600,000 troops. The U.S. Forces were supported by 55,000 British, while the Germans were attacking with about a half million troops of the Fifth and Sixth Panzer Armies. The Battle of the Bulge has become identified with the fight for Bastogne. Such is misleading, because it was not just the holding of Bastogne that defeated the Germans. More important was the repulse of the German attack further north and at St. Vith after four days of fierce fighting. Nevertheless, Bastogne became a symbol of U.S. resistance and contempt for the enemy following the media's reporting General McAuliffe's response of 'nuts' to the German commander's demand for surrender. The Germans lost 1,000 aircraft, 800 tanks and 100,000 men in the attack, while the Americans suffered 81,000 and the British 1,400 casualties. Winston Churchill called the operation the 'greatest American battle of the war.'

Rad said:

> When the Battle of the Bulge began, we hurried to Belgium to set up operations in a small hamlet near Tongres (Tongeren). The trip was a nightmare. The roads were icy, and snow was falling heavily, visibility was poor, and armed Germans in GI uniforms, fluent in English, had infiltrated the area. I was at the head of our convoy, and when I went back with my driver to check things out (we didn't have two-way radios in those days), I found that half of our vehicles were no longer with us. We spent the rest of the night looking for them. We were stopped a couple of times at roadblocks in nervous confrontations with GIs who, to us, could just as well been Germans, and they weren't sure about us either. We found the rest of the company in Liege.
>
> After the Battle of the Bulge, I learned that the Second Armored Division was nearby. So I got a jeep and driver, and we went looking for my brother Leonard, who I knew was in that division. We had not seen each other for over four years. I found him taking a bath, literally, in a house the GIs had commandeered. He claimed it was his first bath in two months. I got permission from Leonard's commanding officer to take him back to a chateau where I was staying in nearby Tongres, providing I got him back within three days. That night, an errant German "buzz bomb" landed in our backyard, making a huge hole, and blowing out the windows. None of us were hurt because we heard the bomb coming and were flat on the floor when it hit. If it had landed a few feet closer, we could have both been killed. Our meeting in combat provided a bonding between my brother and me that grew tighter through the years.
>
> We advanced through Europe. I was in charge of finding suitable quarters for our company as we moved along to keep up with the forward deployed units. This house-hunting duty had its hazards, as my advance party and I would sometimes find ourselves in precarious situations. Once, I unwittingly entered a village being bombarded by German artillery. Upon recognizing the situation, we ducked under a house for cover where we joined several other GIs. The Americans had been in the area for a few days and told us that, based

on their experience, the shelling would probably end in about an hour, which it did. As we were leaving, some German 88s zeroed in on our jeep, but we were able to quickly speed out of range. We were in Mainburg, about thirty-five miles north of Munich, when the war ended.

Rad and the 672nd Engineer Topographic Company were in the European Theater of Operations for thirteen months and earned three battle stars. No one of the company was killed in action, but there were seven wounded. It wasn't the Germans who sent Rad to the hospital at Camp Mourmelon, France, just days after the end of the war. It was pneumonia, with attendant infections. He ran temperatures that reached 105 degrees. Without the benefit of 840,000 units of recently discovered penicillin, he would never have made it home. Nevertheless, he recovered and set sail for the States out of Marseilles on 2 November 1945 aboard the SS *Elgin Victory*. In the midst of heavy seas in the North Atlantic, the ship began sinking as it was taking water around the propeller shaft. The ship limped in to Bermuda for repairs with the help of a destroyer and a sea-going tug.

The grand arrival back to American shores was at Newport News, Virginia, where they were met by a band playing 'Sentimental Journey.' Rad's wife, Terry, met him at Fort Dix, where he was processed out of the Army of the United States into the U.S. Army Reserve on 30 January 1946. So began a rewarding thirty-five-year stint in the Army Reserve until retirement at age sixty in August of 1981.

When Rad opted to join the U.S. Geological Survey in August 1949, shortly after graduating from Hofstra College and doing some graduate work in mathematics at Columbia University in New York, he embarked on a distinguished career.

At the Survey, Rad initially worked as a researcher in photogrammetry, and then moved into successively more responsible positions to become the Survey's associate director. As second in charge of the Survey, he shared with the director in the management of 13,000 employees and annual budgets that reached three quarters of a billion dollars. During the ten years in this position, he was the chair of the executive committee of the Survey and often acting director.

Rad reflected: "Managing the operations of earth scientists was a challenging but rewarding task. They were some of the finest people you could ever meet and very dedicated to their respective sciences, but when it came to administrative and organizational matters, such as getting pre-approvals and working within the system, they were difficult. It was not uncommon for them to spend funds that were not in their budgets, expecting that the front office would somehow come up with the wherewithal and justify their expenditures. Which we always were able to do, but it took a lot of juggling."

During Rad's tenure, the U.S. Geological Survey was responsible for the topographic mapping of the United States and its possessions, for geological and geophysical studies of the earth including volcano and earthquake investigations, for studying and collecting fresh-water data from rivers, streams, lakes, and underground aquifers, and for the management of leases on federal lands and the Outer Continental Shelf for the extraction of minerals, oil, and gas. It was also involved in studies and distribution of data from earth-resource satellites. Just prior to his retirement in 1979, Rad was named the cochairman of an international committee with the long title of 'Soviet American Working Group on Prevention of Environmental Pollution During Well Drilling, Production, and Pipeline Transportation of Oil and Gas.' Rad's counterpart cochairman was an official of the Soviet Union. The assignment required that Rad head delegations of American petroleum and gas experts on trips to the Soviet Union and host Russian delegations during reciprocal visits to this country.

Rad recalled:

> Dealing with the Soviets was difficult. When they visited us here in America, we showed them details of our operations in the Gulf of Mexico, Texas, and California. But when we went to the Soviet Union, they did everything possible to keep us from seeing what they were doing. All they seemed to want to do was entertain us at festive parties that lasted for hours. When we traveled from point to point it was always at high speeds and in the darkness of night. When I insisted that they change these tactics or that we would stop the reciprocal visits and end the exchange, they did shorten the banquets, transport us from place to place in the daylight at more reasonable speeds, and show us more details of their operations. I was particularly appreciative of the shorter meals, because I was running out of subject matter for the obligatory toasts. Every dinner involved a half-dozen toasts. After toasting our joint efforts in World War II, outer-space programs, and our current efforts of cooperating in the oil and gas fields, the subject of toasts became pretty thin gruel. We finally realized the reason for their behavior; they were embarrassed to show us their antiquated technology once they had seen our contemporary U.S. operations. The industry experts in our delegation estimated that their technology was about twenty years behind ours.

Rad also has stories about how, on an occasion, the Soviets had harassed him in his hotel room in Moscow by calling in the middle of the night to come down and pay his bill (which was prepaid). There was the time they would not let his delegation board a British Airways flight out of Moscow, insisting that they fly instead on the Soviet airline, Aeroflot. He is also convinced, on the basis of much circumstantial evidence, that the Soviets were responsible for breaking into his home in Silver Spring, Maryland, while he and Terry were attending a reception at the Soviet Embassy in Washington. The senseless harassment took many shapes. Once, for a visit to an offshore platform in the Caspian Sea, the Russians were going to transport the Americans on a naval vessel which would have taken four hours one way, instead of a forty-five minute helicopter ride. When Rad refused to board the ship, a helicopter was provided. Such was the life of an American in an American-Soviet joint project during the Cold War.

The June 1975 'Report to the President by the Commission on CIA Activities within the United States' (commonly known as the Rockefeller Commission) included the following recommendation: 'A civilian agency committee should be reestablished to oversee the civilian uses of aerial intelligence photography in order to avoid any concerns over the improper domestic use of a CIA-developed system.' In 1975, such a committee was formed, and Rad was named chairman, a position he held until his retirement.

During his service with the Geological Survey, Rad was also active in professional societies. He became the president of the American Society of Photogrammetry (ASP), and president of the Federation Internationale des Geometres (FIG), an international federation of surveyors from nearly one hundred member countries. Following his retirement, he became the executive director of the American Congress on Surveying and Mapping.

In 1966, Rad was given the highest honor awarded by the Department of the Interior, the Distinguished Service Award, by then-Secretary Stewart L. Udall, who himself had an interesting tour of service in Washington.

Speaking about Udall, Rad said:

> In 1965, shortly after he became Secretary of the Interior, Udall, a dedicated environmentalist, authored a book titled *The Quiet Crisis* that traces in a single narrative the history of the nation's tortuous relationship between man and nature. His hope was that the book would "enable Americans to grasp the relationship between human stewardship of the land and the fullness of the American earth." The introduction of the book was written by John F. Kennedy, who noted that "the crisis may be quiet, but it is urgent," and, "we must do in our own day what Theodore Roosevelt did sixty years ago and Franklin Roosevelt thirty years ago." I was flattered that Secretary Udall inscribed in my copy of the book, "For Wm. Radlinski—One of our top USGS specialists who knows the land as few men do."
>
> Another of my bosses, up the line a bit, was Secretary of the Interior Walter J. Hickel, former governor of Alaska. He was a genuine Horatio Alger

character, one of ten children born to tenant farmers in Kansas who, at the age of twenty-one, had migrated to Alaska with thirty-seven cents in his pocket. In May of 1970, Secretary Hickel wrote a letter to President Nixon expressing his concern about the impact of the Vietnam War on American youth. The opening paragraph read, "I believe this Administration finds itself, today, embracing a philosophy which appears to lack appropriate concern for the attitude of a great mass of Americans—our young people." From that point, the letter became even more critical of the president's policies. Unfortunately for Secretary Hickel, the letter, now famous, was leaked to the press and was in the news for months. Mr. Nixon ultimately fired the secretary over the letter, and Hickel returned to Alaska where he again became governor in 1990. However, he had made an impact in the short time he was in Washington. During his stewardship, it was the studies conducted by the USGS in the late 1960s that convinced the administration that the Alaska Pipeline could be built without any significant damage to the environment.

We made a number of other contributions that continue to impact on America's energy and protection of our environment. The safety of outer continental shelf (OCS) offshore oil and gas operations was greatly enhanced by the USGS when it promulgated new regulations for OCS operations including the design of offshore platforms and pipelines. In the preparation of these regulations, the USGS worked hand-in-hand with industry, the U.S. Coast Guard, other governmental agencies, foreign and domestic, and the Marine Board of the National Academy of engineering with which the Survey commissioned a study on safety of OCS operations. I chaired the USGS's work group on OCS safety and pollution control that recommended these controls.

In 1976, Rad was named an honorary member of the Royal Institution of Chartered Surveyors (RICS), a professional organization of surveyors established in Great Britain under Royal Patronage in 1869. He was only the second American to be so honored in 107 years. In 1963, the Board of Geographic Names named a peak in Antarctica after Rad. Mont Radlinski is 9,020 feet high and about 550 miles from the South Pole. Rad has also been a member of the prestigious Cosmos Club in Washington, D.C., since 1970 and is a registered professional engineer.

Rad joined the U.S. Geological Survey in 1949 in the topographic division doing mostly research and development work. He was instrumental in developing advanced photogrammetric instruments and techniques. In 1968, he was elected president of the American Society of Photogrammetry. He rose through the ranks to become the Survey's associate director in 1969. In 1971, while serving as the acting director of the U.S. Geological Survey, Department of Interior, he was elected to be president of the International Federation of Surveyors, the first time an American was to hold that post. His honors and representation on professional boards, committees, and associations are numerous. He was an aggressive, active leader in his profession, authoring numerous papers that were published in professional journals. In 1973 and 1976, he traveled to the Soviet Union as the head of a delegation to discuss ways of preventing environmental pollution from oil and gas drilling and production.

Rad credits his Army experience, during and following World War II, with providing direction and opportunities that he otherwise would not have enjoyed. One of the benefits is his status as a retired Army reservist that qualified Terry and him for entrance into Falcons Landing. (Because of his seniority in federal service and their early entrance in the community, they would have qualified without the Army association.) They have been active residents, performing much-appreciated volunteer services to the community. Terry has been one of Falcons Landing most accomplished artists with her works being displayed in the hallways of the apartment buildings which serve as resident art galleries. She has also been active as a volunteer serving the residents in the Johnson Center, the home of those who require assisted or nursing care.

Recall that as a man, Rad wanted to shake the dust of Salamanca from his size fourteen boots. However, he never abandoned Salamanca. He maintains a close, intimate relationship with his Polish family there, visiting often, and by writing a quarterly *Radlinski Family News & Record* that dates back to January 1989. In September of 1993, the title and scope of the publication changed to include the Prusinoski side of the family. In large part, Rad, who has left Salamanca, has been the glue to bind this close family together. He manifests great pride in the name Radlinski and has written:

"Names ending in 'ski' became popular in the fifteenth century when Polish nobles began to use surnames as a means of distinguishing individuals of the same name. Originally, only nobles could have surnames and only the surnames of nobles could be formed by adding 'ski'. This custom changed, however, as the nobility became weaker and wealthy peasants began to use surnames. 'Ski' is distinctly Polish, while names ending in 'sky' are usually Czech, Jewish, Russian, or Ukrainian. There are many exceptions, but this is true more often than not."

Rad has been the chairman of the editorial board of the in-house publication, *Falcons Landing News,* and was elected to serve on the residents' council as the vice-chair.

"Falcons Landing is the ideal place for us to spend our final years," Rad said. "It provides us with elegant, total care, secure communal living where we can remain active and engaged. Our move here has been one of our wisest decisions."

12

George Ureke

George's Ureke's father, John, with a second-grade education and no ability to speak English, immigrated from the small village of Colmosul Mare, Romania, to Chicago, Illinois, in about 1904. He planned to stay a few months to earn enough money to buy a farm and home in Romania. However, John changed his mind about returning to Colmusal Mare and about 1910 he sent for his wife, George's mother, Linca, to come to the new country. She left their two young

1.   George Ureke died before the drafting of this profile. The majority of quotations herein (with some minor editorials) and the photographs come from *A Personal History*, by George Ureke, January 1, 1997, and *Falcons Landing News*, May 2000. Both may be found in the Falcons Landing library. The text has been reviewed for accuracy by Colonel Ureke's widow, Carol Stolldorf. All photographs come from *A Personal History*.

sons in Romania with her parents. A third son, George, was born in 1919 at home in Chicago into a family that would eventually include five children.

The Urekes led a rustic life in a farm-style house in what is now the middle of Chicago. The house had a wine cellar, vegetable garden, chickens, a cow, and a goat. They lived essentially as the family had lived in Romania. The Urekes converted from Eastern Orthodoxy to Baptist, because there was a Baptist church where the services were conducted in Romanian. By 1922, George's father graduated from being a laborer to owning his own cement contracting company.

John S. and Linca Rusu Eureke

In 1927, eight-year-old George saw a biplane fly across the fields of Chicago, and he was hooked. He wanted to be a pilot. (In May of that year, Charles Lindbergh made his famous solo trans-Atlantic flight. George read his book, *We*, three times.) The 1929 stock market crash led to the Depression and the loss of John Ureke's business. The family went "on relief." George Ureke joined his father in pushing a cart through the streets of Chicago, picking up metal, glass, paper, and anything of value to be delivered to a junkyard, where it would be weighed and bought by the pound. George also sold magazines for $3.15 a week. By age eleven, George had begun caddying on Saturdays and Sundays, earning the princely sum of a dollar for eighteen holes, bringing home as much as two dollars a day.

George was known to be very bright but a problem child prone to be disruptive. He taught himself to play the trumpet. Probably having inherited the talent from his father who played the *fluiera*, (a fife-like instrument that was played by Romanian shepherds),

At age sixteen, George organized a band called "The Five Rhythm Lads," playing Saturday night dances for five dollars each a night. His earnings went to his mother. Besides playing the trumpet, he became the band vocalist and started skipping classes, preferring to spend the bulk of his time with the band and in his school music hall. He flunked a grade in high school.

Ureke and Trumpet, New York, 1936

Later that year, having completed only a year and a half of high school, George left home. His father, tortured by alcoholism, had become abusive. He was given fifty cents by his mother as he left. His plan was to somehow work his way to New York and onto the popular CBS radio show, Major *Bowes Amateur Hour*, an amateur talent contest. Contestants who won three times (by vote of the audience) earned cash awards, scholarships or parts in one of the three stage shows that toured the country. If the performance was a bust, a large gong was struck and the contestant was banished. George hitchhiked to New York and panhandled in the city. He did make an appearance on the Major Bowes show, but the show was rigged. Instead of having a shot at winning one of the prizes, the show's producers paid him fifty dollars to purposefully botch his performance by hitting a sour note while climbing the scales on his trumpet. He got the gong. After that appearance, he made a profession of going to neighborhood theater amateur hours and going through the Major Bowes show routine by deliberately hitting a loud, sour note and getting the gong. Each of these performances netted him a twenty-five dollar fee, a handsome sum during the Depression.

In 1937, George contracted to ship out on cruise ships as a bellboy. On his fourth trip, having saved about three hundred dollars, he jumped ship in Puerto Rico with a friend who was a native of the island. When George's money ran out in Puerto Rico, he shipped out again, this time on a molasses tanker as a second cook. He learned to speak Spanish and made and saved a grubstake.

He returned to New York City. There he registered for night school to earn his high school diploma while working as a pressman in a hat-lining factory.

After a stint working in several resort areas, George received a frantic letter from his sixteen-year-old sister telling him that his mother was in a nursing home and that his father had pneumonia. His sister was struggling to support and care for the family. At age twenty, he returned home to care for the family.

George joined the Chicago Flat Janitors' Union, securing a job as janitor for a sixteen-unit building for $160 a month plus a free seven-room apartment. He moved his father, mother, brother, and sister out of the shack in which they were living into the apartment. There was nothing in the house worth keeping. As in all his undertakings, George flourished in the business. He soon was managing twelve buildings, earning $15,000 a year, a most handsome salary in those days.

George wrote:

> One of the buildings I got was a twelve-unit apartment building, extremely dirty and full of foreigners. We went in and cleaned it all up. Dad and I spent three days just cleaning the building from top to bottom. Three days later,

people were throwing their trash out into the courtyard again, so I decided I wasn't going to work on that building every day. I planned to clean it up once every two weeks. I received a phone call one day. The person on the phone identified himself, but it didn't register with me as to who he was. He said that he was at this problem building, and he wanted to see me right NOW! So, dressed in my white shirt, I jumped in my handsome convertible and went over.

"My uncle," the man said, "the priest who owned this building, has died. I'm taking over. First Chicago Realty Corporation is not going to be the manager anymore. I'm going to manage it. I'm coming back here at three o'clock this afternoon, and I want this place sparkling CLEAN!"

"Bull," I said. "I cleaned it once..."

"What did you say?" he says.

"I said Bull! I cleaned it once. I'm not going to..."

He pulled a gun on me, shoved it into my stomach, and it was the biggest gun I had ever seen in my life. My knees began to shake.

"Get in that vestibule," he said. "You didn't understand who I said I was."

When he mentioned his name again, my god! It came to me. The last three days, the newspaper headlines carried his name. He had been arrested for murdering a dry cleaning truck driver for getting into his neighborhood—into his territory. I think his name was Tony Arcaro.

He said, "I just came out of jail. I've been grilled for three days, and I don't mind going back again to be grilled."

"Yes sir, yes sir, yes sir," I heard myself say. "I'll clean it up. I'll clean it up. I'll go home and change clothes and come back and clean it up."

"See that you do," he says.

Well, I got home, and I called Jimmy Jacobs, my union business agent. Thank God he was in the office.

"George," he said, "Don't leave the house. Keep the door locked and don't let anybody in until you hear from me."

I was pretty worried, believe me, and more than willing to follow instructions. About two hours later, I got a phone call, and it wasn't Jimmy Jacobs. It was him—Tony Arcaro.

"This is Tony," he says. "Your union hoods are here in the office. We just struck a bargain. I'm going to let First Realty manage the building, and I won't be bothering you anymore. You can run the building as you see fit."

I said, "Well, thank you very much." I hung up, and I called Jimmy Jacobs and told him what happened.

"That's right," he said. "Don't worry about it anymore."

The union was very strong in Chicago in those days, just as strong as the hoods and maybe even more persuasive.

On November 11, 1940, the twenty-one-year-old George married twenty-year-old Ann Lupei, also of Chicago and also of Romanian descent. They moved into the seven-room apartment with George's family. Their honeymoon days were short lived. On December 7, 1941, the Japanese bombed Pearl Harbor. On June 30, 1942, George Ureke enlisted as a private in the Army. On June 30, 1943, he was commissioned a second lieutenant pilot through the Aviation Cadet Program. Soon thereafter, he left for Italy to fly combat missions in the B-17. George wrote:

They say in war there are no atheists in the trenches. There aren't any in the air flying combat missions either. I had never spent much time praying, but before a mission, all around me, men were praying. And I prayed then too, from my heart, that my crew would come back safely and, of course, that I would return in one piece.

One of the missions that I flew was a short mission to northern Italy to bomb a bridge, a railroad trestle. I only had one squadron of nine airplanes—three, three, and three. I was the leader. Well, to hit a small bridge, we couldn't fly very high. The bombing height was only about eighteen thousand feet. The enemy had anti-aircraft guns on the top of these eight thousand and nine thousand-foot mountains, which made them very, very accurate.

We started the bomb run, and I saw three or four puffs of smoke. I knew what they were doing. They were bracketing two or three shots to see where we were and where their missiles would explode. We were on the bomb run, and I had no control of the airplane. The bombardier, with the Norden bomb sight, was flying the airplane, tipping this way and that, adjusting to drop the bomb. The next three bursts of flak were spaced about three seconds apart, each burst one-half the distance from my squadron. "Oh, boy," I said. "They've bracketed us, and we're going to get it on the next one. We've had it!" I heard the "Bombs away!" Immediately, I started an unusually steep turn, the whole squadron turning with me. As I looked out right where we would have been, the whole sky exploded. A hundred and fifty guns went off. Hundreds and hundreds of shells were bursting right where we would have been in three or four more seconds. I had turned just in time. I think this was the most scary bomb run I ever made, because I could see it all happening, and there were just so few of us. On this mission, nine airplanes all came home—in one piece.

George continued:

Flying a bombing mission out of Foggia, Italy, off Tortorella U.S. Army Air Field, my B-17 got hit by flak—pretty bad. All four engines were still running, but ALL of my flight instruments failed. I had no air speed indicator. I had no instruments to give me any idea of our speed. We were flying in formation. When we arrived over the base at Tortorella, we peeled off, flying the landing patterns in trail formation. I thought, "How can I plan my approach with no air speed indicator?" An idea came to me. "We'll drop back behind the ship in front of us, so that on the final approach, we can establish a rate of closure that our approach would be above stall speed."

Well, in the morning when we took off, the steel mat runway was covered with three inches of slimy mud. It had been raining for weeks. Airplanes taking off and landing just pushed the steel mat deeper into the mud. Every time they took off and landed, more and more slimy mud pushed up on top of the steel mat. As we approached the mud-covered runway, we had three or four inches of thick slime on top of the mat. But, I was not worried about coming in 'hot' until I called for flaps. (The flaps would slow the airplane down and allow us to land at a slower speed.) Kenneth Goodman, our copilot says, "We don't have any. They're not coming down." It was too late to crank them down by hand.

I wasn't about to go around a second time and not know how fast or how slow I was flying. So I decided to land regardless of our speed. Being "hot," we didn't touch down until we were halfway down the field. The airplane in front of us made a normal landing and turned off at a taxi strip about four hundred feet short of the end of the runway. The plane in front of us managed to land short enough to turn to the left onto that first taxi lane. As he turned, he looked out his left window and saw that we were halfway down the field and had not yet landed. He turned to his copilot and said, "Look out that right window. George is going to crash into the gully at the end of the runway." (The airplanes that had hit that gully in the past had all blown up.)

I finally got the plane on the mud, and I hit the brakes—no brakes! In a B-17, you can look out the window and see your wheel. Every time I touched the brakes, the wheels would stop, lock, and we would hydroplane over the mud. I had one choice, something we'd been told in earlier training to try in an emergency—"ground-loop" the airplane! I pulled No. 3 and 4 engines back all the way. I pushed the No. 1 and 2 throttles forward to takeoff power and called for "boosters" to try to turn the airplane to the right. Centrifugal force would tip the left wing into the ground (hence ground-loop). But it was so slimy, that the wheels had no friction to make it turn. The plane just kept sliding forward toward the lethal gully. No. 1 and 2 engines at full takeoff power caused the airplane to spin around while sliding straight down the runway. As it approached 180 degrees, I put on all four engines. There we were, going backwards, toward the end of the runway with all four engines at takeoff power. Well, we stopped right on the very end of the runway and immediately started to taxi back to the taxiway we just passed while sliding backwards.

You can imagine how scared the navigator and the bombardier were, sitting in the nose of the airplane as it approached the end of the runway and then began to spin. This maneuver is one that you can be sure had never been done previously nor will it ever be done again. It isn't something you can practice. I can only say that on that landing, Kenneth Goodwin and I both were the copilots. God was flying the airplane and God made the most unbelievable landing ever in a B-17.

George flew twenty-nine combat missions. It took thirty-five missions to qualify to return to the States. But the end of the war in 1945 cut his tour short, and he sailed home in August. George fought to stay in the Army Air Corps as a reservist, as it transitioned to become the United States Air Force. After excelling in several undesirable assignments, he finally was assigned to the flying billet he had been seeking.

"In 1950, I flew the first 'jet bomber' to carry any kind of a bomb," he wrote. "This was also the first jet bomber designed specifically to carry the atomic weapon. I was among the first Air Force pilots to fly the Boeing B-47 Stratojet."

George passed a high school GED (General Educational Development) test, secured a diploma from his old high school, and started studying business administration at Wichita University. Later, while stationed in Germany, George continued to attend night classes and earned a bachelor's degree in military science from the University of Maryland. He subsequently earned a master's in business administration from George Washington University. Following retirement from the Air Force, he taught business courses at night at George Washington University—not bad for a boy who had left home without a high school diploma. It is a tribute to the opportunities and encouragement that he received while serving as an Air Force officer.

George summarized his academic achievements:

> I didn't graduate from high school in the normal manner. Think of it! I was a high school dropout with only one and one-half years of high school until I was thirty-three years old. Between thirty-three and forty-three, I went to night school two or three times a week. After I got my master's degree in business at George Washington University, I thought I'd work on the Ph.D. Somebody told me it's better to go to another university. So, one or two nights a week, I attended American University. At the same time, I was teaching courses...at George Washington University. I never did a dissertation....

Unable to conceive a child, George and Ann adopted a boy and his sister in 1953. Soon thereafter, Ann conceived and they had three children within a year.

From 1955 forward, George continued to have challenging staff assignments. He purchased and piloted his own aircraft and completed several language schools.

"After twenty-three years of service in the Air Force, I left the Pentagon in 1966," George wrote. "I was forty-five years old. I started to draw my pension. On Sundays, during the summer especially, I often gave multi-engine or instrument flying instructions at different airports in Northern Virginia. I was also flying my twin-engine, six-place Cessna for different people who needed to go to various places on business or because of emergencies. I called my charter service Washington Flying Service. I continued to fly for about seventeen years after twenty-three years of flying in the Air Force."

Once retired, George applied the energy, talents, and sound judgment he had exercised in the Air Force to his civilian pursuits. In addition to giving flying instructions and teaching at George Washington University, he worked in the securities industry to include restarting and becoming president of the National Association of Security Dealers. In two years with the association, he increased the membership from two hundred to over seven hundred members and the income from $400,000 to over a million dollars a year.

In August of 1987, Ann died and was buried at Arlington National Cemetery. At the age of sixty-six, George met a Northern Virginia neighbor, Joan Wallbillich Squires, who had been an acquaintance of Ann. A friendship developed into a nine-year romance before Joan died of a massive heart attack.

In 1997 George Ureke moved to Falcons Landing where he met and wed a widow, the lovely Carol Stolldorf who remains at Falcons Landing as of this writing. In 2002, George Ureke died and was laid to rest in Arlington National Cemetery with Ann. He will be fondly remembered as a gregarious, fun loving, active resident.

George summed it up:

> If I had to do it all over again, my military career and my flying are two things I wouldn't want to miss. When I think of my favorite things in life, airplanes would top the list—airplanes and all my many years of flying. I was an

Air Force lieutenant colonel when I retired. The Air Force was good to me. In no other country in the world could the son of an uneducated Romanian peasant family become a university professor, an Air Force lieutenant colonel, and a jet aircraft commander—no other country in the world. Truly this is a great country. And today, I believe all the opportunities are still there, as much as they ever were.

13

Edwin M. Adams Jr.

What do you do for an encore after you have earned a law degree from the University of Illinois; been selected for the United States Foreign Service; served as a gunnery officer in the Pacific Fleet during World War II; and worked as a legal attaché to a post-war Allied commission that was tasked with obtaining German assets secreted away in neutral companies? After you have been a diplomat in Paris, London, Bern, Washington, The Hague, and Africa? After you have been a director of professional studies at the Foreign Service Institute in Washington and retired from the Foreign Service?

Well, if you are Edwin M. Adams Jr. you establish a lecture series called "The American Character as Viewed by One Who Lives Abroad"; you host a radio pro-

---

1.   Some materials are from the University of Illinois article, "Lawyer-Diplomat-Actor Remembers Alma Mater in Big Way with Gift" http://www.uif.illllinois.edu/public/InvestingIL/issue12/art04.htm All photographs are from the files of Mr. Adams.

gram that includes a presentation of "Venice, My Love," which would become an NBC television program of the same name and would earn you the Gold Cross of "Knight Honor of the Italian Government"; you write four television shows on the social responsibility of industry; you do a series of TV dramas and numerous commercials; you appear in twenty-four Hollywood movies in minor roles as a congressman, banker, and doctor, and as a priest so many times (seven) that you thought you had been ordained. Your motion picture credits would include *First Monday in October, Airport 1975,…And Justice for All, Mirror Image*, and twenty more.

After Ed moved into Falcons Landing in 1997, it would seem he might have been ready to retire. But it only gave him the time he needed to write a novel, published in 2004, titled *Petty Destiny*. A paragraph from the book tells the story line: "Within the past month, (it was July 1952) the Colonels had overthrown King Farouk and nationalized the property of British citizens. Sir John Gordon, Lady Mary's husband, the wealthiest of those British citizens, faced his financial losses by committing suicide. Now Lady Gordon, in addition to losing her husband, and her vast wealth as a result of the new government's action, had been given three weeks in which to leave the country.[2]"

How Lady Gordon deals with the connivers who would rob her of what remains of her heritage presents many twists embedded in the mysteries of a colorful Egyptian setting.

"When we were selecting the title of the book, my publisher questioned why I should have chosen the title *Petty Destiny*," Ed recalled. "They felt that it would have been more appropriate if I had chosen a reference to a verse or a line from poetry or classical prose. To counter their opposition, I recited to them these lines from a work by Lord Byron:

> O Rome! My country! City of the soul!
> Orphans of the heart must turn to thee,
> Lone mother of dead empires and control
> In their shut breasts their petty destiny.

"I had made my case, and they accepted my title. And the characters of the book are based, in very large part, on people whom I have known both in and out of Egypt."

Ed is multitalented, having achieved distinction on stage, screen, radio, and in print. In March 2002, Ed entertained his Falcons Landing friends with a brilliant

---

2.   Edwin M. Adams, *Petty Destiny*, (XLibris Corporation, 2004) p. 13.

half-hour discussion of Shakespeare, preceding the presentation of a one-act play titled *When Shakespeare's Ladies Meet*. He spoke for forty minutes quoting lines from *Hamlet, Romeo and Juliet, The Merchant of Venice, Anthony and Cleopatra*, and others, without notes.

A descendent of an uncle of President John Adams, Ed was born on September 28, 1914, in Gridley, Illinois. His father was a successful country doctor, and his mother taught high school English and mathematics. His mother and father had known one another but a short time before their lasting, happy marriage. Ed had a sister who was seven years older. She earned a bachelor's degree at the University of Illinois and a master's in sociology at the University of Chicago, where she married an academic.

Ed recalled that his brother-in-law, a rather snobbish intellectual, told him one time that he couldn't understand how he, Ed, a respected, retired United States Foreign Service officer, could demean himself by appearing in TV commercials for automobiles. "Well, I am not dedicated to it in the way I was to the Foreign Service," Ed replied, "but it is fun, and that is the reason I do it. And, oh yes, one other thing…" Ed then told him to look on the top of his bureau where he had a substantial residuals check from his appearance in such commercials.

After viewing the healthy figure on the check, the brother-in-law said, "Well, they do make it attractive, don't they?"

Ed's early schooling was not memorable. He was a good student at both Gridley lower and high schools before transferring to Morgan Park Military Academy in Chicago, Illinois.

"I transferred to a military academy, because my father thought that I would get a better education at Morgan Park," Ed said. "I was always the last one chosen in pickup games of football and basketball. I remember one hurtful time when I was chosen for a team only after someone said, "Well, we'll take Ed as long as we can have two other guys to make up for it." I was a rather puny child, but I got over that. I wasn't an athlete, although I did win a silver medal for weight lifting in high school, and I became a pretty good swimmer and tennis player."

Ed attended the University of Illinois for seven years. In 1936 he finished undergraduate school with a double major in political science and drama. He graduated from law school in 1939. His father was a third-generation physician, and it was assumed that this was the career that he would pursue, but he wanted to do something different and was encouraged to take up law, notwithstanding his talent and inclinations for drama.

Ed told how he almost followed a different route:

Just about everyone in our family were physicians, but I didn't want to become a doctor, since so many of them were short-lived as a result of the demands of their profession. But my family wanted me to be a professional, and I think I was kind of pushed into the law. There was a time, while I was still in law school, when I almost abandoned the law to go to Hollywood.

In 1939, Warner Brothers was doing a search of Big Ten schools for potential actors. You will recall that 1939 was the year when that wonderful film *Gone with the Wind* was released, and other studios were searching for novel ways to beat the company that produced that film, Metro-Goldwyn-Mayer. A Warner Brothers team was interviewing candidates from all the Big Ten schools who were or had been majors in drama. Now it was something of a challenge for me to get from Champaign, Illinois, to Chicago. My father had died while I was in school, and my finances were typical of the Depression. At any rate, a number of us University of Illinois drama aspirants submitted our photographs and resumes, and two of us were invited to give an audition at the Blackstone Theater along with other young men from Big Ten schools. There were a number of producers, directors, and the like on the panel, sitting in the seats in front of the stage. As each of the candidates was called, they would appear on stage and would be told "Do something." Well, they would "do something" for a minute or so, reciting poetry or Shakespeare, and would be interrupted with the statement, "Thank you very much, that will be all; we will let you know." That meant the end for them; they had not been selected. When my time came I did the soliloquy from Hamlet,

> To be, or not to be—that is the question:
> Whether 'tis nobler in the mind to suffer
> The slings and arrows of outrageous fortune
> Or to take arms against a sea of troubles
> And by opposing end them...

Well, they didn't stop me. They let me do the whole soliloquy.

One of the producers called from the seats, "Oh so you think that you're a John Gielgud do you?" I said, "No, sir, I can't match John Gielgud's expertise or professionalism, but I can match him in ambition." Well, they told me to stay there for a bit. The result was that they selected only two of us from the Big Ten schools, the other being Klusman Parks, also from the University of Illinois.

I called my mother with the good news. I told her that they had made an offer to pay all my expenses to go to Hollywood for six months, to be interviewed there, take screen tests, and if we were both agreeable I would get a contract. If it didn't work out after six months, they would return me home. My mother, who was an intelligent woman with good judgment, said something that made sense: "Edwin, this is March, and you are graduating from law school in June. If you take this offer, you would be leaving law school for just a chance at Hollywood." I agreed. She went on: "Do you think it is wise that you leave the university after seven years and our having invested all that money in your education? What will happen if you go to Hollywood, it doesn't work out, and then you come back to school?" I told her I would have to do the third year over again. She talked me out of the Hollywood option.

I called Warner Brothers and explained my predicament and asked if I couldn't enter their program in September, after I graduated from law school and had taken the bar exam. The man was furious. He told me, "Young man, there are people from all over the country who want this opportunity, and you're turning it down? No, you can't come in September. If you don't want it now, it's never." So, I turned down the opportunity to give Hollywood a try and opted for the law instead.

Klusman Parks went through the program and became a star in Hollywood. They changed Klusman to Larry, and he appeared in forty-three movies and a number of TV shows before dying in 1975. One of his best performances was his 1946 portrayal of Al Jolson in *The Jolson Story*.

"Klusman visited me one time here in Washington and said, 'Ed, you made a mistake to turn down the Hollywood offer—you could have had the same parts I was given.' I often thought I would write a book with the title *The Road Not Taken*, a title already used. Nevertheless, I passed the bar exam and practiced law, one way or another, for the next thirty years."

Ed's first job out of law school was in the legal division of the State Farm Mutual Automobile Insurance Company at their corporate offices in Bloomington, Illinois, where he earned the princely sum of $125 a month. The salary proved to be a comfortable income for him at that time.

"I felt blessed," Ed recalled. "Remember, this was 1939; the Depression was in full swing, and people just out of law school often couldn't find a job. I was one of the few law school graduates at that time who had a job that paid money. There were many who went to work in law firms merely for the experience and received no pay."

The salary was enough to finance a three-week trip to Hollywood and Vancouver on the elegant Santa Fe Chief train. Ed visited all the Hollywood studios and saw what he had missed by choosing a career in the law. From Vancouver, he took the train across Canada and saw the magnificent Canadian Rockies on his way back to Bloomington.

"I was comfortable, able to live a good life, travel, buy a new car, but I knew that the life with State Farm in Bloomington was not going to satisfy me," he said. "I knew that if I stayed there in Bloomington that I would never have a chance to see the world. Remember, this was before Pearl Harbor. In my searching, I became interested in the U.S. Lend-Lease program.

The Lend-Lease program was authorized by the Neutrality Acts that were passed from 1935 through 1941. The legislation permitted the United States to provide defense supplies to Allies without going to war with the Axis powers. The principal recipient of this assistance was Great Britain, but the help also included the Soviet Union, China, and about thirty other nations. By the end of the war, the balance sheet found that the United States had loaned over $35 billion to the Allies. Except for the Soviet Union's debt, almost the entire amount was paid off by 1960; the USSR's repayment was spread out over a longer term.

Ed said:

> So, I had seen California, the West Coast, and Canada and knew that I couldn't stay in Bloomington the rest of my life. I had to see the rest of the world. So I wrote a letter to the president of the United States, Franklin Delano Roosevelt, stating that I knew that I could be of help in the Lend-Lease program. I gave my credentials, and lo and behold, I received a letter from the Department of State that told me that the president of the United States was interested in me, and would I please come to Washington, D.C., for an interview. Mine must have been a good letter. I took time off and went to Washington to meet with the State Department representatives. I suppose I was interviewed by some fairly important people, and the subject of the Foreign Service came up. I didn't know that there was such a thing as a Foreign Service. I knew that there was a civil service, but nothing of the other professionals who staffed the State Department.
>
> I asked the people at State please not to tell the State Farm people that I had applied for a job. I said, "I believe that it's my responsibility, and that I should be the one to tell them." Well, when I got back to Bloomington, Mr. Fletcher Coleman, the vice president of State Farm, called me in and said, "Ed, I understand that you have applied for a job with the State Department, and they have told me that they want you." That was the first that I had heard that I had been accepted at State. But he went on to say, "Ed if you stay on at State Farm, you will have a beautiful home at Country Club Place (Country Club Place representing big estates and elegant living), and your children will be able to go to the very best schools. You will have a very comfortable life here, and you will progress at State Farm." I told him that all that was most appealing, but that I would never get to see the world. He replied, "If you don't like that other world, you can always come back here." So I moved to Washington, I did get to see the world, and I have never regretted my decision.
>
> Soon after my move, Pearl Harbor was bombed, and we were at war. The State Department had several intelligence divisions, and I was assigned to one of them. We were working on a program maintaining "The Proclaimed List of Certain Blocked Nationals." It was a listing of those businesses in Latin America that were doing business with the Nazis. The United States and U.S. cor-

porations were prohibited from doing business with them. The program was to be a deterrent to businesses that might otherwise have done business with the Axis powers.

The list to which Ed refers was also known as the "American Black List." It was the result of a President Roosevelt directive of July 17, 1941, that required the secretary of state to prepare a list of persons and firms working with or for Axis nations in activities deemed detrimental to the interests of national defense. Those on the list were denied the privilege of trading with the United States. The Division of World Trade Intelligence of the State Department was given the responsibility for the program under the supervision of Assistant Secretary Dean Acheson. Subsequently it became the Division of Economic Security Controls. The list and its strictures were terminated July 8, 1946.

Ed recalled:

I was assigned to the Brazil unit of the operation. After six months on the job, I was in charge. I was one of the few lawyers in the State Department in those days who wasn't a graduate of Harvard or Yale, and I was often reminded of my "inferior status" of being from a state university by body language and social innuendo. I remember going to lunch with our group one day, and I remarked that the lobster I had been served was excellent. One of my Harvard colleagues told me, "Ed, you're from the Midwest. You wouldn't know a good lobster from a bad lobster." I had my satisfaction in that in a space of six months the gentleman who put me down as a flatlander became my assistant, and I was writing his proficiency reports.

My experience in the State Department was fascinating, but there was a war going on, and I wanted to serve in the armed forces. I had a deferment by virtue of my position at State, but I had it waived. There was an office of naval officer procurement on F Street in Washington. I learned that one could go there and take a physical and mental examination and go through an interview, and if you passed all of those you might be able to get a commission in the Navy. So I went through the procedure and was told that I had met all the qualifications. I was instructed to return to my office, and that in four to six weeks I would be notified and be sent to Pensacola for commissioning and training.

I waited and waited and heard nothing. So I called the Navy office one day, and a young lady answered the telephone who was rather snippy with me. What ultimately transpired was one of the funniest things that ever happened to me. When I asked her if I had been accepted for commissioning, she said, "I don't know whether you got it or not." I asked her who would know. Now I want to point out that I was talking on the telephone, rather excited, and wasn't listening as carefully as I should. She said, "I suppose Adm. Randall

Jacobs knows." I didn't catch the significant word "admiral" in her reply. To me, Randall Jacobs was a file clerk who maintained files on such things. So I told the young lady that I thought I should call Randall Jacobs, and she said, "Why don't you just do that?"

Well, because of our work on intelligence matters, we had a direct line from the State Department over to the Department of the Navy, so I called and asked to speak to a Randall Jacobs. The operator must have said, "Admiral Jacobs?" and over the telephone I still wasn't making the distinction between "Randall" and "Admiral." I said yes, and she said, "Who are you?" I told her that I was Edwin Adams from the Department of State, and she said, "Oh, you're from the State Department?" and connected me to his office where I spoke to a secretary, and another secretary, and then another secretary until finally Randall Jacobs came on the phone. Now, I suppose he said, "This is Admiral Jacobs," not Randall Jacobs. I still thought this was the man with the files, so I said *"Mister* Jacobs, (and my addressing him as "Mister" must have curled his hair) my name is Edwin Adams, and I have applied for a commission in the Navy, and I would like to know if I had received it." He said, "You *what?* Young man, do you know that there are men all over America who have applied for commissions in the Navy? You're the first one who ever got to me. How did you do it?" So I told him that I worked for the Department of State in the intelligence branch, and that we had a direct line to the Department of the Navy, and I knew that he was the man with all the files, and I thought that he would be able to check them out and tell me. He said, "This is unbelievable. I'll do it." I asked if he would call me back then. In an exasperated tone, he said he would. I told him not to call back before 2:30, because I had a luncheon appointment, and I gave him my telephone number and asked if he would call me back. He said, "Yes, yes, I will do anything you want Mr. Adams. Just ask me. Anything you want! I will call you back."

At 2:30 the phone rang, and he was on the line and said, "This is *Mister* Jacobs," emphasizing the "mister," which I didn't get at all. I asked him if I had received my commission, he said, that yes, I had and that I would get orders to go to Pensacola, but that I had better be prepared for very tough training, just like boot camp. Still calling him "Mister" I told him I didn't mind the tough training and deeply appreciated all the help he had given me, and that if I could ever be of help to him that he should call me. He told me that I was going to be trained as an aerial gunnery officer, and I said, "Oh, that's fine. I want to go overseas. Can that be arranged?" He said in an exasperated tone that I thought was hardly necessary, "I don't know where you are going after this. All I know is that you are going to Pensacola."

Well, I went through gunnery school in Pensacola and, to my disappointment, my first assignment from there was to Purcell, Oklahoma. I thought how can the Navy have a facility in the middle of the country? Well Purcell turned out to be quite nice, and I became interested in the daughter of the skipper of the base. She invited me to have dinner with her family one evening, along with a number of other people. During the conversation, the subject came up as to how each of us had become associated with the Navy. I told the party how easy I had found the process, and how all you had to do was contact one of the people in the Department of the Navy, and he could get all the information you needed. I said, "He was very helpful to me. He had all the files and told me everything I wanted to know." The skipper, Captain Clapp, thought that was interesting and asked me who that individual might be. I told him Mister Jacobs. Captain Clapp said, "My God, Adams, that man has stripes up to his elbows! He's an admiral!" That's the first I knew that the man I thought was a file clerk was in fact an admiral.

Vice Adm. Randall Jacobs was a graduate of the class of 1907 from the Naval Academy. He had served in the Atlantic during World War I. He was the chief of naval personnel during his exasperating encounter with Ed Adams. Notwithstanding the frustrations of his responsibilities of dealing with Ed and other civilians about to be converted to sailors, he survived World War II. He died in 1967 at the age of seventy-two and was laid to rest in Arlington National Cemetery.

Ed recounted another humorous moment from his career:

> I went from there to Hawaii, to Eniwetok and Kwajalein. Now I had a talent for mistaking people who were in authority for lesser lights. When we were to leave Hawaii for our duty stations, I boarded a ship at Pearl Harbor. The first evening I was standing at the rail talking to someone in the blackout, and I asked him if he knew where we were going, that now that we were at sea it wouldn't hurt to be told. He told me that, yes, he knew, and that we were going to this tiny island called Eniwetok that we had just taken from the Japanese. I said that it was a good thing that they didn't have to rely upon me to get us there, because I didn't have the slightest idea where we were. My being a Navy officer, he had every right to expect that I should know something about navigation. I told him I knew nothing of the subject. We shook hands and went our ways into the darkness. The next day around 11:00 I heard my name being announced over the loud speaker system to report immediately to the bridge. I thought, "Oh my God, what have I done to be called up like this? Had I broken some naval rule?" I was just a landlubber learning about naval rules and the like. Well, when I got to the bridge, of course, there was the man I had talked to at the railing of the ship the night before. He said, "Ensign Adams, I understand that you don't know anything about navigation. We are going to be in transit about ten days on a circuitous route to avoid Japanese submarines. You report up here for lunch every day, and I am going to teach you navigation." Well, you can imagine the ribbing I got from the other naval officers. My benefactor was Capt. Clarence Day Lee. We became fast friends, and I often had dinner after the war with him and his wife.
>
> I was in the Pacific for a little over a year, and then the atomic bomb was dropped, and we didn't have to invade Japan. I don't know of anyone who

was overseas at the time who had any reservations about our dropping the bomb on Japan. We were getting ready for the invasion, and we were going to be part of it. We were relieved that we would be spared that.

Eniwetok and Kwajalein are atolls in the Marshall Islands of the Pacific. They are each composed of small islets surrounding a lagoon. They were taken from the Japanese in amphibious assaults by U.S. Marines in February 1944 and established as U.S. naval bases. In 1947, they became proving grounds for missiles and atomic weapons.

"There was not much excitement on these atolls," Ed recalled. "There was a shortage of water, but we swam every day in the Pacific. The most exciting thing that happened was when we had a typhoon on Kwajalein. When we had these heavy rains, we would strip down and stand at a corner of the tent and benefit from the water cascading down the tops to get a rudimentary shower. We flew missions against Japanese island strongholds such as Truk, but I was never in any major peril during this time."

After the war in 1946, Ed returned to the States for duty as a lawyer terminating Navy industrial contracts for products that were no longer required.

Ed said:

> While negotiating the terms of one of these contracts, for the first and last time in my life, I was offered a bribe. During the negotiation of termination of one of these contracts, an executive for the firm told me that I was invited to spend some time at the Waldorf Astoria with a feminine companion at his expense so that we might discuss the terms of the contract termination. I was young and not cynical enough to be offended, nor wise enough to report the attempt. I told the gentleman that I wasn't supposed to do that and declined his generous offer.
>
> I was mustered out of the Navy in 1946 and returned to the State Department for a great assignment with the Council of Foreign Ministers. It consisted of the Allied foreign ministers—Anthony Eden from England, Molotov from the Soviet Union, and others. The mission of the council was to decide the fate of those countries in Eastern Europe which subsequently fell under the dominance of the Soviet Union. I was not a major player on the council; I was the low man on the totem pole. I was in charge of documents for the American group. I was still learning the art of diplomacy, but it was a great place to learn.

The Council of Foreign Ministers was aptly named. It was composed of the senior diplomats from the United States, Britain, France, and the Soviet Union who met to attempt to resolve political disagreements in the World War II post-war period. Between 1945 and 1972, they crafted peace treaties with Bulgaria, Italy, Romania, Finland, and Hungary. In 1946 they resolved the controversy over the status of Trieste. In 1954, they convened the Geneva Conference that addressed the resolution of the Korean War. They prepared the way to the agreements on German reunification in 1959, and in 1972 they provided for West and East Germany to gain entry to the United Nations. In the first meetings, there were conflicts between the United States and the Soviet Union over issues such as council procedures and the role of the United States in Japan.

Ed recalled:

> During these meetings I was able to watch these powerful, historic men at work. I remember that throughout one of the sessions, Molotov of the Soviet Union was assumed to be unable to speak English. Everything said to him, and that he said, went through an interpreter. Then, one session, he pointed to the wording in one of the papers and stated in perfect English that it was not correct in that it referred to a "document" when in fact it should be termed an "instrument."
>
> There was a Russian Foreign Service officer who was my opposite number who never joined us younger diplomats during our after-hour meetings for dinner or cocktails. So the French member of our group encouraged me to see if he wouldn't join us one evening. I asked our Russian friend if he would, and he told me that, no, that he was too busy to join us. So, I challenged him and said, "You're not allowed to meet with us. You're afraid to." He told me that such was simply not true. After much discussion he accepted the challenge and excused himself to go speak with his superiors. He was gone for about forty-five minutes and came back, obviously shaken up, and said, "Yes, they told me I could go out with you." So our international group did go out for dinner with some attractive ladies who worked with us. He had a ball—a wonderful time. We went to a New York City restaurant where they had aspiring opera singers serving as waiters who would sing as well as serve. The Russian enjoyed it so much, and it did my heart good to see him released from the restraints he lived under. After that evening, we never saw him again. Evidently, in the eyes of his superiors, he had been compromised. He was returned to Moscow.
>
> I returned to Washington from the council assignment in New York. Back at the State Department, I was assigned to a team conducting the Allied-Swiss negotiations to return monies that the Nazis, such as Hitler, Himmler, Goebels, and Goering had hidden away in Swiss banks as their reserves in the event of a collapse of the Third Reich. We wanted to divert the plunder to the postwar support and recovery of nations such as Belgium, the Netherlands, and England. There were four foreign service officers in each of the Allied groups, and I was one of the four Americans. I spent four years with the group living in England, France, and Switzerland. We had a lot of down time between meetings, since the Swiss would cancel meetings without giving

notice. It was easy for the French and the English to go back to their offices by train, but impossible for me to do so. Therefore, I had a lot of time on my hands to enjoy Europe while waiting for the Swiss to call the next meeting. I must say that I learned to know the various parts of Switzerland very well during the hiatus between meetings.

Switzerland resisted the Allied attempts to recover the booty that the Nazis had invested with them. They viewed the Allied effort as the bullying of a small nation by a consortium of larger powers. The Swiss protested that their actions during the war and the receipt of Nazi funds were proper business operations on their part. They considered the fortunes taken out of Western Europe during the war by the Nazis as being acceptable war booty. Over many years and after lengthy negotiations, the Allies persevered, and there has been a small restitution of funds.

Ed said:

> From Switzerland, I was assigned to the Netherlands for over two years where I was the economic attaché. From there I returned to Washington where I went to work on the Italian desk on economic matters again. There seemed to be a proclivity to assign lawyers to economic tasks.
>
> It was 1954, and Clare Boothe Luce, who was the ambassador to Italy, had been called back to Washington for consultation with John Foster Dulles who was the secretary of state at the time. I saw her in the hall and was inclined to introduce myself to her, which would not have been out of line, because I was much involved in matters of mutual concern, but I didn't. She had a presence and was a stunningly beautiful woman. The next day, she called a meeting of representatives of the Treasury, State, Defense, and the CIA who were working on economic problems in Italy. During the meeting I probably talked more than anyone, because, frankly, I think I probably knew more about the situation there than did the others, because I had been working that problem for some time.
>
> When the meeting was over, she said, "Mr. Adams, I would like to have you stay for a moment." Then she said that she was going back to her home in New York the next day, which was Friday, where she was going to meet her husband, and that she would like me to spend the weekend with them. She said, "You fly up Friday evening, and I will have my car meet you and take you to our home at 450 Fifty-Second Street." I knew the address because Greta Garbo, whom I had admired greatly ever since I was about twelve years old, lived in an apartment in the same building. When you got into the elevator of the building, you discovered that each stop was a separate apartment. The Luces had the top three floors, Garbo had the floor right beneath them, and Valentino, the designer, had the floor beneath Garbo. Garbo was reported

as having an affair with Valentino. I was hoping that I might have an opportunity to meet Garbo, but I never did.

At any rate, I flew up to New York, and Mrs. Luce's limousine was waiting for me. We had a wonderful evening. The financier Bernard Baruch was there. When I read later that Bernard Baruch and Clare Boothe Luce were having an affair, I found it laughable. He was much older than she and treated her like a daughter. The whole weekend was wonderful, and I returned to Washington Sunday night. I felt that Henry Luce, Clare Boothe Luce, and I had become friends.

Ed was forty years old when he met Ambassador Luce, and she was eleven years his senior. She was an American icon—beautiful, possessed of an immense talent, wealthy, and, as one of the leaders of American conservatism, politically controversial. She served in Congress from 1942 to 1946, was one of America's premier playwrights, a wartime journalist, editor of the magazine *Vanity Fair*, a socialite, diplomat, and spouse of Henry R. Luce, the publisher of the *Time-Fortune-Life-Sports Illustrated* empire. It was her second marriage, the first, to a man twenty-four years her senior that ended in 1929 by divorce, but a marriage that produced her only child, a daughter. Clare Boothe Luce was born in New York City of a father who was a businessman and violinist and mother who was a dancer. She attended elite schools in Chicago, Memphis, and France. She and Ed had much in common. Her first serious ambition was to be an actress, and his was to be an actor. She excelled in each of her careers. At the time of Ed's meeting with the ambassador, she had only partially recovered from the tragedy of her life, the loss of her nineteen-year-old daughter, a student at Stanford University, in an automobile accident. She found solace in a conversion to Catholicism. She played a major role in the adoption of a resolution that settled the dispute between Italy and Yugoslavia over the United Nations drawing of the territorial lines in the city of Trieste. The resolution gave the city to Italy and the surrounding area to Yugoslavia.

In 1954, Ed had joined a distinguished group of Clare Boothe Luce's friends and acquaintances that included such as Dwight D. Eisenhower and other world leaders. She had a way with words, describing Vice President Henry A. Wallace's freedom-of-the-air policy as "globaloney," and Sen. Wayne Morse's conduct as the result of him being "kicked in the head by a horse."

"When I got to work on Monday, I learned that the prime minister of Italy, Gaspari, had died," Ed recalled. "President Eisenhower called Ambassador Luce into his office and told her that he really should attend Gaspari's funeral, but that it was impossible for him to do so, but that he would like her to go in his stead;

that she would fly to Rome in his plane. She telephoned me and asked, 'Mr. Adams, is your passport in good order?' I told her it was, and she said, 'How would you like to fly to Italy with me today? We'll represent the United States at De Gaspari's funeral and spend a few days in Rome and fly back here next week.' I replied that I'd be honored to do that. We were the only two passengers in the president's plane with twelve attendants (waiters, cooks, etc.)."

Alcide De Gaspari was probably the most influential politician of post World War II Italy, having led three governments from 1948 to 1953. He died August 18, 1954.

Ed described the trip and events that stemmed from it:

> When I boarded the plane, Ambassador Luce was already aboard and was sitting at a table with four seats. I was not under the impression that we had a close relationship, but that I had just been the beneficiary of a wonderful weekend with her and Mr. Luce. So I told her that I could do cartwheels and handstands to entertain her on the trip or I could go in the back of the plane and just disappear. She told me that I was to sit down with her at the table, and that we would visit all the way to Europe. We had a marvelous time because she had found a Foreign Service officer who knew the theater in New York—and the theater was her first love. And, I did know the New York theater. She had had four hits on Broadway. Most people remember *The Women*, but she had other hits as well. But we didn't just talk about the theater; we also talked about business and Italy.
>
> We stopped in Newfoundland to refuel and were guests at a dinner that was hosted by the senior American naval officer there, an admiral. During the dinner it was necessary that Ambassador Luce protest a put-down by a Canadian colonel who had obviously over-imbibed by reminding him that, as ambassador to Italy, she outranked a four-star general, and that when she was younger, she could rely on the stars in her eyes to make her impression, but that now she had to rely upon the stars on her shoulders.
>
> We attended the De Gaspari funeral and flew back to Washington in the president's plane. On the return trip, she asked me if I would like to be posted to Italy. I, of course, said that I would like that very much. Several days later I received orders to report to Rome, and there I was put in charge of a program to forestall the export of military equipment from Italy to the Soviet Union. It was a nothing job that I didn't have very long before I was moved to jobs where I could be more productive. There, I negotiated the establishment of the U.S. Aviano air base (or for it to continue, I've forgotten which it was); the status of forces agreement with Italy; the agreement that permitted Fiat to manufacture the Sidewinder missile for all of NATO forces. I negotiated the agreement to place the Titan missile in Italy. I was put in charge of the Dwight Eisenhower visit to southern Europe in 1959, which was considered quite an accolade for me.

I had been deeply involved in the positioning of the Titan nuclear missile in Italy and had a difficult time with my Italian counterparts, because they simply didn't want the missiles there where they could make the country a target for a Soviet counter- or preemptive strike. I had used up all my political capital with my Italian associates over the issue. During his visit, President Eisenhower called me into his office, just me, the two of us, one-on-one. It was a long, leisurely visit. He said, "Mr. Adams, I understand that you are having difficulty with the Italians in putting the Titan missile into the country." I told him, yes, it was proving quite difficult. He said, "Stop, give it up, don't work on that any more. We don't need them." He said that we have nuclear armed submarines all over the world, the Italians don't want these land-based missiles in their country, and we don't need them. I told him that I was greatly relieved, and that I would draft a telegram back to the Department of State telling them that you have authorized us to stop the negotiations. I drafted the telegram, showed it to the ambassador and the president, and sent it off to the Department of State. Two days later, we received a message from State signed by John Foster Dulles telling us to continue with the negotiations, to continue as we had been instructed to do earlier. I believe that Eisenhower left the conduct of foreign affairs completely in the hands of Dulles. One must assume that the president and the secretary did discuss it, or I would not have been told to continue the negotiations. We eventually did put the missiles in the southeast corner of Italy near Taranto.

While I was in Rome I became quite friendly with the people who worked in the Cinecittà and became friendly with the film actress Martha Scott.

Cinecittà was Italy's Hollywood, started by Mussolini in 1937 as a means to get the Fascist message to the world. By 1943, with the fall of Fascism, it was a mordant industry, having been plundered by the Germans and bombed by the Allies. However, from 1951, it quickly returned to prominence in filmdom offering benefits of excellent, cheap labor, a favorable exchange rate, and good weather. Within a few years it was dominated by American film companies and boasted the residences of some of the top Hollywood stars, including Deborah Kerr, Robert Taylor, Audrey Hepburn, Gregory Peck, Ava Gardner, and Elizabeth Taylor, to name but a few. Their lifestyles made it a lively place and fertile ground for the press. Hollywood made twenty-seven films at Cinecittà during Ed's stay in Rome in the early fifties. Martha Scott was a distinguished professional actress who was at the height of her career during this period. She had been nominated for an Academy Award for her first film appearance in the 1940 production of *Our Town*, in the role she had played on Broadway. She continued to work in television through the 1980s and died at the age of ninety in 2003.

Ed recalled:

Martha was acting in the film *Ben Hur*, where she played the role of Charleton Heston's mother. Charleton Heston, his wife, and Martha were at my house for dinner any number of times, and Martha and I maintained our friendship for years until she died.

I had rented a house in Rome on the edge of the Roman Forum. There was an agreement that I could have the house as long as no one wanted to buy it, and that it could be shown to prospective buyers. One evening I came home, and there was this gorgeous woman sitting on the sofa. The real estate agent said, "Mr. Adams this is Miss Swanson." I was stunned. She was so beautiful, and although she was fifteen years older than I, she looked younger. She offered her hand, I took it, and after a long pause I said, "Miss Swanson, will you have dinner with me tonight?" She laughed, and after examining me carefully said, "Yes."

She moved in next door to me. Her cook was off on Saturday nights and mine was off on Thursdays. So I would have dinner at her house on Thursday nights, and she would have dinner at my house on Saturdays for about a year. She didn't much care about going out to dinner, because, in those days, people would swamp her asking for her autograph. Not too long before this she had starred in the movie *Sunset Boulevard*, and she was at the top of her fame. There was a place out in the country where we would go that was more private and where they had a wonderful orchestra. She loved to dance. And, of course, I took her to a number of affairs at the Embassy where she always made a grand entrance. She was a star, and she never let anyone forget it.

I once told Miss Swanson how beautiful I thought she was, and she became quite upset. She told me that her beauty, which she didn't deny, was an accident of nature. She did have many more qualities that were equally or more admirable. She was a brilliant woman who could talk intelligently on almost any subject. Not only was she a consummate actress and comedienne, but she also sang, produced films, and was a costume designer. She believed in reincarnation and that we went through nine rebirths in our existence, each time returning as a better person until the tenth stage. She flattered me by telling me that I had reached that tenth stage.

Gloria Swanson was unique. She made the transition from silent films to "talkies" effortlessly. She was the epitome of the Hollywood star, earning and spending fortunes and romancing the most famous figures of the day. Miss Swanson had a towering ambition and, early in her career, in 1922, she was quoted as saying, "I have gone through a long apprenticeship. I have gone through enough of being a nobody. I have decided that when I am a star, I will be every inch and every moment the star! Everybody from the studio gateman to the highest executive will know it." How prophetic. She was married seven times and had a well-publicized, lengthy affair with Joseph Kennedy, father of the president, who financed a number of her film ventures. She was born at a military base into a military family in San Juan, Puerto Rico, on March 27, 1899, as Gloria May Josephine Svensson. Her first appearance in a film was in 1915 as an extra. Her last film was *Airport 1975*, which was made in 1974 and in which Ed played a bit part. During that span of almost sixty years, she appeared in seventy-two movies and produced five. She was nominated for three Oscars as a leading lady and authored a book, *Swanson on Swanson*, written in part as a counter to charges made by Joseph Kennedy's wife, Rose, about her relationship with the president's father. Gloria Swanson was eminently quotable. Particularly appropriate for the residents of Falcons Landing is of one her bon mots: "I think all this talk about age is foolish. Every time I'm one year older, everyone else is too."

Ed talked about his decision to retire from public service:

> I was eventually transferred back to Washington, as we Foreign Service officers always are, and I was made economic advisor for the Bureau of African affairs. I spent the next three and a half years being in Africa, not stationed there, but spending the bulk of my time in African countries. I covered the continent from east to west and north to south. Most of my time was spent on inspection tours. I saw lots of Africa. I was made director of professional studies at the Foreign Service Institute. I was then offered the job as deputy chief of mission for Morocco by my good friend Ambassador Henry Tasca, but I felt that it was time for me to retire. He told me, "Take this job, Ed, and in two years you'll be an ambassador." I told him, "Yes to go on to the Cameroons. I'll retire."
>
> I was in my late fifties when I retired. You know, they try to give you some help to find another job when you retire from the Foreign Service, but I told them that I wanted to do something entirely different. I didn't want to do anything which was even remotely related to government, economic development, or related to the law or diplomacy. I wanted to do something in the theater.

Ed Adams in the role of a butler

I was at a dinner one evening, and there was a lady there who was producing a show titled *Passport* that was to be aired out of American University. She told me that with my background I would be ideal to host the show. She said that they were going to do interviews with ambassadors and cultural attaches all over the world and talk about travel in their countries. So, to make the story short, for three years I was the host on the show interviewing these diplomats.

I also wrote a number of television shows. One of them was "Venice, My Love," which I wrote for NBC and for which I received an award from the Italian government, Cavaliere Uficiali dal Merito, or in English, Knight of Honor. I also wrote for my radio program, "Naples and the South," "Tuscany and the Hill Towns," and others I have forgotten, and some that were not about Italy. These were all written and produced here in Washington. Then I finally got an agent and appeared in a number of films—nothing big, just bit parts. One of the best parts that I had was in the movie *First Monday in October*, in which I played the role of a priest. I also had some good parts in television. Do you remember the TV show *Women and the Law*? I played the role of a shyster lawyer in those series. I loved that role.

Since I have moved to Falcons Landing I have had several offers to play a role in a movie, but I have turned them all down. I retired when I moved here in 1997. I had been living at 2540 Massachusetts Avenue on Embassy Row in Washington, and I loved it there. I knew that it would be prudent for me to move, I was getting old, in my eighties, and had had a heart attack. So I looked at retirement communities all over the country and came to the conclusion that Falcons Landing offered more for me than any of the others. At that time, they were taking people from the Foreign Service. We have had five ambassadors live here.

This profile of Ed Adams cites but a few of the close friendships he has nourished during his interesting life, but, by his personal intent, it mentions no romances. "A gentleman doesn't tell," he said. There is a photograph of a lovely woman that rests in a prominent place in his apartment. The photo is that of his fiancée who, some years ago, was the victim of a violent death in Guatemala. It is difficult for him to tell the details.

"What do I do now?" he mused. "Well, I have given a session on Shakespeare to our community and have written a bit of poetry, some of which has been published in our Falcons Landing newspaper. I am recovering nicely from an automobile accident that reminded me of my mortality. I have written my five hundred-page autobiography to be published after my death, all done at the insistence of Clare Boothe and Henry Luce. I have written that single novel, *Petty Destiny*, which is being considered by BBC in England for a future film."

Ed wrote this poem when he was twenty-three years old. It has been published in the *American Book of Poetry*:

Cycle

Ere long a child from womb is born
Puberty with all its scorn
Arises in a childish breast
To take away from mother rest
The laughter, joy and glee of innocence.

Youth filled with lust of love and living
Always taking never giving
Sees a maid to plight his troth
Plucks a rose from a full plant's growth
And ushers age.

Death falls upon the one or other
Leaving one a suffering lover
Then as the egg to worm to moth
Results in beauty's apparition
So are we who plight our troth
Born again for death to render grief
And joyless nights and days
Unless a grandchild fosters on our hope.

14

Bernard E. Trainor

Lt. Gen. Bernard E. Trainor, USMC (Retired), prefers to be called "Mick" and has never been fond of the name Bernard, tolerating it only when used by his parents. He has no clue why his parents selected the name Bernard, other than they were married in Saint Bernard's Church in New York City. While still a youngster growing up in the Bronx, he encouraged his friends to call him "Mickey" after his boyhood hero, Mickey (Himself) McGuire of the *Toonerville Folks* (sometimes known as *Toonerville Trolley*), a single-frame cartoon, drawn by Fontaine Fox, that was popular from 1908 to 1955.

---

1.   This profile is based on interviews on July 6 and 13, 2005. All photographs are from the files of General Trainor except for the Fontaine Fox Toonerville Trolley cartoon.

The Mickey McGuire character was the toughest little gang kid in his neighborhood. He wore ragged clothes, sported a derby, and smoked a pipe, as shown in this 1937 cartoon. Film actor Mickey Rooney's first stage name (he was born Joe Yule Jr.) was Mickey (Himself) McGuire, and he performed in the role of Mickey McGuire in over fifty silent films before changing his name to Rooney. In 1995, the strip was honored in the Comic Strip Classics series of U.S. postage stamps.

In the photograph of Mick Trainor that heads this profile, he unconsciously emulates his boyhood idol by smoking a pipe and wearing ragged combat utilities and flak jacket, and a derby-like helmet, while being a true tough-guy Marine second lieutenant in the trenches of Korea.

Fontaine Fox, July 2, 1937

On September 2, 1928, Mick was born to Joe and Ann Trainor, both American-born of Irish descent, in an ethnically divided neighborhood in the Bronx of New York City, where there were Poles on one street, Jews on another, Irish on still another, and so on. His Whelan grandparents immigrated from County Wexford in the 1880s while the Trainors were from County Monaghan. Joe Trainor worked for the same company for sixty years first as a fruit auctioneer on the New York City piers, and later as a manager, a service not performed since World War II, following the growth of the supermarkets that replaced the middle-man auctioneer through direct purchase from the wholesaler. Joe was an auctioneer for many years, rising at four in the morning to start the auction at eight, a job he relinquished when he became a manager. He was a good ball player, pitching semipro baseball until his arm gave out. He served in World War I in an Army motor transport battalion. Mick and his brother Joe inherited their father's stage presence. Both sons became entertaining raconteurs and fabulous dinner companions. With the good public transportation system in New York, the family never owned a car and never considered one necessary. Joe Senior died of a stroke at the age of seventy-four. Ann survived him for many years, to the age of ninety-six, maintaining her home in New York until she moved to Maryland to live with Mick's brother in her final years.

Young Joe was the more malleable of the two Trainor boys and the better student in grammar school and high school, while Mick was busy living the life of his boyhood hero, Mickey (Himself) McGuire. Joe joined the Navy V-12 program during World War II, was commissioned an ensign on August 1, 1945, and remained in the Reserves, achieving the rank of captain before retiring, while working at his more than thirty-year career with the Central Intelligence Agency. While Mick may have been an underachiever while attending Roman Catholic grammar and high schools, he was always a worker. He earned his work papers during the Depression at the age thirteen.

In those years, the vendors who roamed the baseball stadiums hawking peanuts, programs, and the like were called "hustlers." It was an apt term; not only was the system designed for them to hustle, while working on commission, but it also encouraged them to be hustled by a management that was not dedicated to good labor-management relations. The first game that Mick worked while selling hot roasted peanuts was the 1942 World Series between the Saint Louis Cardinals and New York Yankees. The hustlers were required to wear the management uniforms that were specifically designed without pockets to discourage pilfering. When he was still a neophyte in the business, he laid his pay for the day—a considerable sum of seven dollars—on a bench while he changed out of his uniform. The lights went out, and when they came on again, his seven dollars had vanished. It was a lesson one learned in the hustlers' profession. Mick always had a job as a youth. Some he quit; once he was fired because another boy offered to work for less money, and another time he was fired for insulting his employer.

Mick's mother contracted tuberculosis while Mick was still young and went through a year of treatment while the two boys and Mick's father tried to maintain the household.

When Joe joined the Navy, Mick itched to enter the Marine Corps, but he had to wait until he graduated from high school. Then, over the reservations of his parents, he enlisted in the Marine Corps in 1946. He went through boot camp at Parris Island, South Carolina, where he would serve as a general officer some years later. Out of boot camp, but still in his Mickey McGuire mode, he found himself in the brig for three days on bread and water for being involved in a soldier-Marine brawl aboard a train returning from leave in New York. The brig made a lasting impression on him.

Private Mick Trainor, USMC

In November 1946, his mother sent Mick a clipping from the *New York Times* that told of the inauguration of the Holloway Plan, which augmented the 1926 Naval Reserve Officer Training Corps program with a scholarship adjunct that led to commissioning in the regular components of the Navy and Marine Corps. (Sixteen and two-thirds percent of any graduating class was eligible to opt for commissioning in the Marine Corps.) At his mother's prompting, Mick told his first sergeant of his interest in the program, and the first sergeant made the necessary arrangements for him to take the qualifying examinations. Mick took the examinations, and in the hectic pace of a Marine's life, forgot about it.

Some weeks later, he was told to report to the commanding officer, never a good omen for a private. The first sergeant ushered him into the commanding officer's office where the CO began to question him about his background and his interests and aptitudes. Finally, he said, "You really don't know why I called you in here do you? Well, I am interviewing you to determine your qualifications for acceptance into the Naval ROTC program." The interview must have gone well, because Mick was accepted into the program, discharged as a Marine and commissioned as a midshipman in the United States Navy.

Mick had a choice of schools to which he might be assigned and was leaning toward applying to Notre Dame where they had a strong NROTC program in addition to a fabulous football team. However, in the preschool training period he met a salty Marine sergeant, Gerry O'Keefe, who advised him that the best school for the two of them to attend would be Holy Cross, a Jesuit undergraduate school established in 1843 in Worcester, Massachusetts, one of the premier liberal arts colleges in the country.

O'Keefe and Mick became roommates and lifelong friends at "The Cross." It was here that Mickey McGuire Trainor experienced an academic epiphany that resulted in an impressive academic and intellectual record. The transformation ultimately led to: a master's degree; completion of coursework and orals for a doctorate in international relations; posting as a Marine Officer Instructor; becoming associate professor at the University of Colorado in the NROTC program that had afforded him his commission; being director of education at the Marine Corps Development and Education Command; and, after his retirement, military correspondent for the *New York Times*; director of the National Security Affairs Program of the Harvard University John F. Kennedy School of Government; and the author of a number of professional articles and two books on the Iraqi wars.

Mick was commissioned in the regular component of the Marine Corps upon graduation in June 1951 and, like his counterparts from the Naval Academy and other officer procurement sources, attended the Basic School in Quantico, Virginia. In December 1951 he shipped out for war to join the First Marine Division in Korea, where he served as an infantry platoon leader with Charlie Company, First Battalion, First Marine Regiment. He tells us this about joining his unit in Korea[2]:

> The Second Platoon CP (command post) was not much. It was a cave dug into the back slope of the hill and covered with tropical shelter halves left over from the war in the Pacific. As I trudged up the trail, I was met by the current landlord standing in front of it. He was all smiles and greeted me warmly. His arm was in a sling from last night's wound. A scruffy little Marine wearing a big grin stood just behind him with a backpack at his feet. I assumed it was the lieutenant's gear. My predecessor introduced himself and handed me a map and an overlay. With a smile, he pointed over his shoulder to the north and said, "They're that way." Reversing the direction of his hand he continued, "I'm heading that way." With that he motioned to his grinning companion, and the two of them disappeared down the trail I had just come up. A terrible loneliness overcame me.

---

2.   Bernard E. Trainor, "On Going to War," Quantico: Marine Corps Association *Marine Corps Gazette*, 1998.

I entered the CP to a decidedly indifferent welcome from a committee made up of my platoon sergeant, a red-headed company guide, two radio operators, and a pair of Navy corpsmen. They had been on the line for a couple of weeks, and their appearance showed it. As I soon learned, the duration on the line could be measured by the intensity of red-rimmed eyes and black pores. Introductions were exchanged, and I was directed to "the lieutenant's bunk."

After studying the map and overlay of our position that my predecessor had willed me, I expressed interest in walking the lines. "Be my guest, Lieutenant," said my platoon sergeant. Then, with the clear indication that he had no intention of accompanying me, he waved his hand toward the entrance of the shelter and said, "Just follow the communication trench." I ventured forth, "to check the lines."

It was deadly silent, and light snow fell as I made my way to the forward slope and into the fighting trenches. Periodically, a head would emerge from one of the fighting positions and glance at me before returning to obscurity. I completed my survey and retreated back down the communication trench. The hospitality with the platoon bunker was only a few degrees warmer than the outside temperature. I was being studiously ignored.

In the ensuing days, I got the feel of the place, experienced slithering down the slopes on patrols, and lying, snow-covered, in ambush. Communications improved between my platoon sergeant—his rank was gunnery sergeant—and me, and the other members of the platoon were no longer treating me as the man who wasn't there.

My platoon was assigned a supporting fire role in a night raid on a North Korean position. I made a study for the spot to establish a base of fire that would best cover the raiding party to and from the objective. I discussed it with the gunny, and he seemed unusually reticent. The two of us went forward to reconnoiter the position, and I said, "This looks good to me Gunny. What do you think?" He was looking straight ahead at the distant, snow-covered hills, and without looking at me said, "I guess so, Lieutenant, you're the platoon leader." I had arrived! In that moment he relinquished command of the platoon to me. While I had won my bars at Quantico, I won the privilege of command on that hill.

His name was Gunnery Sgt. Harold Wagner, a native of West Virginia. After our shaky start, we became close during our time together. In March of 1952, the First Marine Division moved to the west coast of Korea to face an expected Chinese spring offensive that never materialized. We began what is now called 'the war of the outposts' that lasted until the end of the war. In it, Wagner was killed. He took three burp machine-gun slugs in the belly while on a patrol near a place called "The Hook." We pulled him and the other casualties back through the wire. Wagner was dead by that time. Before his body was hauled to the rear, I had the privilege of closing the lids over his lifeless eyes, ending the service of a good Marine—preceded and succeeded over the years by legions of others.

In the move to the west coast of Korea, Mick's platoon, Charlie Two, was directed to occupy Hill 159, which was held by a South Korean Army unit. There was to be a relief, in place and a passage of lines, always a tricky business, especially between units coming from different organizations more or less from different nationalities.

Mick recalled:

We were silently wending our way up a narrow trail on the back side of a hill when I spotted figures hurrying down the hill on either side of the column. Suspecting they were the South Koreans we were to replace, I hissed at the Korean interpreter on loan to me for the relief of lines, 'Find out who they are!' No sooner was that said when the familiar sound of burp guns broke the silence from the crest of the hill, followed by the bellow of a Marine behind me who was hit. In a nano-second it was clear what had happened. The Chinese, noting unusual activity in the lines of the South Koreans we were relieving, had sent out a reconnaissance patrol to see what was going on. The ROKs (Republic of Korean troops) saw them coming, we were late, and they had no interest in a firefight just when they were being relieved. So, they simply headed down the hill for the rear. The Chinese were now on the position and firing at whatever was coming or going on the slope below them. At that point I issued the shortest five-paragraph combat order of my career, "F—it, let's go!" As if by magic, the squads and fire teams dropped their heavy packs, spread out, and assaulted, the BARs (Browning automatic rifles) gaining fire superiority as we drove forward. It happened just like the endless assault drills we had practiced while in reserve. Like the functioning of the human hand, each finger moves independently, but all work in harmony to achieve its objective. A well-trained unit, with perfect trust in one another, operated the same way. It wasn't much of a fight. The Chinese were firing high. They had found what they came for and were faced with a platoon of pissed-off Marines coming at them, and they scurried down the far side of the hill.

It was well after midnight when the platoon took up a hasty defense in the ROK trenches. The 'relief of lines' was late and inelegant, but complete. We had one man per fire team go back down the hill to bring up the packs. It was not long before the outraged Marines came back up the hill with the news that most of the packs had been snitched by the ROK soldiers on their way to the rear. The loss of those packs was no small thing. Everything we owned was jammed into the "willie peter" (waterproof) bags: parkas, sleeping bags, rations, spare ammunition, personal effects, and, in my case, binoculars. We were in for some cold and hungry days.

During the three years of the war, fifty-three thousand Americans died in Korea. The majority of them were killed in the static, trench warfare phase while the peace talks ground on at Panmunjon. During that time, Charlie Company did its share of duty on outposts, the main line, in night raids, and counterattacks. Many a good Marine was killed in the process. Those of us who survived were blessed with a combination of good luck and survival skills. We were pretty damn good to boot, and in the spring of 1952, when I was informed that my MOS (military occupational specialty) had been changed from an apprentice lieutenant infantryman 0301 to a fully qualified 0302, I felt elated. More than that, I felt that I had earned it.

When Mick's tour in Korea ended, he was assigned to the Second Marine Division at Camp Lejeune, North Carolina, where he served as an assistant plans and operations officer with the Eighth Marine Regiment. In June 1953, he was assigned duties aboard the heavy cruiser, USS *Columbus*. The assignment reunited him with a ship he had sailed on during a summer cruise as an NROTC midshipman. On this 1953 assignment, Mick served first as executive officer and then commanding officer of the ship's Marine detachment. During this tour he shared a stateroom with the ship's first lieutenant, Bill McDonald, now a retired Navy captain who also lives at Falcons Landing. Following Sea School at Marine Barracks, Portsmouth, Mick reported aboard the *Columbus*:

> It was a glorious day in May when I drove through the gate of the Charles-town Navy Yard in Boston and caught my first glimpse of my new duty station for the next two years. I admit to a thrill seeing her again. She was an impressive and formidable greyhound of the sea.
>
> There are a hundred good stories that could be related about the life at sea and ashore while I served on the *Columbus*. As a preamble to one, it should be pointed out that the ship's skipper, Capt. Luther K. Menlo, was a genuine war hero, the possessor of two Navy Crosses, the nation's second-highest award for bravery. He may have had an excessive taste "for the drink" as we Irish would say, but he was a gentle man with sleepy eyes, and he always appeared to be apologetic about his appearance. He was a good commanding officer, and the crew adored him. The captain's executive officer was as meticulous as Captain Menlo was casual. The XO was a Jack Armstrong type who thought he would become chief of naval operations by birthright.
>
> While anchored in Guantanamo Bay, the skipper invited his XO to go ashore to partake of the Cuban libations before they were to attend a reception in the admiral's quarters. The XO was not much for drink, but he could hardly refuse his boss's invitation. So the two of them went ashore, attired in colorful polo shirts, pastel slacks, and, significantly, argyle socks. Upon their return, the XO needed a rest to recover from the afternoon's drinking marathon paced by his skipper. When the time came to go ashore for the admiral's reception, reasonably sober, he dressed quickly to join the captain in his gig. Upon arriving at the boat landing, they started to step ashore when the captain drolly called his XO's attention to an oversight. "J. D., is there any reason

you're not wearing your shoulder boards?" The XO, looking at his shoulders bereft of boards and therefore any rank insignia, was both mortified and furious, while the captain sauntered off to the reception alone. The XO turned on the gig's coxswain, "Why didn't you tell me I wasn't wearing shoulder boards? Why, man, didn't you tell me?" The shaken seaman, in a stressed and contrite voice replied, "Sir, I didn't notice." J. D. yelled, "You didn't notice? You didn't notice? How could you not notice?" "Commander," came the reply, "to tell the truth, I was too busy looking at your argyle socks."

Mick had more than his share of the requisite tours of duty at Headquarters Marine Corps. His first was an assignment to the personnel department where he served until 1958. Then he was named an exchange officer with the British Royal Marine Commandos. Under that program, the United States sent a Marine to England to train for a year, and England sent a Royal Marine here for the same period. Now a captain, and after a period of rigorous commando training in the United Kingdom, he commanded a company in Forty-five Commando, Third Commando Brigade on Malta.

Mick said:

> You started your tour with the Royal Marines by doing a tour of their bases to see what they did. Then you went through a staff course with Royal Marine captains who were preparing for promotion. There I learned how they were organized and functioned and made many good, long-term friends. The physical part came with the six-week commando course that three Canadians and I took with the enlisted Marines. We went through a winter warfare course, cliff assault school, and special boat school, all rugged stuff. Now we U.S. Marines never gave command of any of our units to the Royal Marines who were exchanged to the Second Marine Division at Camp Lejeune, North Carolina. However, the Brits did give us the privilege of command. So I was given command of Alpha Company of Forty-five Commando of the Third Commando Brigade on Malta where they were assembling for operations to quell an insurgency that was going on in Cyprus. They had to engage in a bit of prestidigitation to change my citizenship in the records from U.S. to Canadian, but that didn't seem to cause a problem for them.
>
> I learned an awful lot on that tour, especially about small-unit operations and reconnaissance that stood me in good stead later on in Vietnam. It was my experience in the Royal Marines that gave me the insights to promote the "Stingray" concept. (The concept involves small reconnaissance teams that would go deep into enemy-controlled areas to identify and direct artillery fire and air strikes on targets. The technique has become more sophisticated with the advent of new technologies to include "painting" of targets with lasers to make them identifiable to aircraft.)

The Brits have this wonderful sense of humor and understatement....As I was winding up my tour of duty with the Royal Marines, I paid a courtesy call on the commanding officer of the training unit to which I had been assigned. During our conversation he said to me, "Trainor, do you remember that little Irish recruit, Hannigan, who was in your group?" I told him that I did, and he continued, "Well, I received a letter from him in which he said that he would not be back, thank you. However, he was grateful for the training that he had received courtesy of Her Majesty's Government, his battle kit, and number three rifle that would be quite helpful and would be put to good use in his service as a terrorist in the Irish Republican Army." To cap off the story, the commanding officer leaned forward toward me and said, "Cheeky what?" It was so British.

It took me several experiences before I fully grasped how I was to fulfill my officer duties in leading British troops. On more than one occasion I, completing the seven troop leading steps we American Marines had been taught, went among the troops myself to supervise the completion of a task. On these several occasions, a color sergeant would present himself to me and ask, "May I help you, sir?" What he really meant was, "What the hell are you doing here?" I would tell him that I was about to oversee the completion of the assigned task, and he would reply, "The officers are in the wardroom sir." I believe I learned that what the British soldier and Marine wanted of their officers was that they be brave, be inspirational, and stay out of the way.

The British aviators were given a "Blood Chit" that was a bit of silk that had the imprint of a Union Jack on it and, in the language of the area of operations, it identified the bearer as being an aviator in the service of the Crown and, if he should be in distress, that a reward would be given to anyone who returned him to friendly forces. The Brits were quite pleased with Sandy, one of their helicopter pilots, who had made his own "Blood Chit" that read, "I am a British officer. I cannot stand pain. Do not hurt me and I will tell you everything I know." I really doubt that he ever carried that, but it made for good wardroom humor.

When I returned from England, Peggy and I were married. Peggy was born in Chicago but was reared in upstate New York, which meant that we could speak the same language. She has been the good trooper through the two tours I spent in Vietnam and my travels as a military correspondent in war zones. One wonders sometimes if we give the medals to the right people. It was a union that led to four wonderful daughters, all of whom have led interesting, challenging lives. They have all been competitive swimmers and runners, and some have run marathons. All are married, but we have only one grandchild so far. Cathy is the eldest; she is married and lives in Falls Church, Virginia. Theresa and her husband live in the District. Saxon and spouse live in Los Angeles. Clare also lives in Southern California, in Santa Monica, with her husband and baby, Theodora.

Following his detachment from the Royal Marines, Mick returned to the Marine Corps' operating forces, the Fleet Marine Force, where he served successively as a company commander in reconnaissance, antitank and infantry battalions of the First Marine Division. In the early 1960s, he rejoined the Naval ROTC complement, this time as a Marine officer instructor in the unit at the University of Colorado where he was awarded the faculty rank of associate professor. Mick then attended a series of schools before being posted to Vietnam in 1965 to serve in an unconventional warfare unit, the Studies and Observations Group (SOG) that was conducting war against and in North Vietnam. SOG operations remained highly classified until publicly recognized in 2001 with the award of a Presidential Unit Citation for heroism. Mick returned to the States, taught in the Marine Corps schools, became a "Distinguished Graduate" at the Air Force's Air War College where he received the university's Anderson Memorial Award for politico-military thought. It was 1970, and now a lieutenant colonel, it was time for Mick to return for a second tour of duty in Vietnam where he first commanded the First Battalion, Fifth Marines and subsequently the First Reconnaissance Battalion. He had the honor of returning the latter's colors to the United States and presenting them before the president, Richard M. Nixon, as part of the First Marine Division's homecoming parade in 1971.

Mick recalled:

The First Battalion, Fifth Marines (1/5) CP was on Hill 34, southwest of Danang. One of our jobs was to maintain a company on ten-minute alert as a quick-reaction force. The alert force was saddled with the detested code name of "Pacifier." (The thumb-sucking torment directed at its members by Marine artillery neighbors on Hill 34 led to some serious intra-service combat.) We Pacifiers, reacting to hard intelligence, most of which came from radio intercepts and periodic reconnaissance sightings, would zip off by helicopter to attack identified Vietcong (VC)/North Vietnamese targets.

There was hard intelligence that a VC cadre meeting was to take place at Truong Son, a hamlet at the southern foothills of the Queson Mountains, a haven for the VC/NVA. The 1/5 Pacifier team landed in a dry paddy adjacent to the hamlet and caught the enemy by surprise. A short-running gun battle ensued as a half-dozen VC headed for the hills. Most got away, except one gent in black pajamas. He cut across the paddy in full view of a firing line of Marines on full automatic. Not one of them hit him! The disgusted fire team leader, Lance Corporal Reynolds, screamed, "Cease fire, cease fire." Dropping his M16, Reynolds ran down the VC and tackled him. Reynolds dragged the little fellow back, waving the captive's pistol in triumph. The prisoner was turned over to the First Marine Division intelligence translator, and it was discovered that he was Nguyen Loi, the VC intelligence chief for the Quang Da Special Zone.

Loi was an intelligence jewel. But he was tough as nails and totally resistant to interrogation. At first, his only concession to our intelligence crew was to accept food, drink, and cigarettes. That is until they found that he was entranced with the sexy films that the troops were showing on the screen in the rear area. Evidently, Loi had never seen such blatantly bawdy entertainment, and he liked it. Considering his resistance to the earlier blandishments by his interrogators, it was amazing to see him break down and be almost eager to provide valuable information, as he became an avid movie fan, willing to trade information for a season movie pass.

Loi revealed that the headquarters of the Quang Da Special Zone was hidden in a draw on the southern slopes of the Quesons. We Marines of 1/5 (First Battalion, Fifth Marines) received orders to find, attack, and destroy the VC headquarters. I approved a plan for a two-company operation. Company A, commanded by Capt. Tony Zinni, would land by helicopter in the low ground at the bottom of the draw. (Zinni later went on to be commander in chief of Central Command as a four-star general before he retired in 2000.) Company B, under Capt. Art Garcia, a tough old mustang, would land on the high ground above the draw. The helicopter assault began. and immediately upon landing, Alpha Company came under fire. Zinni, among others, was hit. The captive VC, Loi, who was providing direction in the attempt to locate the well-hidden CP (command post), panicked as he heard his name being shouted from among the rocks that were sheltering the VC defenders. Loi was evacuated along with the wounded; he was too valuable an intelligence source to lose in the firefight that continued through the night.

As the sun rose the following morning, morale was not good, as there was the sense that we were blundering about the bush searching for a CP that was not going to be found. As the battalion commander, I was almost ready to pack it in as a job not very well done. However, my enthusiasm was rekindled by the surprise arrival of Maj. Gen. Charles, F. Widdecke, the division commander, who, during the afternoon of the second day, dropped in from the sky. Full of optimism, he inspired a renewed effort by telling me that 1/5 "would stay in these goddamn mountains until they found the goddamn VC headquarters!" Then, as mysteriously as he arrived, he flew off to torment some other poor soul. The only other thing to drop out of the sky that day was a heavy rain that made the troops that much more miserable.

The third day started out much the same as the previous two. Marines were still climbing over rock slides, fallen trees, and through the undergrowth, looking for the "goddamn VC headquarters."

Now, enter PFC Hughes who, while a good Marine, was not particularly gung ho. Hughes kept a fuchsia-colored Frisbee in his pack. Out of sight of his fire team and squad leader, he tossed the Frisbee to another Marine to initiate a game of catch. It sailed over the head of the intended, landing in a bush covering a small hole. Taking out his K-Bar, the Marine probed at the hole, which grew bigger and bigger. They had found an entrance to the VC command post! The hole was one of many entrances and exits of the cave that was an extraordinary feat of primitive engineering. It must have taken years to excavate. There was an elaborate system of bamboo conduits—some carried water, some were designed to evacuate and dissipate the smoke from cooking fires. We found an estimated twenty-seven tons of rice. For all the years of operating in the Quesons, nobody had an inkling of the cave's existence.

The pièce de résistance stood against the wall of the main chamber. It was a filing cabinet made up of used U.S. five-gallon coffee cans set on their sides and bound together with communication wire. In the containers were the personnel and pay records, complete with photos, of all the VC agents and double agents in the city of Da Nang and the whole of Quang Nam Province.

The find was kept secret because of the incriminating data that was found on South Vietnamese officials. A Navy Unit Citation was awarded to 1/5 for finding and capturing the intelligence treasure. I don't have any idea what happened to Loi. Perhaps he's a movie producer in Ho Chi Minh City. The Frisbee-er, PFC Hughes, is probably a lawyer somewhere in middle America, and I wish him well. You might say that in the final analysis, sexy films and frivolous Frisbee-ing can produce redeeming military if not social value.

Each Marine division has a reconnaissance battalion, and the employment of the battalion is dependent upon the needs of the division, the nature of the terrain, and the mission. Seldom has it been employed as a unit, but rather, its elements are normally committed to small efforts in support of division intelligence or in support of maneuver units. In Vietnam, the battalions were invariably used in support roles deploying small units into enemy areas to gather information. It is always a dicey affair requiring a high order of skill, patience, and discipline. It is not work for the faint-hearted. Mick had served in reconnaissance during peacetime and was a logical choice to assume command of the First Reconnaissance Battalion after the combat death of the former commander, Lt. Col. Bill Leftwich, who had been awarded the Navy Cross in a previous service in Vietnam. (His widow, Jane, is on the waiting list to move to Falcons Landing.)

Mick said:

> During my tour as commanding officer of the Recon Battalion, we ran 203 deep reconnaissance missions. We took pride in being the "eyes and ears" of the division. I personally flew on twenty-eight day/night emergency extracts of recon teams. In all, we suffered only one killed in action and a half-dozen wounded during the period. The key to our success was meticulous planning and savvy, well-trained troops. All our missions were high-risk but high-payoff operations. Every time I stepped off a chopper after an emergency extract, I shouted our mantra, "Cheated death again!"

Not only did our teams secure information on enemy dispositions and operations, but we also called in fire missions on targets of opportunity. Our teams operated either on foot from a platoon patrol base established in the bush or were inserted by chopper from our CP adjacent to the division headquarters. We never operated in developed or populated areas, which gave us two advantages over other infantry operations. First, the mine and booby-trap danger was minimized. Second, all we encountered in these areas were hostiles, so we had no trouble identifying the enemy.

All our officers, NCOs, and men were seasoned volunteers who underwent a vigorous training program there in our area. Our teams were normally made up of seven Marines, a front and rear point man, a team leader (officer or NCO), a corpsman, two radiomen, and a "blooper" or M-19 man. (An M-19 is a portable, shoulder-fired grenade launcher.)

A Marine Reconnaissance team being extracted using the SPIE technique

Physically and psychologically, recon teams were at a theoretical disadvantage. They were normally outnumbered and out-gunned if they made contact and could not break it off. This theoretical danger was offset, however, by the high state of training of each team, the stealth with which it operated, and having the advantage of the initiative. During my command of the Recon Battalion, no team was ever ambushed; on the contrary, it was our teams that did the ambushing. One of the great psychological advantages which made our recon Marines confident in the bush was the almost religious devotion of the Marine helicopter community to their well-being. Team helicopter inserts were made with surgical care and precision to give the team the best chance of avoiding detection, and helicopter crews worked through exacting details with teams prior to a mission. The teams were confident knowing that heaven and earth would be moved to help them if they got into trouble, and they were sensitive to the incredible risks that the chopper pilots would take to get them out of a tight spot. When it was not possible to land a helicopter in the extraction area, there was the "Special Purpose Insertion and Extraction" alternative, also known as SPIE. As a result, a team normally did not ask for an emergency extract unless they really had an emergency.

After this second Vietnam tour, Mick was ordered back to Headquarters Marine Corps where he again served as a joint plans officer. Mick was promoted to colonel and was subsequently assigned to his hometown, New York City, as director of the First Marine District that made him responsible for recruiting and reserve matters in the Northeastern states. When he was selected for promotion to brigadier general in 1976, he was returned to Parris Island, where he had undergone recruit training thirty years earlier. Following his tour as assistant recruit depot commander, Mick returned to Quantico as director of the Marine Corps Education Center, in the rank of major general, and when promoted to lieutenant general became the deputy chief of staff for plans, policies, and operations and Marine Corps Deputy to the Joint Chiefs of Staff before retiring in 1985.

Mick said:

> As one might expect, there are always some bumps in the road of life, and I have had my share. Back in 1984, while still on active duty, I delivered a speech at the Naval War College in Newport, Rhode Island. In my remarks I said that as the Soviets continued their naval buildup, a confrontation between them and the U.S. Navy was "almost an inevitable probability. A Washington reporter in the audience reported my statement the following morning. That would have been the end of it, except that a TV journalist shouted to President Reagan as he was boarding the presidential helicopter asking him if he agreed with the Marine general who said that conflict with the Soviet Union is inevitable. Once aboard the aircraft the president turned to an aide and asked, 'What was that all about?' Soon the statement became international news, and one headline read words that said that an American general had said nuclear war with the Soviet Union was inevitable. When the

president heard the full story, he concluded that my remarks were taken out of context, and he called the commandant of the Marine Corps to say so.

The president's call reassured me, but it did not relieve my widowed, Irish mother, and she worried. The president learned of her anxiety and sent her the following letter:

THE WHITE HOUSE
WASHINGTON

August 27, 1984

Dear Mrs. Trainor:

I have been informed by a mutual friend that you are concerned still over the news headlines which appeared in June concerning your son's comments at the Naval War College. First, let me tell you that I have the greatest regard for Lieutenant General Trainor. The headline that day and most of the news stories were in error. Mick's views concerning the challenges of the military in the future are totally in accord with my own views. We tried very hard to correct the erroneous interpretation of what was said but were unsuccessful, as sometimes is the case with the media. I thought the evening news was so distorted that I called General Kelley to ensure him that I totally supported your son.

Incidentally, I am well acquainted with Mick's distinguished service record and his background. You should be very proud of him and I share your pride. I thank God every day that men such as him continue to fill the highest leadership positions in our military. And I thank God for mothers like you whose example and prayers provide a constant source of strength and inspiration.

God bless you always.

Sincerely,

Ronald Reagan

When Mick retired, one would think that he was prepared to relax and enjoy the fruits of his strenuous labors. But that was not going to happen:

My last job in the Marine Corps was that of deputy chief of staff for plans, programs, and operations and Marine Corps deputy to the Joint Chiefs of Staff. You can guess how little free time you had in a job like that. So I had no plans at all as to what I would do after I retired from the Marine Corps. The first month was really fun, because I started to make visits to Civil War battlefields. But then, out of the blue, I got a telephone call from Craig Whitney, an executive of the *New York Times* who asked if I might be interested in serving as the *Times'* military correspondent. They had been searching for someone for two years to take over that job that had once been held by Hanson Baldwin and is rather unique to the *Times*. To make a long story short, we came to terms, agreeing that we would go through a trial period to see if I liked the job and if they liked what I could do. It worked out, and it was fabulous. I got to travel to hot spots all over the world, see first-hand the wars of the period, and get my views published. I spent about half my time outside the country. We had an agreement that my role would be to produce mostly analyses with but little reporting, which gave me much more latitude in what I wrote.

Libyan designs on neighboring Chad in North Africa date to the early 1970s when Libya's "Brotherly Leader and Guide of the Revolution," Muammar al-Qaddafi, began to actively support the Chadian rebels. In 1975, Libya annexed a 70,000-square-kilometer area in northern Chad, a landlocked country that is mostly desert. In December 1986, Chadian troops attacked and routed a thousand-man Libyan outpost at Fada where a large number of Libyan tanks were destroyed and captured. In March of the following year, Wadi Doum, a Libyan air base that was defended by five thousand Libyan troops, ringed with extensive minefields and supported by the Libyan Air Force, was captured by about a thousand Chadians riding in pickup trucks armed with machine guns and antitank weapons. It was a total rout of the Libyans, as they suffered a staggering number of casualties running through their own minefields to escape the primitive Chad onslaught. Mick relates an interesting aside that the Chadians, attacking in their Toyota pickups, had been told by their leaders that if they drove through the minefields fast enough, they would roll over the mines before they exploded. Of course that was not true, and there were many trucks and Chadian troops that became casualties. But the confidence that speed ensured their safety added to the energy of their assault.

A Chad truck that didn't make it through the Libyan mine field

In early 1986, the *New York Times* sent their military correspondent, Mick Trainor, to cover the events following the Libyan rout.

Mick wrote:

> It was clear from the outset that this was not going to be anything like Palm Springs when I arrived in the capital of Chad, N'Djamena. I found the hotel and its food to be a disaster. But two weeks later, when I was in the desert, I thought of N'Djadema as being a luxury.
>
> Those two weeks were spent in what seemed to be an endless pursuit across the Chadian desert, retracing the advance of Chad's fierce northern warriors, the Gorans, as they chased the Libyans into northern Chad's Tibesti Mountains. My life as a Marine had prepared me to live in the field under difficult conditions, but this was different. During my war-fighting days as a Marine, there was always something to eat and drink. Here in the desert, as a war correspondent, that wasn't the case.
>
> The trip to the battlefield started aboard a military supply flight from the capital to a military base at Kalait, an oasis 560 miles northeast of N'Djamina. We then transferred to the rear of a malevolent Fiat truck that was bereft of shock absorbers, and started what seemed like an endless bounce over the roadless terrain.

The Fiat truck on the Chadian desert

The journalists in the desert with Mick on the far left.

The other passengers on the trip were a congenial group of American, British, and French journalists of both sexes, and bags of millet that were destined for the frontline troops. The sun baked us during the day. At night we shivered in the cold. I partially solved my problem with the cold nights when we came across a Bedouin who had tethered his camel and was kneeling in prayer on an old French army blanket. I bought the blanket for thirty-five American dollars. I think that was what he was praying for.

Relentless dust storms stung our eyes, clogged our nostrils, and coated our tongues. Our throats were parched for long periods for lack of water. We started each day's travel before dawn after being served a small cup of hot sweet tea which appeared to be a normal day's ration for our Chadian hosts. Each day we would set out on our bone-jarring torment on the Fiat flatbed across the desert the cartographers have named "Tchad Inutile" or Worthless Chad. An apt name. In fairness, however, we were treated to some of the most spectacular views of dun-colored oceans of sand transfigured to escarpments of ochre, salmon, and saffron hues. We progressed to gray flatlands which faded into the shimmering horizon that gave way to rock-strewn stretches dotted with scrub brush reminiscent of the California High Sierras. During the second day of our journey, I thought that surely, Las Vegas or the Hoover Dam must be just over the horizon, but I would have settled for a McDonald's. But it was just vast stretches of emptiness. We wondered why anyone would fight over possession of this desolate land.

At noon we would halt and try to escape the blast-furnace heat and crawl under the truck for shade. Then as the afternoon wore on, we would be aroused from our heat-induced stupor and bump along on our journey to travel well into the night. It was then that we were treated to spectacular sunsets and gorgeous skies alive with stars.

We often had cause to question the legendary native ability to navigate the unmarked desert, because it was obvious that there were times when our driver was lost.

He would never admit that he had lost his bearings even when I could establish it undeniably with my compass. There were times when we became anxious that we could become monuments to his folly as all that would be found of us would be sun-bleached bones covered by the drifting sands.

We had some anxious moments. On occasion, we got stuck in the sand, we had a flat tire, and, most frightening of all, we ran out of gas. None of this bothered our driver who appeared totally unconcerned—all of this was to be expected. He was not responsible for maintenance or supply; his job was just to drive. When we ran out of gas, he found a comfortable place to go to sleep, notwithstanding the barrage of curses directed at him in several languages. There was near panic from some of our French colleagues that was not made better by mindless stiff-upper-lip admonitions from a British journalist. I was reassured that our cargo of millet bags would save us, as they would be missed, even though we would not. I was confident that someone would come looking for our party if not to rescue us, but to save the millet. That's what happened, but not until we reached the point where we were sipping water from the radiator of the truck to slake our overwhelming thirst.

Eventually we reached the oasis at Fada, where in the shade of a thorn tree, we rested and were fed a welcome meal of camel meat, boiled millet, and sweet tea. It was the first food we had since leaving N'Djamena three days earlier. We were grateful for it.

The journalists first meal in three days is led to the kitchen

A MiG-21 bombing of Wadi Doum, the battlefield being visited by the correspondents

There was evidence of the grisly battle of the Chad desert all about us, and we set to doing the work of journalists. The group took hundreds of photos, and our notebooks were crammed with our impressions. We visited Bir Kora, the graveyard of a formidable Libyan armored task force, Wadi Doum where we were bombed by the Libyan Air Force that was attempting to destroy the arms and vehicles that had been abandoned by them in the rout, and Faya Largeau, the completely intact political capital of the northern desert which had also been abandoned by the Libyans. We had stories galore but no access to a telex, and we were anxious to get back to the capital so we could file our stories. We didn't look forward to another seven-day trip in that Fiat truck across the desert. But our prayers were answered when we heard the sweet drone of airplane engines. One of the wag journalists gave us a laugh with his cries of relief, repeating, "Boss, da plane, da plane!" It didn't take us long to board the aircraft for our flight to what we now considered the luxury of N'Djamena.

After five years with the *Times*, Mick joined Harvard to lead its National Security Program within the John F. Kennedy School of Government. It was during that period that his third (or fourth) career as a TV military analyst took root, a career, that, as of this writing, is still active. However, his principal preoccupation is writing, both his second book on Iraqi wars and other articles and memoirs.[3]

"I had been to Iraq to cover their war with Iran, so when Desert Storm, the first Iraqi war, commenced, I was one of those who had some insights into their capabilities and operations," Mick said. "I appeared at a symposium at Georgetown University on the subject and later received a telephone call from an ABC executive who asked if I would be interested in doing some TV analyses of the situation there. I accepted and was teamed with Peter Jennings. I moved from ABC to NBC and finally MSNBC and now, periodically, with PBS. I keep busy at what I facetiously describe as being a national security dilettante."

Mick and Peggy Trainor have made the transition from Lexington, Massachusetts, to Northern Virginia easily. They are rather recent arrivals at Falcons Landing, joining the community in the spring of 2005. Peggy would be an asset to any community. Mick is a great raconteur and interesting commentator on national security affairs, both great contributions to the community's social gatherings. He is a good and loyal friend. As is true of many residents of Falcons Landing, he has rubbed shoulders and sat in council with some of the best-known figures in American political and military circles, and that can be heady stuff. Yet Mick has never abandoned his origins and has always stayed close to longtime friends, including some with whom he attended grammar school.

Mick can sometimes be guilty of a bit of Irish blarney. For example, he claims to have been responsible for the successes of the New England Patriots football team (2004 world champions) and the Boston Red Sox (2004 world champions) when he and Peggy were living in Lexington. "But my work was done there, and it was time to work my magic in D.C.," he said. And thus he takes credit for the success of the Washington Nationals who were sitting at the top of the tough National League East Division when Mick and Peggy moved to the Washington, D.C., metropolitan area. Perhaps he does have the luck of the Irish. Just don't call him Bernard!

---

3.   The first book was: Michael R. Gordon and Bernard E. Trainor, *The Generals' War* (Boston: Little, Brown and Company, 1995).

15

William Oller

Bill Oller with model of Frigate USS Constitution he was building

There is a group of men at Falcons Landing who spend two to four hours a week making furniture and other conveniences used within the community. They normally divide into two work groups. The larger group is directed by Rear Adm. William Oller, USN (Retired). The smaller group currently is captained by Brig. Gen. Bain McClintock, USMC (Retired). Both Bill and Bain, by any standard, qualify as professional cabinetmakers.

Bill described his interest in furniture making:

> I likely inherited my woodworking aptitude from a grandfather who was a professional cabinetmaker and a father who had, at least, an interest in the art. My interest in designing and making furniture goes back to my early teens and to the purchase of a lathe at the age of fourteen. Our two teams of woodworkers have left our mark on Falcons Landing, from a large, 320-slot internal mail center, to a credenza in one of the staff offices, to file cabinets and containers,

---

1. Profile is drawn from interviews starting July 29, 2004.

to name but a few of the pieces of furniture we have designed and built in our well-equipped workshop.

However, woodworking is my avocation, not my vocation. I decided to be a sailor at an early age. I graduated from high school in Lancaster, Pennsylvania, and after a two-year stint in a local college, enrolled in the Naval Academy, to graduate in the class of 1947. The Lancaster McCaskey High School was good to me, for it was there that I met and, in time, married Doris Greenleaf. It was my best decision in a career that required many decisions some of which had a direct impacted on the economic health and national security of the United States and the way we Americans live our lives.

Bill's life is replete with anecdotes from the positions he has held from the command of Navy Supply Centers to being director of the Navy's automated systems. Nevertheless, if we focus on the years 1972 and 1973, we find a series of events that affected the lives of every American living at the time and, to a significant degree, the lives of those who followed.

Bill recounted:

> In November of 1972, I assumed command of the Defense Fuel Supply Center (DFSC) of the Department of Defense Logistic Agency (DLA).[2] Eight months later, in July of 1973, the DFSC was designated the manager of all U.S. military bulk petroleum. It was not a popular decision in all quarters. The military services were being shorn of their authority and responsibility to manage their own bulk fuel resources. It upset the systems and routines of commercial suppliers. The centralization of authority for the purchase, maintenance, and allocation of military bulk fuel channeled enormous authority and responsibility into a single government entity. The Defense Department is the largest single consumer of fuel in the United States, consuming about 80 percent of the federal government's use.[3]

With the ultimate support of the chairman of the Joint Chiefs of Staff and others, Bill was able to plan and organize to make the transition to an integrated system work. He did so with a minimum of stress on the providers and users. Bill said:

---

2.   On January 16, 1998, the DFSC was renamed the Defense Energy Support Center (DESC), and its duties were expanded to include the consolidation of all the department's regional energy efforts.

3.   Elizabeth G. Book, "Pentagon Needs Accurate Accounting of Fuel," *National Defense*, March 2002, http://www.nationaldefensemagazine.org/article.cfm?Id=750

If I thought I had walked into a buzz saw with the creation of an integrated Defense petroleum supply system, it paled in comparison with what was to follow. Less than a year after I had taken the reins of the DFSC, on 17 October 1973, the thirteen-nation Organization of Arab Petroleum Exporting Countries (OPEC) imposed an embargo on the sale of oil to those nations that supported Israel in its October 1973 Yom Kippur War with Egypt. (Seven of the OPEC nations were Arab.) The Middle Eastern states were furious that the United States had provided emergency supplies that permitted Israel to withstand the Egyptian and Syrian military forces. Prior to the embargo, the United States and other industrialized nations took for granted that they would have access to cheap and plentiful Middle East oil. The United States' use of energy had become profligate. Oil consumption in the United States had more than doubled between 1950 and 1970. The OPEC embargo was a serious blow to the U. S. economy and was a threat to its security.

Arab motivation for the embargo was not entirely punitive in retaliation for the support of Israel but also economic. The OPEC cartel raised the price of its oil throughout the Western World. There was also a political facet to the OPEC embargo. The OPEC states hoped to bring political pressure on those industrial countries that drew heavily on their Middle East national resources. For years, the U.S. Department of Defense had been relying on these overseas petroleum resources for over 50 percent of its needs. The 1973 embargo was the first oil-supply malfunction to precipitate a major price increase and a global energy crisis. How serious was the oil crisis? The retail price of a gallon of gasoline went from an average of 38.5 cents in May of 1973 to 55.1 cents per gallon in June of 1974. The U.S. importation of oil from Arab states dropped from 1.2 million barrels a day to only 19,000 barrels. In January of 2004, thirty-year-old British government documents were released that revealed that the United States considered invading Saudi Arabia and Kuwait to wrest from them the control of their oil resources. In a lesser crisis, some six years later, President Jimmy Carter called an Arab oil embargo, "the moral equivalent of war."

"Fortunately, I had been given ten months to shake down the newly integrated bulk fuel supply system prior to the OPEC embargo," Bill recalled. "That meant that I was not fresh to the task of buying, transporting, storing, and allocating petroleum products worldwide for the entire federal government. I had almost a year's experience of managing the huge inventory of petroleum stocks for the Department of Defense. Nevertheless, in late 1973, we had a lot of hard problems to solve."

In November of that year, he was a major player in the Department of Defense's invocation of the Defense Production Act of 1950 that gave Defense first priority in the claim on domestic petroleum production. The action diverted an additional 300,000 barrels of fuel per day from domestic to defense needs. The OPEC embargo had hit the Department of Defense hard, because it depended on overseas petroleum resources for 50 percent of its fuel needs. The invocation of the 1950 act did not go into effect without a fight. William E. Simon, the newly appointed energy administrator, ordered the Department of Defense to give up 1.5 million of its 19.7 million barrels of aviation fuel for use by U.S. domestic airlines. Secretary of Defense James Schlesinger protested and claimed that such a loss would "weaken our defense posture and leave Defense supplies almost 30 percent below the amount required for military war reserves."[4] It was a classic competition for resources between the military and civil sectors. As a compromise, Simon reduced the amount Defense must release from 1.5 million to 900,000 barrels of aviation fuel.

"As one might expect when a single authority is charged with the responsibility for purchasing and allocating scarce, very expensive resources, there were many conflicting priorities that had to be resolved, and there were more consumers and producers dissatisfied than those celebrating their good fortune," Bill said. "Nonetheless, throughout the crisis, we were always able to meet the essential needs of the Defense establishment. There was *never* a petroleum supply failure within the Department of Defense."

Bill was able to witness OPEC lifting the embargo in March 1974. However, there were long-range impacts on the petroleum supply system both within the civilian sector and the Defense establishment. The price of energy continued its upward spiral while the dollar lost value in world markets. Energy costs were the single greatest factor in producing the soaring inflation of the 1970s in the United States.[5] However, the careful management of the petroleum procurement and distribution system by those such as Bill Oller avoided a complete disaster, and perhaps even war.

But the oil embargo did change the way Americans lived and viewed their consumption of energy. A national speed limit of fifty-five miles per hour was imposed. An "energy czar" was named, a move that ultimately produced a new cabinet-level Department of Energy in 1977. A limitation on the price of "old"

---

4. Capt. Chris L. Jeffries, "Defense Policy in a World of Limited Resources," http:// www.airpower.maxwell.af.mil/airchrinicles/aureview/1975/jul-aug/jeffries.html
5. "1973 energy crisis," from Wikipedia, the free encyclopedia, http://en. wikipedia.org/wiki/1973_energy_crisis

oil was established. Year-round daylight savings time was decreed and shortly abandoned. Americans became more aware of how profligate they had become in the consumption of energy, and national campaigns to save fuel with catch phrases such as "Don't Be Fuelish" found their way on stickers across the country. Renewable energy sources such as wood, solar, and wind power became more attractive. Recycling of materials became standard. The international consequences also were significant. America recognized that Russia and China were not the only threats to its security and prosperity. There came the realization that Third World Nations could represent a threat if they united and withheld their valuable resources.[6]

Bill retired from the Navy in 1977 to work in the commercial petroleum industry in senior executive positions in Houston and Fort Worth, Texas, and New Orleans, Louisiana. He continued to have an impact on the lives of Americans as he managed the modernization and filling of the 1976 Strategic Petroleum Reserve program wherein crude oil was stored in underground salt caverns along the coastline of the Gulf of Mexico. He subsequently was hired to upgrade and automate a major U.S. refined products pipeline serving the entire eastern half of the United States.

"When I retired from the oil industry in 1990, I established Maxwell Woodworks Inc. to fulfill commercially my lifelong attraction to the art of cabinetmaking," Bill said. "After making a thorough research of the retirement community options available, Doris and I moved to Falcons Landing in May of 1996. We were pioneers, being the second family to move into a house. The moves into housing were not as simple and easy in those early days as they were later. We early residents battled red clay mud and dust and architectural glitches. The first staff community services manager left. Doris stepped up to fill the void as a volunteer. They chose the right person."

The energetic Doris Oller proved to be as talented as her husband and instituted programs such as bridge, poker, billiards, excursions, theater, concerts, arts and crafts, music, dance, drama, and computer instruction. Her reach for volunteers within the community was so ubiquitous that she later wrote, "I soon noticed that the residents were trying to avoid me in the hallways." The Ollers are so active in the community that periodically they leave Falcons Landing for a vacation to "rest up" from their local labors. If they demonstrate great pride in Falcons Landing, they have earned the right to do so. There is no couple that has contributed more to the happy circumambience of the community.

---

6.   Wikipedia, opcit

16

The Builders: Charles Buckingham and Hans Driessnack

Air Force Comptroller publication announces relief of Buckingham by Dreissnack

U.S. Air Force photo

There would be no Falcons Landing without the heroic efforts of Lieutenant Generals Charles E. "Buck" Buckingham and Hans H. "Whitey" Driessnack, both retired from the U.S. Air Force. The two, while very different in character,

---

1. Profiles are based on interviews with Charles Buckingham and Hans Dreissnack during and after May 2004.

had similar career patterns after completing their training and early flight assignments. Friends characterize Buckingham as being dynamic, open, blunt, forceful, intelligent, and strong-willed. They characterize Driessnack as being solicitous, discrete, thoughtful, intelligent, intense, and resolute. In July 1981, Whitey Driessnack relieved Buck Buckingham as comptroller of the Air Force when Buckingham retired with thirty-two years of service.

Buckingham went from the military academy to become a bomber pilot. Driessnack was commissioned out of the Syracuse University Reserve Officer Training Corps, and soon thereafter applied for flight training to become a fighter pilot. In the middle of their careers, both began to focus on the management of U.S. Air Force systems. Their decisions led them to successful careers in programming, research, development, production, procurement, and supporting systems.

These distinguished officers were each asked what motivated them to make the sacrifice of a substantial period of their life in retirement to make the dream of Falcons Landing a reality. There was no potential for profit. There was no promise that their efforts would be met with success, much less gratitude or appreciation. They were both fully employed in second careers. Their self-conscious responses to the question of motivation were couched in very different terms. However, there were common elements. Neither would be so intellectually arrogant as to ascribe his motivation to the basic urge to create. Neither would be so self-serving as to describe his efforts as the basic urge to do good. But it seems that these two factors were behind much of their determination and perseverance to see Falcons Landing through to fruition. At some point in the planning for the construction of the community, they must also have recognized that they had assumed an obligation to those who had invested in the project. They must have felt the tug of responsibility to those who were relying on spending their mature years in the comfort of a special community of companions who had similar experiences and backgrounds. Finally, underlying all other reasons, there was the dedication to the Air Force institution and its officer corps.

The two were particularly suited for the task. Their Air Force careers had qualified them to plan, implement, and manage a program of these dimensions. They had managed Air Force programs that involved hundreds of millions of dollars. They knew the details of finance, procurement, contracts, and construction. Just as importantly, they had the personnel skills to direct the efforts of those who would assist. Nevertheless, there were plenty of bumps along the road.

Here's how it all started. On July 1, 1984, a lunch-bunch group of twelve retired Air Force officers, led by Col. George W. Johnson, invited Whitey Driessnack to discuss the potential for establishing an Air Force retired officers' community in the Washington, D.C., area. The group was convinced of the need for such a facility, but it had no clue as to how to proceed.

The first bump on the road came when they learned that it would not be possible to secure formal Air Force approval and support for a Washington area facility. Driessnack convinced them that, given the circumstances, it would be fruitless to continue to seek formal Air Force support for their project. Furthermore, if they were to be taken seriously by any authority or enterprise, a legal corpus must be organized. They asked Driessnack if he would be willing to undertake that task. He agreed to do so.

Driessnack recognized that he needed a board of able, committed people with management experience. The first two people he approached were Buck Buckingham and Brig. Gen. Bohdan Danyliw. Buckingham had been retired from the Air Force for about six years and had financial and large-project experience. Danyliw was a former staff judge advocate at the Air Force Systems Command, retired from the Air Force, and had a lot of contract experience. The board was subsequently filled by seven other retired Air Force officers and an Air Force widow. The members of the board possessed a wide range of talents and experience that would serve the organization well in the many challenges soon to be faced.

Driessnack had retired from the Air Force as assistant vice chief of staff a year earlier and was committed to a job with United Technologies Corporation (UTC). He had been assigned duties there not unlike those of an inspector general, traveling to UTC facilities around the country, troubleshooting, and sharing management techniques. Notwithstanding his busy schedule, he agreed to serve as chairman and president of the first board of directors.

Buckingham was working in a second career as an assistant to the vice president and general manager of a major corporation. He accepted the position of chairman of the Air Force Retirement Officer Community (AFROC) Finance Committee. (In subsequent years, he would be the vice chairman and chairman of the board.)

Danyliw was a partner in a large law firm. He ultimately became, along with Whitey and Buck, a member of the board's executive committee. He undertook the task of incorporating the Air Force Retirement Officer Community, Washington, D.C., in the Virginia and drew up the bylaws in late 1984.

Col. George W. Johnson, who was interested in every phase of the program, was elected vice president. He, along with the assistance of retired Air Force Lt. Col. Bing Binge, managed the AFROC office at Andrews Air Force Base. In recognition of his early efforts to establish an Air Force retirement community and his management of the AFROC office, the Falcons Landing health center with assisted living and skilled nursing was named the Johnson Center.

Both Johnson and Binge, among the earliest occupants of Falcons Landing units, began soliciting memberships in AFROC by sending out fliers from the AFROC office. Soon 1,400 members were accepted who placed $1,000 each in a non-interest-bearing deposit to secure a priority number for eventual entry into the proposed retirement community. The interest from the $1.4 million covered the founding of a benevolent fund and the board's operating expenses.

A memorandum of understanding was negotiated with the Marriott Corporation to develop the community. A site was selected at Fort Washington, Maryland. Then came another bump in the road that challenged the perseverance and skill of Dreissnack and Buckingham. Two of the Fort Washington site neighbors opposed the zoning of the area for the facility. Their objections led to two years of litigation before the rezoning was ultimately upheld. Another setback came when Marriott, experiencing difficulties in a troubled economy, withdrew from its commitment. At this point, AFROC had assumed obligations to the membership that had made $1.4 million in deposits. The motivation to create, to do good, to benefit the Air Force officer community, had been reinforced by the obligation to the membership to persevere. If there had been any doubts about their proceeding, the recorded history does not show it.

There was an aborted approach to join with the Army to build a facility adjacent to The Fairfax retirement community in the vicinity of Fort Belvoir, Virginia. Several meetings were held with other community developers and financial groups. After a lengthy search, the board, still led by Dreissnack and Buckingham, entered into an agreement with Haskell Community Developers and Force Financial. A thirty-three-acre site on the Algonkian Parkway in Potomac Falls, Virginia, was selected from among fifteen possibilities. The rest is history.

Whitey Driessnack with his F84G in Korea, 1953
Photo courtesy of Dreissnack

Neither Buckingham nor Driessnack came from a privileged background. Driessnack was born in 1927 in Yonkers, New York, into a family that would include four children. In 1914, his father, in an American port while sailing as a German merchantman, signed off his ship, paid his five-dollar "head tax," and five years later became an American citizen working as a tool and die maker. His mother emigrated from a German farm community in 1921. She met his father through local German social activities in Yonkers, New York.

Driessnack graduated from Groton High School in Yonkers in 1945 and enlisted in a Navy program that obligated him for a period of victory in the war, plus six months. He served for one year. He was following an older brother's trail that included service in the Navy's V-12 college program. Driessnack served aboard the USS *Kearsarge*, CV-33, a newly commissioned aircraft carrier that was on its shakedown cruise while home-ported in Brooklyn, New York.

Whitey the sailor
Photo courtesy of Dreissnack

He was discharged from the Navy in August 1946. With the assistance of a football scholarship, the GI Bill, and money he had saved in the Navy, he enrolled in Syracuse University to major in civil engineering. His football days were numbered; he tore cartilage in his left knee and had to give up basketball and football. He found crew a satisfying substitute and rowed four years at Syracuse with a crew that took second place in 1947 in the highly competitive National Regatta at Poughkeepsie, New York.

Driessnack would have enrolled in the Navy Reserve Officer Training Program (NROTC), but it was not offered at Syracuse. He enrolled in the newly activated Air Force program instead, augmenting his scholarship and GI Bill with the $27 per month he received from that quarter. He had jobs within and outside the university, including a job in the dining room. That proved to be his most productive employment, because it was there that he met coworker Gloria Magel, a native of Wyomissing, Pennsylvania, and later his wife. Driessnack was cited as a distinguished graduate when he completed Syracuse and was commissioned a second lieutenant in the regular Air Force in March 1951. He and Magel were engaged upon his graduation. His first assignment was as a base civil engineering officer, but it took only one orientation flight for him to be hooked on flying, and he entered flight training at Hondo Air Force Base, Texas. Gloria earned a master's degree in library science and worked for the New York Public Library on Fifth Avenue in New York City for a year.

While Magel was visiting Driessnack in Texas in 1952, the couple was convinced by friends that they should be married—right then. They made the short trip to Nuevo Laredo, Texas, paid a fifty-dollar fee, made their lifelong commitment, and moved into government quarters. Driessnack describes the single barrel of household effects that his wife brought to their new quarters. He does not dwell on the fact that his few possessions could be stored in a duffle bag.

In February 1953, Driessnack left for Korea where he flew twenty-five combat missions as a fighter pilot. The Korean experience is best told in his words:

> My baptism under fire came in Korea in 1953. On one of my first missions, I would be hit without ever having seen the guns that had taken me under fire and without knowing that they had damaged my plane.
>
> I was flying F-84s out of K-2 in Tageau. Our primary mission was close air support and interdiction. I had arrived during the winter, and the Korean landscape was bleak and uninviting. We flew over snow-capped mountains and empty rice paddies. I initially thought that this was going to be a miserable, uninteresting tour. How wrong I was.
>
> During that first month of my tour we had a strike mission on a Korean bridge that was on the enemy's main line of resupply. I was flying in the number two position. When I rolled in to start my bomb run, inexplicably, my aircraft rolled over. I thought I had hit the jet wash from the lead aircraft. I righted the aircraft, adjusted my run, and dropped my ordnance on the target. When I rejoined the flight, my flight leader radioed, "It looks like they got your number early." Upon inspecting my aircraft, I could see that I had taken a direct hit through my left aileron. It was this hit that had rolled me over. The flight home was a struggle, but the landing was routine.

In July of '53, our squadron was tasked to destroy another bridge, this one at Huichon in northern North Korea. One flight of four would approach the bridge at low level, attacking from the north. The squadron commander led that flight, and I flew the number three position. There were three other flights of four fighters that were to fly "flak" suppression to give the lead flight a fighting chance to get to the bridge, deliver our ordnance, and get out again. Timing and coordination were everything. We were on our low-level approach to our bomb run when the flak suppression attacks began. However, despite these suppression runs, once we were in the target area, I thought every gun in North Korea must have been shooting at us. After the first two aircraft dropped their two one-thousand-pound bombs, the sky was filled with the resultant debris along with the flak. I adjusted my course, aimed for the abutment of the bridge on the river bank, and as recorded by the gun camera of the number four aircraft, I got a bull's-eye, hitting the abutment, squarely dropping that end of the bridge.

I pulled back on the stick until I was in "red out," climbing for altitude out of the maelstrom of flak and debris. We couldn't believe our good fortune. With all that rubble in the air over the objective area, not only did no one get shot down, but neither did we sustain any damage. The angels were flying with us on that mission.

Driessnack maintained his flight status in fighter aircraft until his promotion to major. The remainder of his career was diverted to the business of Air Force business. Along the way, he secured a master's degree in business administration, attended the Naval War College, and completed the advanced management program at the Harvard Graduate School of Business Administration.

The Driessnacks took the advice they were offering to hundreds of potential residents and moved into Falcons Landing in June 1996. The following years have not been idle. Not only were they builders of the community, but they have generously volunteered their services. They have been at the vanguard of the maintenance of the community's standards and lifestyle.

◆   ◆   ◆

Photos courtesy of Buckingham

Buck Buckingham was born in Chicago, Illinois, into a family of three children. He was raised by a heroic, single mother who brought them through the Great Depression. Buckingham was an enterprising lad who worked hard, starting with his first job as a salesman of the *Radio Guide*, earning a penny and a half on the sale of each copy. He caddied and was much influenced and encouraged by a world-class amateur golfer who became his father figure. He graduated from Woodruff High School in Peoria, Illinois, where an English teacher taught him not only his lessons but also the virtues of discipline and diligence. His high school honored him with a Distinguished Alumni Award in 1999.

Buckingham became an Air Force enthusiast early in life after he saw a movie that featured life at the Military Academy, an experience that was reinforced by his first flight in an airplane for which he paid a dollar. He was determined that he would fly in the Army Air Corps. He attended Bradley University in Peoria from 1941 to 1943, winning an appointment to the Military Academy at West Point through the office of Everett Dirkson, then a representative and later senator. He graduated from the academy in 1946 with a bachelor of science degree and pilot wings.

In January 1946, Cadet Buckingham met and was smitten by Gloria Doyle of Floral Park, New York. He was the beneficiary of a blind date arranged by a friend of Gloria's sister. He first thought that she was a college coed, but after he proposed, she admitted that she was a senior in high school. They married on June 6, 1946, immediately after his commissioning. The union produced five children—four boys and a girl—and has garnered them thirteen grandchildren and three great-grandchildren. They also hosted three nephews off and on for three years.

Lt. Gen. Buckingham began his pilot career as a second lieutenant in the Army Air Forces, later to become the United States Air Force. His early assignments were typical. He completed bomber pilot training in B-25s at Enid Army Air Base, Oklahoma, and was assigned to the Strategic Air Command as a B-29 pilot in the 509th Bombardment Wing at Roswell Army Air Base, New Mexico, in late 1946. At that time, the 509th was the only wing equipped and trained to drop atomic bombs. The Enola Gay and one other B-29 from that wing dropped the atomic bombs over Hiroshima and Nagasaki. Buckingham's assignment to the 509th was short-lived, because he was selected to go to Sandia Base for weaponeer training. He had hoped to return to the 509th but was kept at Sandia to train weaponeers, aircraft commanders, and assembly personnel in monitoring and assembling the atomic bomb. In 1949, he was transferred to Carswell Air Force Base as a B-36 copilot and weaponeer. He participated in the Operation Ivy test series, which involved the largest ever atomic bomb dropped from an aircraft at the test site on the Eniwetok Atoll in the Marshall Islands in the Pacific Ocean.

It was November 16, 1952. Two weeks earlier, the first thermonuclear weapon had been detonated in the same area. Because there were no aircraft equipped to drop a ten-megaton thermonuclear super-cold liquid bomb weighing more than fifty thousand pounds (code-named "Mike"), it was mounted twenty feet off the ground and was detonated on the island of Elugelab. It obliterated the island with a force 450 times the power of the atomic bomb that fell on Nagasaki. It left a crater 164 feet deep where the island had once been. The atomic bomb dropped from Buckingham's aircraft was in the kiloton range and was code-named "King." Buckingham described the drop:

> We started training for the "King" drop during July 1952 at Carswell Air Force Base in Fort Worth, Texas. About a year before that, I was the Eleventh Bombardment Wing adjutant. As all rated pilots in the Strategic Air Command were required to have duty on a crew, I was assigned to the wing standardization crew as the copilot (third pilot) and weaponeer. The aircraft commander, Lt. Col. Roy Showalter, was someone I had known for three years. As his right arm, I wrote a B-36 crew procedures manual used throughout the wing.
>
> Our crew was selected for the "King" drop based on the expertise that existed within the crew makeup and our CEP (Circular Error Probable) average during bomb drops at various ranges. The fifteen-man crew consisted of three pilots, two flight engineers, three bombardier/navigators, two radio operators, and five gunners. In addition to our aircraft crew, we were assigned thirty maintenance specialists who would deploy a day ahead of us to the Kwajalein Island, our base of operations, in early October.
>
> Our training consisted of multiple replica bomb loadings and drops, simulated bailouts, and water survival techniques. The aircraft commander and I received specialized/refresher training at the base Special Weapons Lab. The integration of the maintenance crew into our daily activities gave us an excellent understanding of each individual's capabilities. We felt that one individual was not living up to our expectations and were about to relieve him when he performed a very heroic act. The heavy rain, preceding a tornado that swept across the Carswell airfield on Labor Day, washed the wheel chocks away. This, combined with the effects of the tornado, caused the B-36s to slide and roll into each other, which resulted in a substantial amount of damage to all except our airplane. At the warning of the storm, the individual we were about to relieve manually set the wheel brakes. His action kept the aircraft in place during the storm even though the wheel chocks washed way. Needless to say, we kept him with us for the duration of our mission.
>
> We departed Carswell on 4 October, stopping overnight at Travis Air Force Base, and left the next morning for a non-stop flight to Kwajalein arriving on 6 October. We continued our training, flying simulated bombing runs over the target area, and supervising the loading of the bomb by the mainte-

nance crew. Because of the heavy damage caused by the tornado to B-36s at Carswell on Labor Day and the lack of knowledge that existed at that time on structure mechanics, the officials in charge of Operation Ivy were concerned that the blast from the bomb would cause catastrophic damage to our airplane. Therefore, serious consideration was given to having a B-47 drop the bomb, as it was a faster airplane and would be farther away from the blast than ours could be. We were not concerned and were able to convince the authorities to let us go ahead with the mission. Early on 14 November, the bomb was wheeled out, completely shrouded to prevent anyone from observing the four antennas that would enable an expert to predict the height at which the bomb was set to detonate. The bomb, affectionately called the "Fat Man," was 128 inches long, 60 inches in diameter, and weighed 10,800 pounds with approximately 5,000 pounds of TNT surrounding the nuclear core area. After two hours of preflight planning, we took off precisely at 0800 hours and leveled off at 8,000 feet. At that time, I went out into the bomb bay, opened up the nose of the bomb, and extracted a long steel chain that had been inserted to minimize any collateral damage from a TNT explosion should we crash on takeoff. I then took the nuclear core out of its container, inserted it into the bomb and closed up the nose. We climbed to 42,000 feet and headed for the target area. On arrival over the Eniwetok Atoll target area, we encountered a thunderstorm. After conversing with Operation Ivy officials via radio, the aircraft commander aborted the mission and headed back toward Kwajalien. After descending to 8,000 feet, I again entered the bomb bay, opened up the nose, pulled out the nuclear core, and put it back into the container. I then inserted the steel chain. While doing this, Operation Ivy officials asked, "Is the chicken out of the basket yet?" When I finished closing up the nose, they were advised that the chicken was out of the basket. After landing, we supervised the maintenance crew while the bomb was being unloaded and returned, along with the container with the nuclear core, to the guarded storage area.

The next morning, we repeated the process. This time, other than some isolated clouds, the weather was clear enough to drop the bomb from an altitude of 42,000 feet. Immediately after the drop, the aircraft commander made a forty-five-degree bank to the left and leveled off 135 degrees away from the bomb drop heading. Each of us quietly said a prayer that the blast effect would not damage our airplane. The bomb exploded at the preset altitude of 1,500 feet over the target with a force of 500 kilotons. We were approximately seventeen miles away with outside temperature at minus sixty degrees, when we felt a blast of hot air come through the airplane. That pushed the aircraft up 2,000 feet. Our prayers were answered; there was no damage to the aircraft, and we arrived safely back at Kwajalien and began preparing for the trip back to Carswell.

The next day, we loaded up the bomb bay pallets with scooters, Noritake dish sets, and other items purchased at the base exchange. On the way home, we stopped at Hickam AFB in Honolulu. On arrival we were met by a customs agent who said, "Don't tell me I can't come on board the airplane, because it is classified 'Secret,' as I have a 'Secret' clearance." It turned out that a group of weather B-29s arriving the day before from Kwajalien had refused the customs agent permission to inspect their aircraft as their aircraft were classified "Secret." By the time we landed, he had checked and had the proper clearance. In addition to going through the aircraft, he made us off-load all four bomb bay pallets, put everything on a truck, and take it into Customs for a detailed check of our luggage and other possessions. It took us six hours to clear through Customs and to reload the pallets. Fortunately, none of our purchases was confiscated.

We spent the next day relaxing and sightseeing. We departed Hickam on November nineteenth for the flight back to Carswell. After being away from our families for forty-five days, we were all glad to be home.

Less than a year after his participation in Operation Ivy, Buckingham started the long, successful series of assignments of doing the business of the Air Force. His assignments took him to U.S. Air Force Headquarters; to Chateauroux, France, for service as a staff procurement officer with the inspector general; contracting officer with the French Air Logistics Office; and Chief of the Procurement Division for the Air Material Force, European Area. He earned a master of business administration degree at George Washington University and completed the Industrial College of the Armed Forces as a Distinguished Graduate. Before he became Air Force comptroller, he served as chief of staff for Air Force Logistics Command at Wright-Patterson Air Force Base in Ohio.

One of the highlights of his management career came as a lieutenant colonel when he developed a financial management program for weapon systems what would ultimately be used throughout the Department of Defense. It was a program he had developed while working with the eight associate contractors of the Minuteman System Program Office. His experience and education in the management of Air Force systems have paid huge dividends to the entire Defense Department. His experience and education have also paid huge dividends to the Air Force Retired Officers Community.

Gloria Buckingham was reluctant to leave their home in Great Falls, Virginia, to move to Falcons Landing, but she became a convert once they joined the community in September 2002. Her husband has continued to contribute to the success of the community by serving as chairman emeritus of the AFROC board and president of the residents' council. He has led the effort to secure necessary legislation in the Virginia Commonwealth Legislature to enable Falcons Landing to continue to provide services essential to the local community and to its future financial well-being. The entrance to the center of the Falcons Landing community is a large, handsome reception area. It was recently named the Founders

Hall, as a tribute to the enormous contributions and inspirations of Buck Buckingham, Whitey Dreissnack, and Bohden Denyliw.

Falcons Landing fronts Algonkian Parkway. It is a four-lane, beautifully landscaped, divided highway. From the far side of the parkway, there is an impressive view up the hillside of the six brick buildings surrounded by thirty duplexes and twenty manor houses. It is more than the home of some five hundred retirees. It is also a monument. It is a monument to the skill, perseverance, and dedication of the many who have made major contributions to building and sustaining the facility. Mostly, however, it is a monument to the selfless labors of Whitey Driessnack and Buck Buckingham. It is the last community in which many of the residents will live, and they will do so with a compatible, social group, in comfort, security, and contentment. Thank you Whitey and Buck.

17

Anjelina Likia Oneke

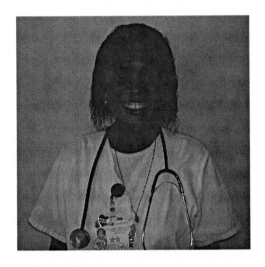

Anjelina Likia Oneke is a refugee from Southern Sudan and is employed at Falcons Landing as a certified nursing assistant licensed by the Virginia Board of Health Professions. Her odyssey from the bush of Southern Sudan to Falcons Landing started during the First Civil War (1956–1972) and extended through the Second Civil War, which began in 1983 and is continuing. Anjelina is an attractive, intelligent, articulate woman with a broad, ready smile and laugh. She has a good command of the English language, delivered with a slight lilt, characteristic of her native tongue, Ma'di. Hers is a tale of courage, fortitude, love, faith, endurance, and the lure of America and the opportunity in this great land.

Sudan is the largest country in Africa with an area about one-quarter the size of the United States, and a population of about forty million. It is in Northern Africa on the Red Sea, and its principal neighbors are Egypt to the north, Chad

---

1.   Profile is based on a series of interviews starting in March 2005.

to the west, Ethiopia to the east, and Uganda to the south. Black ethnics represent 52 percent of the population, while 39 percent are Arabs and 6 percent belong to the nomadic Beja tribe in the northeast. Seventy percent of the population is Sunni Muslim, 5 percent is Christian, and the remainder might be termed indigenous religions. Sudan gained its independence from the United Kingdom in 1956, and for all but eleven years (1972–1983), it has been involved in a bloody civil war characterized by institutionalized starvation, genocide, mass rapes, kidnapping, and persistent attacks on civilians. The atrocities have been tolerated and, many times, promoted by the government in Khartoum. Over a tenth of the population has been displaced within Sudan and to neighboring countries. More than 180,000 people have been killed. The number dead from starvation and disease brought on by the wars has not been established, although there is an estimate that, at the turn of the twenty-first century, 300,000 Sudanese died in the single area of Darfur in two years. Other estimates have placed the death toll at 2.5 million people with two million of them being from south Sudan.[2]

In the broadest of terms, the Sudanese civil wars have aligned the Muslim Khartoum government against southern rebels who are mainly Christians and animists. The conflict is complicated by the struggle for the control of oil, the differences in ideology, and ethnicity. Anjelina has survived this horrible chaos and personal injury and her determination and dedication to her family and others celebrates a triumph of the human spirit.

Here is Anjelina's story in her words:

> My name is Anjelina Likia Oneke. I was born in 1965 in Southern Sudan in a town called Nimule (on the border with Uganda about ninety miles southeast of Juba, Sudan). I grew up in a Christian home and belong to the Ma'di tribe. I have six brothers and three sisters, and I am the youngest child in the family. My father, who has died, was not an educated man, but he was very kind and humble. Not only did he take care of his own family, but he cared for others who needed help as well. I have kept the name of Oneke, which is my family name—my father's name—to honor him. My mother is still alive and living in Uganda. She was a good, hard-working woman who took good care of her children during very hard times, when our lives were often threatened. She went through grades one to three in school, speaks a little English, and writes well in the Ma'di language. She has been a counselor to the Ma'di community.

---

2.   CIA Factbook, www.cia.gov/cia/publications/factbook/geos/su.html

The year that I was born, war was being fought in Sudan between the Muslims and the Christians. The Muslim Arabs from the north have found our country very hospitable and rich in minerals, good soil, and even oil. They were very strong and we were weak. Many of us were Christians, which provided another reason for the war.

We people of the south are poor, humble people; we didn't have guns to defend ourselves. So at the outbreak of the war, when our lives and freedom were threatened, many of us fled south to the refugee camps in Uganda. Ten of our family, that is, my mother and her nine children, walked over two hundred miles through the bush to Gulu, a small town in north central Uganda where there was a UNHCR (United Nations High Commissioner for Refugees) refugee center. We walked through hard country, from bush to bush, where we hid from wild animals, rebels, and the government army. If any of those had found us, they would have killed us. My mother had a hard time protecting us as we moved from bush to bush, and it was luck if we found something to eat and drink. My mother was cut badly across her legs in the high saw grass that is found in that part of our country. In the last days of our difficult journey, when we were only two miles from the Uganda border, my older brother had to carry her on his back.

My father remained behind in Sudan to care for his uncle who was dying of leprosy. During our absence, the government soldiers came and accused my father of being a spy, and when there was a struggle while he was trying to escape from them, they cut off his thumb. Our uncle died in about four or five months, but it was about a year before my father could join us in the refugee camp in Uganda.

The seeds of the civil war in Southern Sudan were sown a decade before Anjelina was born, dating back to a mutiny within the Sudan Army in the 1950s. In 1955, immediately preceding the British granting independence to Sudan, the SDF Equatoria Corps mutinied. The corps, which consisted mainly of enlisted men from the Christian, animist south, was led by Arabian-Muslim northerners. The mutiny was in protest of the Arab-led government's reneging on the promise to create a federal system that represented all the Sudanese. Northern troops crushed the rebellion, the corps was disbanded, and the mutineers, with many of the local police who had supported them, took to the bush to fight against the Khartoum government. While the mutineers posed no serious threat to the central government, hundreds of northern officials, teachers, and bureaucrats living in the south were massacred by the rebels. Khartoum responded in kind.

In the decade of Anjelina's birth, there had already been about half a million people who had died either as a direct or indirect result of the war. Harassed by the northern forces, hundreds of thousands of southerners either hid in the bush or escaped to refugee camps in bordering countries such as Chad and Uganda.

Neighboring countries in the region supplied arms to the rebel forces. The principal rebel faction in the south as of this writing is the Sudan People's Liberation Movement (SPLM), started in 1983 and led by John Garang, a Christian Dinka educated in the United States. Garang earned a Ph.D. in agricultural economics at Grinell College in Iowa and is a graduate of a U.S. Army company commanders' course at Fort Benning, Georgia.

There were hundreds of thousands of refugees in the United Nations camps in the vicinity of Gulu, Uganda. Anjelina's family was in the Unyama camp from about 1966 to 1973.

"It was a hard life for us," she said. "There was little for us to eat, so my mother went to work, not for money, but for food to feed us. She was able to earn enough cassava, millet, and other basic foods to keep us alive. The first war lasted for about ten years, ending in 1971 when there was a peace agreement. They are now again at war."

Uganda, while more secure than Southern Sudan, was hardly a hospitable place for the Oneke family and the thousands of Sudanese who took shelter there. A civil war was being waged in Uganda by a rebel group, the LRA (Lord's Resistance Army), originally dedicated to establishing a state based on the Ten Commandments. Its leader, Joseph Kony, reportedly has recently converted to Islam and become a Muslim. The LRA was known for abducting more than twenty thousand children from their families, forcing the boys to become soldiers and taking the girls as concubines.

But the Sudanese children in Anjelina's camp were intrepid and sometimes outwitted those adults who would take advantage of them. Anjelina recalled:

> While we were in Uganda, many people worked for a very rich man named Tamanya of the Cohali Tribe who treated the people badly. People would work for days without pay and having nothing to eat. One time, we children were playing near his fields, and Tamanya came and offered clothes if we would work in his fields. We had no clothes, and, of course, we felt we needed them; so we agreed to work to weed his sweet potato field for him. I was the youngest of the children who entered into the agreement. We were excited about it because Christmas was coming, and here was a chance to earn some presents. Our parents gave us permission to work for Tamanya because they didn't believe he would cheat a bunch of children, who are special and protected in our part of Sudan. So the group of us children worked for eight hours in the man's fields. But when it came time to pay us, he refused and kept putting us off until we could see that he had no intention of giving us what he had promised.

So we started to plot against him. Our first plan was that we might throw stones at him. But we decided that wouldn't be wise, because he had a gun, and we were afraid that he would shoot us. So we planned that we would go into his fields early in the morning and pull up his sweet potatoes and let them lie there on the ground, which we did. Fortunately, a heavy rain came after we had done our dirty deed and washed out all our footprints so he couldn't tell that it was a group of children who had been in his fields. He was furious, but there wasn't anything he could do about it, and he never suspected us. Our actions were enough to encourage the community to confront the man about not paying them. It led to a big meeting between the Sudanese refugees and the Cohali tribesmen to discuss how Tamanya was taking advantage of us. From that time on, he paid us for our work, and we got our clothes.

After the first war ended, and it was fairly safe in Southern Sudan, we applied to the United Nations representatives to return home. The UN provided a truck to bring us back, but it was still a long, hard journey through many land mines before we got to our village, Nimule, and I was able to start school.

Before the war, the missionaries had come to our village and had built a concrete and brick church and school that went from first to sixth grades. During the war the building had been damaged, and the roof had been torn off, so our parents rebuilt the church and school so that we could start our classes. Our family lived in three grass huts. We had no electricity and cooked our meals outside in pottery pots over open fires. Our men hunted in the forest; my father was a farmer, and we raised cattle and goats. Besides going to school, we children had chores to do. I cared for the younger children in our family and in the village, cleaned our house and compound, ground sorghum and corn with stones, and I cooked.

We used the cows and goats for our dowries. Dowries can be as large as fifty cows and fifty goats that the men have to pay for a wife. Getting a bride in Sudan is expensive, and maybe that's one of the reasons that there are so few divorces among our people. Our livestock made up our wealth, our daily food, and our special feasts. People would sell their livestock to pay for school fees. They would slaughter their cattle and goats to feed guests at burials and other rituals. Before long, my family owned about a hundred and fifty cows, a hundred goats and lambs, fifty chickens, and ten ducks. Each of the animals had their own fenced yard and house.

I was the best student in our school, so when I graduated from elementary grades, I was qualified to go to Bullock middle school, which I attended from 1979 to 1981 in the nearby town of Juba. From 1981 to 1984, I went to high school where again I did well. When I finished high school, I was eligible to go to the university, but my parents couldn't afford that. There were a lot of children at home, and while my parents wanted me to continue my school, it wasn't possible. So instead of going to the university, I went to work as a bookkeeper at a soft-drink factory owned by an Indian.

I got married in 1983 when I was eighteen and my husband, Dominic Felix Maku, was twenty-eight years old. I picked my own husband; he was not selected for me. This is the way the system works in our part of Sudan: the boy watches the girl while they are growing up, and he knows her reputation and how she looks. Then, if he knows how to write, he will write a letter to the girl telling her of his interest. She will not say right away that she is interested in him but will tell him that she needs more time, and then she will study him, his character, and reputation. I accepted a proposal from Dominic while both of us were still in school. Dominic's uncle was the director of the local school and had money, so he paid half the dowry. The dowry was in livestock and money, about half and half. I never knew how much the dowry was. We were married in a church by a Catholic priest. Dominic got a job as a government clerk. He was very literate.

By this time, the second war had already started, and the Dinka tribe, the largest ethnic group in Southern Sudan, had taken to the bush as separatist guerrillas to fight against the government's forces. My husband and I moved back to our village, Nimule, from Juba where I went to work as a village social worker. Later, we returned to Juba where I worked as a bookkeeper in a factory. Many Sudanese in the south fled their destroyed villages and became refugees. By 1987 my husband and I had one child, a son, and we were living in Juba when that city became a victim of the war. By 1990, the situation had become very dangerous and hard. We decided that we had to leave Juba to fly to the capital in Khartoum. We had an uncle by the name of John Brown, who was a lieutenant colonel in the army, who helped us. We flew to Khartoum with nothing, just my husband, my son Angelo, and a nephew Godfrey, who had been separated from my brother's family during the war.

Anjelina and her family joined the thousands of Sudanese who were classified as Internal Displaced Persons or IDPs. Huge numbers of displaced persons were generated by civil war, drought, famine, and the lack of government assistance that bordered on genocide. The bulk of the displaced persons were from the south and west Sudan. The Kharthoum government seemed to consider the displaced persons intruders, bereft of civil rights or support. Support for displaced persons came mainly from United Nations agencies and non-governmental organizations (NGOs). Anjelina said:

We were in a displaced persons camp in Khartoum. But I had a goal and a plan; someway, we would escape from Sudan. I sold some gold bracelets I had, and we bought a small hut there for fifty Sudanese pounds, where we lived for two months. Khartoum is in a desert, so we couldn't build the same kind of grass building we built in Nimule—in this desert you built them with adobe walls. The roof was made with a tarpaulin provided by the NGO people. We made a plaster that you use to cover the tarp, and the roof had a hole so that you could build a fire in it. Since we were in the desert, there were no trees or grasses to be used to build a house. So the four of us were living in this hut with not enough food, no money, and no hope. We had no way that we could farm or raise livestock.

Then the government decided that they didn't want all these displaced people around Khartoum, so they destroyed our camp. I was pregnant with our second child. On the twenty first of February 1992, the government came in with bulldozers and crushed all our houses, and we fled. In one hour, in our encampment of six thousand refugees, twenty-one people died—in just one hour. The NGOs tried to protect us, but there wasn't much that they could do. They told the government people that we were innocents, that we had committed no crimes, that we were Sudanese with the rights of citizens, and that we should be helped, not driven out of our homes. But the government wouldn't listen.

The Muslim government and the NGOs then helped us move to Jebel Aulia, about forty miles south of Khartoum, where there is a dam across the Nile.

The Jebel Aulia camp was populated mostly by Christians of the embattled Southern Sudan. It was an area bereft of vegetation, industry, and sustaining agriculture. There was no access to shelter, food, or potable water in the torrid desert, a desert that could turn bitter cold during some seasons. The area is without natural shelter, which makes it particularly hazardous during the rainy season.

We had some six thousand families there, and life was very hard. There were no sanitary facilities, and there was much disease, with many people dying. We had to walk five miles to the River Nile to get water, and I was eight months pregnant, carrying water on my head back to the family. ADRA (Adventist Development and Relief Agency International), one of the NGOs, dug a well, and my husband and I built a small hut out of empty sacks. We were barely surviving. There were three days in a row when we had nothing to eat at all. But the NGOs established a health center, and things started to improve a little.

My husband finally found work in a poultry farm. In April of 1994, I started to work as a community health worker for the French Medecins Sans Frontieres, one of the medical relief programs. My job was to keep statistical and health records on the community and to encourage people to come to the health center. Some of our Sudanese people preferred the primitive African way and had to be coaxed into going to the western doctors. I would give health counseling and make home visits to inspect sanitation conditions and teach families how to dig slit trenches for human waste. I instructed people how to avoid and treat malaria, diarrhea, chickenpox, and measles and how important it was to be vaccinated against diseases. The treatment of and avoidance of HIV and AIDS were an important part of my work. I was one of the leaders of the native staff working there at the health center.

In May of 1998, a series of epidemics broke out including cholera, measles, chickenpox, and diarrhea. I collected all of the statistics relative to the epidemic and drafted a report that was sent to Amsterdam in the Netherlands. A team of three Dutch men came to inspect the situation. They stayed three days and made a report to Khartoum and to others outside of Sudan as they tried to help us. I think that the Dutch report was the reason that the government came to suspect that I was working against them.

On August 20, 1998, following the al-Qaeda bombings of the United States embassies in Kenya and Tanzania, the Al-Shifa pharmaceutical factory in Khartoum was destroyed in a U.S. cruise missile attack. The U.S. administration's rationale behind the strikes was that there was evidence that the factory had been used to manufacture chemical weapons for al-Qaeda.

The Khartoum government said that the Sudanese Christians were behind the American bombings of August 1998. The officials took all the records that I had made about the epidemics and the health of the people in the Jebel Aulia camp, suspecting that it could be used as evidence against me on charges that I was supporting the rebels. They arrested me and kept me in jail for six days, and when they could prove nothing, they let me go. But those six days were torment. The jail was underground and very dark. My cell was tiny. I never knew where I was, because when I was brought there, and whenever I was moved, they blindfolded me. The jailers abused me terribly. I was brutally beaten, deprived of water, then immersed in cold water. I was forced to eat a sandwich of sand, and a bag of hot chili powder was placed over my head. They covered my mouth and my nose with tape, and then tried to make me blow until I was unconscious. They did many despicable things to me I can't talk about. But I was lucky—many other Christians who were in the same position as I was in were killed.

We survived those horrible days in Jebel Aulia, but, in 1998, the Khartoum government claimed that my husband was cooperating with the rebels, and they put him in jail. They had no reason to suspect him; that's just the way they would make their war against Christian citizens. They knew that my husband had a group of men who met for Bible study, and that was enough to make them suspicious. They kept him in one of those terrible jails for two years.

At this time, I had five children, including a daughter who was only five months old. I knew that if we were to survive we had to get out of Sudan, and I started making secret plans to escape. Going to Chad was an option, but it would be difficult. After our first experience, I didn't want to go to Uganda again. I figured that the easiest way to escape would be to go to Egypt, then later try to get to Uganda to get my parents, then to find a place to settle. But I was never able to get to Uganda, and my mother and some of my relatives are still there in Ajumani, Northern Uganda, in a refugee camp. I assembled my family of five children, plus my nephew, and we started our escape without my husband, who was still in jail.

We first crossed the desert by car with a driver that a friend had provided for us.

We then went by taxi, train, and steamer through Aswan to Cairo. It was a dangerous trip for us. At the terrible Sudanese border town of Wad Halfa, I was strip-searched but was able to conceal the money that was sewn in my underclothes. If the Sudanese government military or police had discovered us trying to escape, they would have killed us. I kept watch over my children and didn't sleep for five days.

We didn't know anybody in Egypt; we were completely alone; we had nothing. The only advantage I had was that I could speak English, which I had learned in the Christian schools in Southern Sudan. I was fluent in English, and I knew enough Arabic to speak, but not to write it. I had a little money that I had brought with me from Sudan. I had converted some Sudanese piastres into dollars, which is against the law in Sudan, and I sewed the dollars into my underwear, all neatly folded in plastic wraps. There were other Sudanese on the train portion of our trip, and we helped each other the best we could. My plan was to go to a church and ask for help once we got to Cairo.

In Cairo, a Sudanese man and his wife loaned us enough money for a taxi, because all my money was still hidden in my underclothes. They told us where we could find a church that might help us.

God was with us, because when we stopped in front of the church in a taxi, there was a priest coming out of the compound, and I approached him. He was Greek, about seventy-two years old, had lived in Cairo for many years, and was in good health. The children and I were in terrible shape. We were dirty, in rags, and tired, but the priest stopped, and I spoke to him in English. I told him my story—that I had grown up in a Christian home, that I was active in the church, that my husband was still in Sudan, that we had nothing, and had nowhere to go. He took us in, showed us where we could take a shower, and he fed us.

I told my priest friend that I knew that I needed legal status to remain in Cairo, but I only wanted to stay for one or two months to find a way for me to go back to Uganda to find my parents and bring them away from there. He explained to me that there was a UN office in Cairo (United Nations High Commissioner for Refugees Agency—UNHCR) that helped refugees, and that he would take me there. After a few days, he took me to the UN offices to spend the night in the compound, so I could be first in line to get papers from the officers that would give me legal protection. I took my five-month-old daughter with me to spend the night in a cold, uncomfortable place where there were many refugees waiting to be processed. We all got there the night before, so that we could get in the line for the interview the next day. At 5 AM, they took ten people at a time to give them protection papers, but I was number eleven, so I missed it. I left without getting the protection papers but returned that night to try again the next morning. The next morning there were two lines, one for men and one for women. At first I was number two in the women's line, but when they started taking people in, there was such a rush, screaming and pushing by people who weren't carrying a baby and who were stronger than me. I ended up at the back of the line again. I was really worried for the safety of my baby, and I started to scream to protect her. The pushing, shoving, and screaming alerted a man in the high commissioner's office who opened a window and saw the scene below. He came down to where we were, and he started pointing out women who were in the line—one on crutches, an old lady, four of us—and he told us to step aside. I thought, "Oh now we are in real trouble. Are they going to deport us?" However, one by one, they took us into an office, and they gave us forms to fill out and to write our stories. That permitted me to get my interview, and they issued me my protection papers. The papers gave me a status so that I could either stay in Egypt with my children or leave for another country in a legal way.

Some good came of all the confusion at the high commissioner's office, because I was able to tell the person who processed us about how the system had broken down, and that it was only the strongest who could push their way through the crowd to get into the official's offices, and how it threatened the weaker persons. I made some suggestions as to how they could give out priority numbers to the people who were waiting. The officials accepted my suggestions, and the process became more orderly.

At this point I felt that I was free of Sudan, but I needed to get my husband, Dominic, out of the jail and bring him to Egypt. I had kept in touch with a priest in Sudan who was helping me. We raised some money and used it to get access to people who could help us. I got a job with the Joint Relief Ministry in Cairo, and I worked hard at my job and in taking care of my family. It was a busy, busy time for me, as I was working and taking care of these six children, five being mine and one the nephew I adopted. Fortunately, the older children were able to help with the younger ones.

At the ministry, my job was to care for pregnant women and to help with post-natal care. It was my job to coordinate with the hospital. I acted as a midwife assistant and performed duties we called general nursing there but which we call licensed practical nursing here, such as giving health education, giving injections, and administering intravenous feedings, IVs and such. I had received training in nursing from the MSF (Medicins Sans Frontiers) when we lived in Sudan. I soon started doing social work for the refugees, telling them how they should go about getting the documents they needed to be legal, helping them find work, and advising them on other social problems. During all these busy times I had to keep thinking, "Never give up hope for life." I didn't know how to drive, and I didn't have a car anyway, so I used public transportation to get back and forth to work.

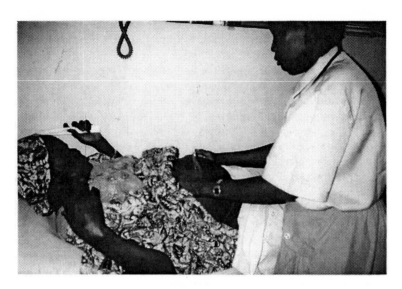

Anjelina the midwife

We were in Cairo for two years. It was not possible to send the children to school, as the tuition was too expensive for me. The Egyptians were not always welcoming to us. It's a very sexist society, and when there are disputes between the Egyptian citizen and the refugee, of course, the authorities always supported the citizen. Their form of the 'N' word was to call us "Chocolates" or "Unga Bunga," which they considered to be insulting.

Some Egyptians cheated us, and some would throw stones at us. But there were also advantages for our being in Egypt. Food and rent were cheap, although we had three large families living in a three-room apartment.

One time my son Richard was eating tuna out of a can, and one of the Egyptian boys threw a stone at him. Richard retaliated by throwing his tuna can at the Egyptian boy and cut him in doing so. The Egyptians boy's father, who was named Mohammed, was furious and tried to break into our house. I had a seventy-six-year-old friend who tried to protect me when Mohammed tried to break down our door. Our building landlord stopped the man, but I was told by one of our neighbors that Mohammed was planning to harm me and my family. I took another way with him. I treated the boy's cut and eventually Mohammed calmed down and didn't threaten us any longer. However, for a woman alone with five children and no male protection living among people who were ready to do you harm, it was a very threatening time for me. There were many Sudanese refugees in Cairo and they were suffering as well. Many found work as housekeepers, but many couldn't find any work, and a lot of them died.

I didn't have enough money to get my parents out of Uganda. But I continued to work to get my husband free from the Khartoum government jail and have him join us in Cairo. At the same time, I applied for refugee status to leave Egypt. One day I was called to the UN offices in Cairo and I was given the choice of going to Canada, Australia, or the United States. I didn't know anybody in any of these places, and I didn't know anything about any of the countries. I asked the UN person as to how I was going to be able to support myself and my children in these places, and they told me that people would help me find work. He told me that I could get work just as I had in Egypt, and that the children would be able to go to school in each of these countries. I chose the United States, because even in places like Sudan and Egypt, they know that America offers you freedom, and you enjoy your God-given rights as a human being.

The Lutheran Social Services purchased the air tickets for the six children and me, and we left Cairo for America on August 28, 2000. We landed in New York and got on another airplane to fly to the Baltimore airport. When we got off the plane, we were met by a representative of the Lutherans and were provided a house and some furniture. The children were really excited to be in America. I was looking for an introduction to the Catholic Church but couldn't arrange one. I contacted the Evangelical Free Church in Annandale, Virginia, and they found a job for me at Target in Arlington, Virginia, where I worked in customer assistance. I took the public bus transportation to and from work, while my oldest son babysat for me while I was in the store. When winter came, we all saw snow for the first time.

I wasn't working in the medical field where I had been trained, so I wasn't enthusiastic about my job. But we were in America, and we were surviving. I couldn't go to work in the health-care community until I was certified by the state. The Lutheran Social Services arranged for my children to start school, with the two older boys going to high school; there were two in elementary school, one was in kindergarten, and one was too young for school. We had food stamps, and the government helped to find a babysitter for me, and that was a big help.

With the help of a Catholic priest in Sudan, my husband was able to escape from prison. He had been in the government jail for two and a half years. He went first to Egypt, where he had to stay for two years. After the 9/11 tragedy, immigration to the United States became very difficult, but our congressman, Frank Wolf, was a help. I also got help from the lawyers at the INS (Immigration and Naturalization Service). In May of 2002, I went to Capital Hill to testify on the problems of the refugees. I told my story, and I hope that I was able to do some good for the refugees who had the kind of experience that I had.

My husband, while in very poor health, but thank God he was still alive, was able to join us in 2003. My mother and father were still in Uganda. I moved from the job at Target to my health-care work here at Falcons Landing on December 23, 2001 with the help of the Lutheran Church. They knew that my background was in health services, and they arranged interviews for me with Falcons Landing. By this time I had learned how to drive.

I love it here. I love the way those in charge treat us. I love working with older people. For me, it is a comfortable place to work. I have much in common with many of the people who live here, because they are veterans of wars, just as I was. I treat our patients with dignity and respect, and I love them. I take care of them just as if they were my own parents, and they treat me as if I were their daughter. Last year I was selected as the best worker among all the staff at Falcons Landing. I was also selected as one of the outstanding health workers in Northern Virginia. At first I worked as a nursing assistant, but after they saw that I had some promise, they sent me to classes to qualify as a nurse practitioner. I was sent to Loudoun Long Term Care for training. I passed the government's qualifying examinations and was given my certificate.

Today, my oldest son Angolo is twenty-one, and my nephew, whom I raised as a son, is twenty-four. My nephew married a Sudanese woman here in Northern Virginia in 2005, and even here in the United States we keep the customs of Sudan, and a dowry of four thousand dollars was paid to the family of the bride. He is going to school at a university in Arlington, Texas, studying to become a nurse, while he is working. He is a gifted musician and plays the guitar at church services. Our oldest son is twenty-one and will graduate from high school this year. He was supposed to graduate last year, but he didn't have enough credits. Remember, he was out of school for two years while we were making our way to America. He will apply to George Mason University when he graduates. He also is a musician and plays the guitar and the drums, but he plays only in the Evangelical Church. Our third child, a son, is now thirteen and in middle school in Annandale, Virginia. Our fourth child is twelve, also a son, and in the third grade in elementary school. Our fifth child, a son, is ten and is in the third grade. And the last one is a daughter, who is seven and is in the first grade.

My husband is currently working at the Ritz Carlton Hotel in Tysons Corner, Virginia, in the laundry. He doesn't like the work, but I tell him that he should keep at it, train, work on the language, and then something better will come along. This is the land of opportunity, and if we continue to work hard, something better will happen. But right now we have to work at it. We have to work to get our children a good education and raise them properly with the right values. It is harder to raise children here than in Sudan, where we had a village to help care for them.

When we first came here I couldn't drive, so when I went to the store I would carry the groceries home on my head while holding the hand of our youngest child, just like we used to do in Sudan. People would look at me and laugh, as if I was doing a really strange thing. One time an African-American man stopped me and said, "Look, a real African lady!" I told him, "Yes, I am a real African lady; my skin is black, and my mind is black." He thought that that was really funny, and he had a good laugh. One time a lady driving by in a car stopped and offered me a ride. I had been warned to never get into a stranger's car, so I told her no. She offered on another occasion, telling me that she was safe, that she was a good churchgoing person, and that there was nothing to fear. So I let her give me a ride. Many people have been very kind to me here, particularly the people from the churches.

After I was here in America, I located my brother in Sudan, with the help of the Red Cross. He is now fifty-two. He and his family had been hiding from the Sudanese authorities for about sixteen years, going from bush to bush often without eating for days. With the help of the relief agencies, I was able to get him, his wife, and the four children still with him out of Sudan—remember, I had one of his boys with me—and they are now living in Alexandria, Virginia. He is also working in a hotel like my husband.

God has been good to us. We are very happy here in America, and we want to become good Americans. However, we also want to keep our culture, and I have been active in that respect. I am involved in three social efforts. One is to protect our culture. Another is to work for the benefit of refugee women and in family affairs. The third is to raise money to send to Sudan and Uganda to support schools there. I have been so blessed; I want to give something back.

18

Jerry Warden Friedheim

On the marble façade of the Newseum, currently under construction on Pennsylvania Avenue in Washington, D.C., the text of the First Amendment to the United States Constitution will be inscribed in letters bold enough to be read from a distance:

---

1.   Profile is based on interviews conducted starting December 2, 2004. All photographs are courtesy of Mr. Friedham.

CONGRESS SHALL MAKE NO LAW
RESPECTING AN ESTABLISHMENT
OF RELIGION, OR PROHIBITING
THE FREE EXERCISE THEREOF;
OR ABRIDGING THE FREEDOM
OF SPEECH, OR OF THE PRESS; OR
THE RIGHT OF THE PEOPLE
PEACEABLY TO ASSEMBLE, AND
TO PETITION THE GOVERNMENT
FOR A REDRESS OF GRIEVANCES

The protection and invocation of First Amendment rights has been one of the major concerns in the professional life of Jerry Friedheim. He coined the name Newseum for this edifice and enterprise that will celebrate and promote an appreciation for the First Amendment and for a strong, free press, in a strong, free country served by professional soldiers and professional journalists.

Some argue that our freedom of the press is different from our right to free speech. In fact, both rights derive from our Constitution's Bill of Rights. America's media has no special rights or privileges not also guaranteed to each citizen and each soldier. Jerry has said, "Our founding fathers understood that a free press and free speech were fundamental to a democratic society. In fact, our Constitution could not have been ratified without the First Amendment."

But within that bedrock essential of liberty, Jerry's lifework has focused on teaching about one indispensable nuance: the *joint* responsibility of the military and the media for freedom's flourishing.

To hundreds of meetings of thousands of military officers he has preached: "A strong free country and a strong free press are inseparable."

You can't have one without the other. No nation ever has; none will.

And so, in several jobs and many places, he has championed contact, compromise, understanding, and professional work between the two constitutional entities. "Your institutions attract very different people with very strong views, but you can and must be adversaries without being antagonists, because if either of you fails, then freedom ultimately fails," he said. He has been fortunate to have had opportunities to pursue his cause as a reporter, editor, Army officer, journalism professor, congressional staffer, assistant secretary of defense, a newspaper association president, and a founder of the Newseum.

"I have been pleased to share this soapbox with others over the years," Jerry said. "I believe the message has been heard, the philosophy embraced. Challenged today in Iraq, the media and the military are working together in ways that are safeguarding troops on the line while providing home-front citizens with unprecedented information at astonishing speed."

Jerry gives much credit for the current success to the system of "embedding" reporters with units, on ships, and at bases long enough for them to form bonds of understanding and respect for the troops, and for the troops to realize that an informed citizenry is one of the things they are fighting for.

"In a way, we had embedding in Vietnam, because we had no censorship, and correspondents were provided transport all over the country, even on General Creighton Abrams' plane," Jerry said.

However, after Vietnam, animosities erupted and the two institutions jousted and griped at each other so much that by the time of Grenada, the troops went without any accompanying correspondents. This led to a series of high-level seminars, conferences, and studies on military and media relations. By the time of the first Persian Gulf War, Jerry and others were recommending embedding to President George H. Bush and Secretary of Defense Dick Cheney. "They tried it sort of halfheartedly," Jerry said, but only the image-conscious Marines succeeded at it. The Army's efforts foundered on shoals of self-doubt and snarled communications. Again, myriad after-action studies resulted, and by the second Gulf battle, it was the military leaders who urged Secretary Donald H. Rumsfeld and President George W. Bush to let them work with media leaders to make embedding work.

It has. America knows what its troops are doing—and what they are not doing. America knows the great good and the occasional misstep. A volunteer armed force remains a part of, not apart from, its citizenry.

"We in the United States have the only free press in the world," Jerry said. "Some of our friends, like Canada, come close; but the British have their Official Secrets Act; and the Scandinavians directly subsidize the 'second' newspapers in their cities; and the Mexican government is often too willing to ration newsprint and telecommunication connections. But these shortcomings are offset by the great progress formerly totalitarian states are making: Poland, the Czech Republic, South Korea, maybe soon Ukraine—while Putin's Russia backslides."

Jerry sees other, less overarching, challenges to preservation of First Amendment freedoms: legalities and technologies.

He sees some judges giving the Sixth Amendment, which provides protection of the rights of the accused in criminal prosecution, preference over the First, as they jail reporters who protect sources. It's not military and media: it is fair trial vs. free press. It is another instance in which no single one of our constitutional rights can be allowed to drive other rights from the field. Jerry explained his beliefs:

> Our rights coexist. Democracy demands comity and compromise. Liberty demands tolerance and flexibility. Soldiers, reporters, and judges must all function for freedom to function...and function with common sense not confrontation.
>
> Of course, lawyers and journalists must work together to preserve decorum and an atmosphere in which justice can be done. Judges must control officers of the court and court procedures. But, too often, the current trend seems for some judges to try to reach out of the courtroom in an attempt to control the reporter's typewriter, the newspaper's library, and even history itself.
>
> What else is it when a judge tells a newspaper not to print history from filed clippings, or even to deny people across town the facts their townsmen in the courthouse can read on a "wanted" poster on the very courthouse wall?
>
> And when these absurdities happen, they seem to be based on an erroneous theory that there is an inherent conflict between the First and Sixth Amendments.
>
> There's no doubt that those who look for conflict under every rock can find it, but there is a huge body of evidence—the very history of our country—to show that a free press—and open reporting of judicial actions—are joint, non-conflicting pillars of all our society's freedoms.
>
> It's simply not true that the First and Sixth Amendments must collide to the damage of the accused or anybody else.[2]
>
> At the same time, technology is thrusting forward myriad non-print communications capabilities. They manipulate electrons not ink. Most—like audiotex, videotext, computer data bases, two-way fiber-optic marvels—seem to us more like broadcasting than print. Unfortunately, we are permitting government to regulate such broadcasting.
>
> Unless we firmly confer the "no-regulation print model" of First Amendment protections to tomorrow's information technologies, we may soon have a First Amendment that doesn't apply to the way most of us communicate. Major efforts must be made to bring government to the view that in a twenty-first-century society, deregulation is not just for phones and planes—it must also be for all the ways we express thought in the amazing, light-speed world that is spinning around us. Almost none of that world enjoys free expression; almost all of it suffers under some sort of government regulation.
>
> We might ask ourselves: as we watch walls crumble across the globe, as we witness citizens assemble to demand basic freedoms, as we see dictators retreat, is our world moving toward governments dedicated to the protection of indi-

---

2.   Jerry W. Friedheim, "Newsroom, Courtroom and Country," March 13, 1976, remarks delivered at Regional Meeting of Kansas City Bar Association and Kansas City Press Club, inter alia, in files of Friedheim.

vidual liberties? Or will the new elite's natural penchant for control skew incipient democracies away from toleration of free thought and confine it under government control to include government ownership of all press and media transmission? Will a global sweep of regulated electronic information interchange overwhelm the print model First Amendment, not just in other countries, but here at home as well?

So our own and the world's future First Amendment freedoms need our constant nurturing. Our freedom of the press, upon which free societies depend, can be very vulnerable.

Jerry quotes from an American series of articles titled *Cato's Letters* published in 1772: "Where a man cannot call his tongue his own, he can scarce call anything else his own."

Futurist Alvin Toffler has written and talked about "the information bomb" that has exploded in our midst, and Jerry has mused whether bloggers, the Internet, and other electronic media will someday make newspapers irrelevant in the information industry. Twenty years ago, in speaking to a Georgia Press Association gathering, Jerry said: "Will the information consumers of the future need newspapers? Sure. They'll need newspapers to provide useful data in print—and some of it electronically.

"They'll need us as a:

- Watchdog on government

- Beacon in a murky world

- Marketing voice for goods and services

- Source of entertainment

- Flagger of the important and unpredictable.

- Source of the common knowledge that fashions common interest."[3]

In 2006, Jerry is less certain about the future of newspapers than he was in 1982.

Jerry was born on October 7, 1934, in Joplin, Missouri, to Volmer and Billie Friedheim, both journalists. They worked on a family-owned newspaper. Billie was the society editor. Volmer was an advertising salesman and wrote a syndicated humor column.

---

3.   Jerry W. Friedheim, "Newspapers Today and Tomorrow—Why bother?" *Vital Speeches of the Day*, March 15, 1982, p340.

The young man's lineage traces to the Rhineland, Scotland, Ireland, and Spain. His American ancestors converged on Missouri via New England, Wisconsin, Louisiana, and Arkansas. They included farmers, merchants, a frontier judge, and a lay rabbi. Family names included Warden, Havens, Volmer, Richardson, Starr, Dowell, Green, and Francisco. At the Civil War siege of Vicksburg, one Missouri ancestor, a Union brigadier general, was shot and then died in the Confederate hospital where another ancestor, a Rebel private from Louisiana, was an orderly.

At Joplin High School, Jerry lettered in track, played American Legion baseball, and was a class officer and an officer in the school's Junior ROTC program. He passed the academic and leadership qualifications for a four-year Naval ROTC college scholarship but didn't have the required twenty-twenty eyesight.

While Jerry always wanted to be a journalist, he wavered several times over the years when he twice was offered a regular commission and an Army career. He won several reporting awards as he was progressively a reporter, an editor, a professor, a congressional fellow, a congressional press secretary, a legislative and administrative assistant in both the House and the Senate, and assistant secretary of defense for public affairs. Then he ran the American Newspaper Publishers Association and became the founding executive director of the Newseum, which opened in 1997 in Rosslyn, Virginia. The Newseum is now being moved into an even more imposing structure on Washington's Pennsylvania Avenue in view of the Capitol and the White House.

Jerry's military service started while carrying a sousaphone in his high-school junior ROTC marching band and continued as a distinguished military graduate of the University of Missouri Reserve Officer Training Program, where he was in Air Force and Army programs and where he earned both bachelor (1956) and master's degrees (1962) in journalism. As an undergraduate, he was managing editor of the student newspaper.

In 1956, he married Shirley Margarette Beavers, whom he first spotted as a junior high school cheerleader in Joplin, Missouri. She trained as a teacher at the University of Missouri but mostly raised their three children while doing hospital emergency-room volunteer work. The couple traveled the world in Jerry's jobs and moved to Falcons Landing in 1997 before Jerry's 1998 retirement. Shirley was chairman of the Falcons Landing library in its formative years and a chorus singer and dancer. Shirley died of breast cancer in 2003 at Falcons Landing Johnson Center.

Shirley and Jerry had two sons and a daughter and eventually seven grandchildren. Son Daniel, born at Fort Benning, holds a Yale doctorate, was a Foreign

Service officer, and now works in Miami, Florida, for the Inter-American Press Association. Daughter Cynthia, a graduate of the College of William and Mary, was a USA Today reporter and is now raising two daughters in Colorado Springs, Colorado. Son Thomas is a Tulane-trained architect and a wine shop owner in Dalton, Georgia.

"Grandkids are great," Jerry said, "and I am particularly proud just now of my oldest granddaughter, a high school senior. She was engaged to a Marine lance corporal who was killed at Fallujah, Iraq, and she now plans an Army enlistment upon graduation with college targeted for the Virginia Military Institute."

In 2004, Jerry married a longtime family friend and professional colleague, Jacqueline "Jackie" Grant. Jackie had an exciting Pentagon career in the offices of the Army, the Joint Chiefs of Staff, the General Counsel, and Office of Public Affairs. One of her memorable experiences came when she typed a press release about the USS *Pueblo* that no one in her office was cleared to read. Jerry met her in 1969. When he left the Department of Defense, he convinced Jackie to join him as front-office manager of the newspaper association. Later they worked together when Jackie was coordinator and trainer of the Newseum's 220 volunteers. Jerry said "Love works in wondrous ways, our mission now is to make people happy wherever we are." At Falcons Landing, Jackie sings soprano in the chorus soprano and bowls.

Jackie cradled the "Baby Jesus" (a draped, basket-borne flashlight) in the Falcons Landing 2004 holiday show while her quartet sang a haunting fifteenth century carol. And Jerry sometimes gets carried away with "happy." Twice he has been persuaded to don his street-urchin costume and belt out before a Falcons Landing audience, "All I Want for Christmas Is My Two Front Teeth." "But never again," he mumbles.

After his University of Missouri graduation, he was commissioned in the Army Reserve. At Fort Sill's Artillery School, he ranked first in his officer basic course. He served two active-duty years with the Tenth and Second Infantry Divisions as an artillery officer in Germany and Georgia and remained in the Reserve, achieving the rank of captain, and completing courses from the Industrial College of the Armed Forces and the JFK Center for Military Assistance. The Army might have kept Jerry and changed his career, but when, in 1958, it offered a regular commission to the enthused, young artilleryman, it offered him armor instead of artillery; Jerry said no. He stayed in the Reserve until his civilian Pentagon job working with all the services made it inappropriate for him to be associated only with the Army. Nonetheless, he stayed close to the military services by lecturing on military and media subjects at the service academies, the

Defense Information School, and the capstone courses at the National Defense University.

For six years, in his role of assistant secretary of defense for public affairs, he was the daily spokesman for Secretaries of Defense Melvin Laird, Eliot Richardson, and James Schlesinger. He then served another six years as a consultant during both Democrat and Republican administrations.

His career in journalism and rise to prominence on the American political scene (he served well in three presidential election campaigns) was attributable, in part, to the book he wrote in 1968, *Where are the Voters?* Through an analysis of assembled statistics, he showed where American voters were located by age, occupation, sex, race, education, religion, and party or political persuasion. It became a valuable asset for the practicing politicians of the time. He recalled his career in journalism and politics:

> When I was released from active duty while retaining my reserve commission, we returned to Missouri where I went to work for the *Neosho* (Missouri) *Daily News*, Neosho being a small town not far from my home in Joplin. There is a truism that the way to learn to be a journalist is to work first on a small newspaper where you have to do a little bit of everything. In Neosho I was a photographer, typesetter, ad salesman, reporter, sports editor, and then managing editor. I was also a correspondent for the Associated Press, and later, on the *Joplin Globe*, I was news editor, an editorial writer, and a political columnist.
>
> However, suddenly, Shirley and I were about to have our third child, and we decided that if I were going to support a big family, I would have to move on and up. I was offered a teaching fellowship at the Missouri School of Journalism where I taught copy editing and was Sunday editor of the *Columbia Missourian*. The best front-page, banner headline I wrote there was "Iron Curtain Falls on Berlin." The dean thought it was a bit dramatic, but it turned out to be right.
>
> In the year I spent back in Columbia, Missouri, I had earned a master's degree in journalism with my master's thesis being a historic study of presidential press secretaries. I received a tempting offer to go to Chicago to work on the *Wall Street Journal*. But I also had received an offer to be a Washington congressional fellow of the American Political Science Association, after receiving an APSA award for distinguished reporting of public affairs for my coverage of the 1962 congressional elections. So Shirley, the now three kids, and I packed up and moved to Washington during the Cuban Missile Crisis with sublime confidence and a moving-van bill we had to finance for six months.
>
> Like so many people who come to the capital for a single year of experience or professional education, we never left. As a congressional fellow, you worked

in a representative's and then a senator's office while attending orientation classes all over Washington. It was a great deal for the congressmen, because they didn't have to pay us; the fellowship took care of that. You had to compete to get a position on one of those staffs, and many of us did segue onto a staff as we finished the fellowship stint.

I went to work for U.S. Representative Durward G. Hall, a Republican from my home district in Missouri, a physician, who at times was known as "Dr. No," because the party leadership assigned him to monitor floor debate and to object if anything surprising came up. He was a distinguished Army veteran of World War II, who served six terms, and was a member of the Armed Services Committee. I worked in that office as press secretary, legislative assistant, and, eventually, as his administrative assistant.

Then I moved over to the office of Senator John Tower, a newly minted Republican from Texas, who was elected to the seat vacated by Lyndon Johnson when he became vice president. Tower, an associate professor of political science at Midwestern University in Wichita Falls, had previously run for the Senate in 1960 against Johnson and lost by a substantial margin. But he was known and liked all over the state, because his father was a widely traveled Methodist minister. When Johnson vacated his Senate seat in 1961, Tower beat Bill Blakley, a liberal Democrat, in a special election among seventy-one candidates. At thirty-six, he became the youngest member of the Senate, the only Republican in the Southern caucus, and the first Republican senator from Texas since Reconstruction. He came into the Senate to a cyclone of publicity, and in his twenty-three years in the Senate became an authority on national defense and military affairs. I just started out as a helper around the office, but I was the only one on the staff who had any military experience, except the senator, who had served as a sailor during World War II, and who rose to the rank of chief petty officer in the reserves while serving in the Senate. He was given a coveted Armed Services Committee seat, and I became his military affairs assistant.

The end of Tower's life was an unhappy one, as his nomination to become Secretary of Defense was rejected by the Senate in one of the first examples of the 'politics of personal destruction,' which, to this day, haunts the once-orderly nominations process. The victim was Tower; the real target was President Bush. It was the first rejection of a president's cabinet nominee in more than thirty years. Tower died in a plane crash in 1991 that also took one of his three daughters.

In 1963, several Tower aides were on the staff of Barry Goldwater's run for the presidency. Many people forget that conservative Goldwater thought he would be running against liberal John F. Kennedy, not conservative Lyndon Johnson. Even after the assassination changed the political landscape, we campaigned hard all over the country. As a member of the 1964 GOP Truth Squad, I was the director of research. We trailed the Hubert Humphrey jet across the country providing another side of the story, covering twenty-five thousand miles, thirty-four states and sixty-eight cities. Goldwater knew he would lose and won only six states, but he continued the campaign because he also wanted to realign the Republican Party and, in that, he succeeded.

In 1960, Vice President Richard M. Nixon had made his first bid for the presidency but lost to John F. Kennedy, who was a close Senate friend. In their first TV debate, Nixon argued well but projected badly with a five o-clock shadow and a gray suit, while Senator Kennedy exhibited a vigorous, youthful appearance. President Eisenhower hardly campaigned for his vice president. Nixon blamed Eisenhower for his narrow loss. Two years later, in a stunning blow to his political career, Nixon lost a race for governor of California and, in his concession speech, told the press, "You won't have Dick Nixon to kick around anymore." That turned out to be wrong.

Jerry described that period:

> Then 1968 approached, and Nixon, seemingly in a political graveyard, made his bid for the nomination. Almost everyone thought that he was out of the running, but not John Tower, who was one of the very first to enlist in the draft Nixon movement.
>
> Tower brought me along, and at the age of thirty-three, I wound up as staff director of the Nixon-Agnew Key Issues Committee composed of twenty-five Republican senators, governors, and congressmen who provided the Nixon campaign with issue advice and suggestions. We did in-depth, quick-reaction research and sustained twenty-two surrogate speakers who were active nationwide.
>
> Sometimes I tell students that I was on the candidate's staff for Richard Nixon's first successful presidential campaign. They find that pretty bizarre now, but at the time, and given the likely opponents, it seemed a real good idea.
>
> So John Tower was instrumental in getting the Republican nomination for Nixon in his 1968 defeat of Vice President Hubert Humphrey and third-party candidate George Wallace. In 1972, Nixon defeated Democrat George McGovern by one of the widest margins in history. McGovern was a real war hero, having flown thirty-four combat missions as a B-24 pilot and having been awarded the Distinguished Flying Cross. However, he never used that distinguished record to further his campaign. He was too busy opposing Vietnam.
>
> In November of 1968, Nixon wanted to name his entire cabinet at one time—in December—not really a good idea. The Secretary of Defense position became a stickler. Nixon attempted to enlist Democrat Senator Henry "Scoop" Jackson for the job. Scoop really would have liked to take it, because he was well-versed in military matters, having served on the Armed Services committees in both houses of Congress. He would have been a stellar secretary

of defense. However, he belatedly decided that as a Democratic leader, he couldn't serve in a Republican administration. So, faced with the December deadline, Nixon scrambled to find another candidate.

He turned to Wisconsin Congressman Melvin Laird, a member of the House Defense Appropriations Committee and of our campaign Key Issues Committee, asking if he would serve as the tenth secretary of defense. He would be the first one to come from Congress. Laird thought hard, then accepted. However, knowing that the administration-in-waiting was pressed for a nominee, he dealt from that strength and accepted with the proviso of two key caveats. He told Nixon that he knew how Washington worked, and that he would have to accept some staff from the roster of White House favorites. But he wanted to have his own team. If there was a recommendation from the White House that he didn't want to accept, then he wanted authority to veto that choice. The second caveat was that he would serve as secretary of defense for only four years. Nixon was in a bind for a nominee; he agreed. Laird then took a card out of his pocket on which those terms of acceptance were written and asked Nixon to sign it. Nixon did by initialing it "R N," and Laird used the card to turn away those he felt were not suited for his team.

Friedham with President Gerald Ford

Laird ultimately built a loyal team that was bipartisan, came from all over the country, and agreed to remain with him for four challenging years. That team accomplished many wise, lasting things. For instance, I was with Laird at the San Clemente "Western White House" when Nixon was briefed on and approved the concept of the all-volunteer force.

Laird retained Daniel Z. Henkin as his primary press aide. Henkin was a Democrat but a true DOD professional who had served effectively in the Johnson administration. I was still on a learning curve at this level of operations and so was happy to be named as assistant to Henkin. Subsequently, having learned the ropes, I was nominated by Nixon and unanimously confirmed by the Senate to be the assistant secretary of defense for public affairs, a member of Laird's personal staff, and his deputy for public information, internal DOD information, community relations, security review, and the like. I held that position through three secretaries of defense, through the hard, troubled times of the Vietnam War, the Christmas bombing shortly after Nixon won his landslide reelection, the controversies over the mining of North Vietnamese harbors, POW-MIA tribulations, and Watergate—and into the administration of President Gerald Ford.

There were some difficult times in those years, but we had no problem getting excellent people to staff our press office. For several years, I had talented Air Force General Daniel "Chappie" James as my deputy spokesman. Chappie did yeoman work and provided some good chuckles. Once, anxious to get some younger people on board, Chappie interviewed a woman just off the campus of a fine school. She filled out all the requisite forms to include her former addresses and her known associates. She did just fine, Chappie regaled us, until she came to the last question which read: "Do you advocate the overthrow of the government by force, subversion or violence?" "Gosh" allowed Chappie, "she thought it was a multiple choice question!"

As the war in Vietnam continued, I briefed the press almost every day, including many Sundays. I have told people that the basic fact of life for such a spokesman is that it's not always what you know; it's often what you can remember in time. Things were often murky on the other side of the world, and it was our rule to say of any complex operation, event, or accident: "I am providing you with the first, initial, fragmentary, incomplete, unconfirmed data from the confusing scene of a very complicated, still-evolving, matter. Some of this is almost certainly wrong, but we will tell you more as soon as we know it." This careful caveating inevitably rewarded us with next-day headlines that read, "Pentagon Revises Story," or "DOD Spokesman Changes Account;" sometimes even, "Military Lie Laid Bare." We didn't just come to work on the good days.

Then there was the State Department. Stalwart colleagues all, but a challenge sometimes. Diplomatic niceties burdened the DOD impulse to speak plainly about our people and equipment. Laos we couldn't mention. Not activities of U.S. military personnel there. Not aircrews and aircraft searched for or lost. Not supplies sent. Not South Vietnamese incursions there. Not even exactly where the Ho Chi Minh trail really was. Only State could talk Laos, and they didn't. Finally, to rub salt in our wounds, State sent over to our press briefing a correspondent from TASS, the Soviet "news agency." We were certain that he was a GRU colonel, military intelligence undercover. But he had State Department press credentials, so we let him in. Then he up and asked a Laos question. I looked at him a bit, took off my glasses and polished them, looked at him some more, and answered: "I am neither aware nor unaware of that." He never came back. I still use that answer from time to time around Falcons Landing. People here ask weird things like, "Is the peanut soup worth ordering?"

The daily Pentagon news briefings came about because, during the first Nixon election campaign, there was a lot of political talk about a "credibility gap." Also Laird's predecessors, Robert McNamara and Clark Clifford, did not tolerate the press well. Laird, on the other hand, was a people person, a Capitol Hill maneuverer, and he saw the press as a conduit to the American people. Laird liked reporters. Right from the start, we told the Pentagon press corps that we would be there every day to address their questions on the record. We would not preempt Saigon and MACV's releases on military operations, but we always would be available both in briefings and in our offices.

Laird, himself had more than four hundred on-the-record press meetings. We protected what needed to be protected. We said, "No comment," when necessary. But we were always there. We never disappeared. We often had military experts brief on military matters. On the record. It worked.

In Washington, whoever briefed the press first could set the news agenda for the day. The State Department traditionally briefed at noon and the White House at about 12:30. So we briefed at 11 every morning. We set the daily news agenda. Laird talked to the president nearly every day, and he was confident about what the president wanted and about what his long-term policy goals were. In these hectic times of the drawdown from Vietnam, there was uncertainty whether or not we would persevere in troop reductions, and there was deep concern about the status of our men who were prisoners of war or who were missing. We always knew, even during peace talks, that we were staying the course until our service people who were prisoners were brought home.

The U.S.–North Vietnam peace negotiations in Paris were frustrating and too long. The United States tried both diplomacy and force to end the war, including the eleven-day Christmas bombing of 1972, code named by Laird, "Operation Linebacker II." Neither the bombings nor the mining of North Vietnam's harbors elicited any apparent compromise from the North Vietnamese.

"But eventually Henry Kissinger did come to terms with them, and the phased release of prisoners was tied to reductions of our forces in Vietnam," Jerry said. "Here was where reclaimed credibility counted. When we announced that some thousands of our forces were being withdrawn, we knew that they would be. But the press and the public didn't know—until General Abrams did it on schedule, again and again."

There were 726 military personnel captured during the Vietnam War and sixty-five of them were acknowledged by DOD to have died in captivity. There were 591 military POWs who were returned to U.S. military control during "Operation Homecoming" between February 12 and April 1, 1973. Jerry described efforts to get the prisoners home:

> It is sometimes forgotten that one early plan for the return of our POWs was to have Sweden be the intermediary between Hanoi and Washington. However, the particular group of Swedes that the State Department was doing business with became increasingly difficult and wanted to exercise a control over our people that DOD couldn't permit. Our unwavering, overriding concern was for the health and non-exploitation of our returning troops. We even had carefully selected the ship to transport the prisoners. Then the Swedes refused to let our planes or ships land at their ports. It was a sorry scene played by a supposedly compassionate, friendly nation.
>
> Eventually our prisoners came home under entirely different circumstances with sensitivity, care, dignity, and honor. They went first to hospitals all over the United States. They didn't talk to the press unless or until they wanted to do so—even if the White House suggested it. We sent one of our public affairs representatives to each hospital to assist the returnees. One of my military deputies was on the Gia Lam airfield in Hanoi to see each of the POWs onto our planes, shaking hands with each and ensuring that each had a good start home. We listened from the Pentagon as he called out their names.
>
> It is a source of great pride to me, that in 1973, I was honored by the Aviation/Space Writers Association for our part in bringing home these prisoners of war in the right way.

The association citation reads, in part, "for the sensitive and responsible public affairs direction of Project Homecoming, the return of the American Prisoners of War from North Vietnam."

Jerry sometimes wonders if DOD could get the same cooperation from the press more than a quarter of a century later. He believes that times have changed in the news business, that too many of the electronic press feel they must wax cosmic too much of the time, that things must be represented as bigger than big. He faults the current press for rushing to judgment too often, presenting instant, carbonated news about the bubbles, not the beverage, where exaggeration is thought to equal entertainment and entertainment to equal news; that cliff-hangers are created where there are no cliffs. Events must be "defining moments," or a "hinge of history." The O. J. Simpson trial must be a "turning point in American juris-prudence." Princess Diana's death must be a "watershed event" equal to a Kennedy assassination.

Watergate is the popular term to describe a complex of political scandals that took place between 1972 and 1974. It is a term that has become synonymous with political intrigue. It arose from Nixon's internal fear of "enemies" and out of the national turmoil occasioned by the war in Vietnam. Its flashpoint was the 1970 publication of the Pentagon Papers, a secret study done for Secretary McNamara on the conduct of the war's early years.

"Laird's position was that the papers should be declassified and made public promptly," Jerry said. "The White House and Justice Department said no. And from that point on things went down hill."

Burglars, under the control of some Republican political operatives, broke into the Democratic Party's National Committee offices on June 17, 1972, at the Watergate Hotel in Washington. Their forced entry was discovered by a security guard, and the whole episode began to unravel on the front pages of newspapers across the nation. The scandal rocked the country, and attempts to cover it up led to the downfall of President Nixon.

Jerry told of those times:

> At the Department of Defense we were insulated from the events of Water-gate. We noticed that the White House seemed distracted, and we were receiv-ing oddball requests from the executive offices. We became very careful whom we talked to over there and what we talked about. Presidential advisor Chuck Colson, in particular, was making some strange requests, and I was given the responsibility of screening all his calls to the Department of Defense. I listened a lot. We did nothing he asked.
>
> After Laird left his post as secretary of defense, he was succeeded for a mere ninety days by Washington insider and liberal Republican Eliot Richardson, who moved to Defense from his job heading the Department of Health, Edu-cation and Welfare. In 1973, in the middle of the Watergate imbroglio, he left Defense to become attorney general. During the investigation of Watergate, he refused Nixon's orders to fire Special Prosecutor Archibald Cox, and he resigned his position. He was followed to the office of secretary of defense by James Schlesinger, who moved over from the director of the Central Intelli-gence Agency. Schlesinger was an intellectual academic. He wasn't terribly comfortable with people and was totally different from Laird. He was also totally different from Laird's first deputy, David Packard, whose philosophy of management was to 'walk around' and visit offices in the Pentagon to see what was going on. That worked at Hewlett Packard and at DOD.

Jerry Freidheim with General David Jones, who in 1947, was chairman of the Joint Chiefs of Staff. Both are now residents of Falcons Landing.

Jerry traveled the world to defense meetings with Laird, Packard, and Schlesinger. He recounted:

> People-challenged on occasion or not, America owes a great deal to Jim Schlesinger, and to the chairman of the Joint Chiefs of Staff who served alongside him, Air Force General David Jones [now residing at Falcons Landing]. These two had the sensitive, monumental task of managing DOD and the services during the unprecedented, hectic days of Nixon's impending resignation. Although it never happened, there were those who anticipated that at the final hour Nixon or his White House lieutenants would seek to somehow misuse U.S. military forces to foil the resignation engineered by Congress. Schlesinger and Jones simply, jointly, and privately assured each other that if any inappropriate calls or 'order' came from the White House they would not immediately act but first would consult each other about the best interests of the Republic. Profound stuff.
>
> Nixon never intended it. It didn't occur. But two public servants who were on the hot spot in a time uncharted for our democracy acted wisely and well...just in case. Hats off to both.
>
> So here it was, 1973, and I had been in government service for about a dozen years, and Shirley and I decided that I was never going to make any money in that business. Friends who had been in the same position I was in

told me that I had been at DOD about two years too long. They told me not to worry about the first post-Pentagon job I took, but to take it as a sabbatical and consider this first step a transition. So I went to work with Amtrak for six months as vice president for government affairs. That was a quasi-governmental operation which was totally dysfunctional, and it still is, but it did offer me the opportunity to make a transition into the private sector. I learned that the American Newspaper Publishers Association (ANPA) was looking for an executive vice president and general manager (a title that later changed to president). I applied for the job and was hired by the board of directors. In that capacity, I ran the day-to-day operations of an international trade association that represented 1,400 newspapers in the U.S., Canada, the Western Hemisphere, and Europe.

The association was founded in 1887. Its name was later changed to the Newspaper Association of America. ANPA membership accounted for about 91 percent of the U.S. daily circulation and 84 percent of the circulation in Canada. While there, Jerry founded the association journal *Presstime*, which covered all aspects of the newspaper business, including news-editorial, news research, readership, circulation, and advertising.

Jerry Freidheim with Katherine Graham,
chair of The Washington Post Company

His relations with the luminaries of the publishing world, such as Arthur Ochs "Punch" Sulzberger, publisher of the *New York Times*, Katharine Graham, publisher of the *Washington Post*, and Allen Neuharth, chairman of the Gannett Company, were effective and comfortable. He had met and worked with many of that group while he was in the Pentagon. The job permitted him to continue to work in the media, not as a journalist or editor or bureau chief, but, nonetheless, as a player. Newspapers are businesses subject to the same taxes, human resource needs, and regulatory problems as other industries. Jerry's background at the shirtsleeves level of the industry as a newspaper and wire service reporter and as an editor served him in good stead in appreciating both the large and the more mundane problems of the association members.

"The association business took me all over the United States and the world—again," Jerry said. "ANPA was much like NATO, in that the United States contingent was providing the leadership to a number of countries with a free press who didn't want us to run everything but wouldn't come together without us. We also had a major technical operation doing research and development of new print technologies. The ANPA scientists invented photo-typesetting, ink that would not rub off on your hands or clothing and newsprint wood-pulp substitutes. Importantly, we were also fighting the continual First Amendment rights battles on behalf of the newspaper industry worldwide."

After sixteen years leading ANPA, Jerry moved to the media-oriented Freedom Forum, and with that foundation's trustees, he and Shirley were witnesses in August 1991 to a bloodless revolution in Moscow. Jerry and his two dozen colleagues were staggered when they suddenly saw tanks and troops in the streets of the Russian capital as they were being deployed to suppress a citizen coup against Soviet President Mikhail Gorbachev.

Jerry later wrote this for a professional journal:

> Our first reactions were of disbelief tempered by fright as troops appeared on the downtown streets and T-72 tanks—still in Afghan-war, mottled tan camouflage paint—sped by the Americans' bus, churning chips from the asphalt of Moscow's Ring Road. More worry came as one bus was stopped cold in the middle of the vast square just outside the Kremlin, blocked by the crowds, armored cars, and no-nonsense militia traffic police.
>
> Slipping quickly from the bus, two dozen Americans walked away as calmly as possible down the middle of the street past the Lenin Museum; behind them the army troops shoved empty buses and street cars into barricades blocking all the Kremlin gates.

Things looked dire. It seemed only a question of time until some mistake flashed events into a riot, even gunfire, but it didn't happen. The American 'reporters' moved out to find out why.

They found a coup that never got off the ground.

They found Muscovites grimly but ostentatiously waving from rooftops and construction scaffolding the white, blue, and red flag of pre-1917 Russia. Someone had a lot of those flags stored up.

They found Soviet paratroopers lazing atop their armored personnel carriers, exchanging souvenirs with citizens as if killing time until a parade started, not a fight.

They heard demonstrators ask teenage soldiers if they would shoot their friends, their mothers. "No," said the troops. "No," said their sergeants.

Despite the limited violence from the military (three deaths in Moscow and three in the Baltic States), there were great political pressures being brought to bear, and Jerry and his colleagues had witnessed the start of the end of the dominance of the Communist Party which accelerated the disintegration of the Soviet Union.

Jerry recalled how he got to the Freedom Forum:

You know when you go into the association industry that you aren't going to be able to stay in a senior position for any thirty years. The members of the board of directors who hired you are going to be moving on, and the new crew is going to want to have their own president. So after sixteen years with ANPA, in 1992, at the age of fifty-six, I joined the Frank E. Gannett Foundation, a charitable trust that had a $625 million endowment with annual expenditures of some $50 million. The foundation soon became independent of the company, the name was changed to The Freedom Forum, and it was dedicated to promoting First Amendment, free-press issues. We then searched for a major enterprise that would promote our goals, rather than just building a basketball court here, or helping out a community program there, without any visionary direction. The decision was to establish a unique museum devoted to educating the public on free press matters. We speculated how great it would be to have such a museum in the Washington metropolitan area. Well, we did it. We're doing it. The first result was the $27 million Newseum built in Rosslyn, Virginia, just across the Potomac River from Georgetown. The museum was built immediately across the street from the Gannett buildings, which housed the corporate offices of the newspaper USA Today and other Gannett enterprises. The world's first interactive museum of news opened in 1997 and was a huge success.

Jerry guided the Newseum's evolution and became its founding executive director during the 1992–93 concept development phase, serving in 1994 as Freedom Forum vice president for public affairs and from 1995 to 1997 as the director and deputy director of Newseum operations.

The Arlington Museum was closed in March 2002 while being moved to Washington, D.C. The Freedom Forum is erecting a new, six-level, 215,000-square-foot structure on a 531,000-square-foot piece of property that was purchased from the District of Columbia. The new Newseum, opening in 2007, will have three times the exhibition space as the Arlington facility. The area will also provide office space for the Freedom Forum staff, a 9,000-square-foot conference center, 30,000 square feet of retail space, and 100 condominiums. It will cost upwards of $500 million to build and tens of millions to operate annually. Luckily, the foundation endowment is now about a billion dollars.

"We found a museum designer, Polshek Partnership Architects, who built the planetarium in New York, a large, striking, glass building," Jerry said. "Then we went through the complex routine of getting all the many bureaucratic and environmental and cultural approvals you need to build on Pennsylvania Avenue. And again we signed up designer Ralph Applebaum to update all the exhibits. I still sit on the advisory board for the operation, but I'm relieved of any day-to-day responsibilities."

In 1973, when Jerry left the Pentagon, which he has described in jest as "that wastepaper-shaped building where to err may be human but to repeat is policy," he was awarded the Defense Department Medal for Distinguished Public Service for "faultless professionalism, clear, concise, accurate, and timely information concerning the worldwide activities of the Department of Defense." It was his second DOD Distinguished Service Medal.

At Falcons Landing, Jerry has been busy in the community's choral programs, been on such committees as Fitness, Chapel and Library and been president of the Resident's Council. Jerry's mother, Billie, was a patient at the Johnson Center for two years until her death in 1999 at the age of ninety-five. Jerry describes the community as one of "compassion, comity, and comradeship." He and his wife, Jackie, award-winning equestrienne, are far from retired as they have many outside interests as well as being stalwarts in community activities.

The Friedheim family's hallmark credo is from "Epilogue to Asolandro," the last poem composed by Robert Browning in 1889. It provides some insight into how Jerry thinks and how he would like to be remembered—as the optimist, the warrior, the resolute:

He was one who never turned his back
but marched breast forward,
Never doubted clouds would break,
Never dreamed, though right were worsted,
wrong would triumph,
Held we fall to rise, are baffled to fight better,
Sleep to wake.

19

Alfred Lesesne Jenkins

One can hardly imagine a more varied, interesting life than that of Dr. Alfred
Lesesne Jenkins, who died while resident at Falcons Landing in December of
2001. His birth in September 1914 in Manchester, Georgia, took the life of his
mother, and Jenkins was raised by an uncle and his uncle's wife, who became his
father and mother. Early in life, Jenkins thought he wanted to be an actor. At sixteen, he embarked on a Thoreau-like visit to his Walden, a three-month monastic

1.   This account and all photographs are taken from: Alfred Lesesne Jenkins, *Country,
     Conscience and Caviar: A Diplomat's Journey in the Company of History*, (Seattle, WA:
     Book Partners, 1993), and interviews with those who knew and lived with Jenkins
     in the Department of State and at Falcons Landing.

meditation in the wild pines of Georgia. He took only his vittles, a rifle, his dog, a horse, a tent, and a stack of books that included a Bible from his father's extensive library. This transcendental experience influenced the remainder of his life as he gravitated through studies that earned five degrees (one honorary), a short career as a soldier, services as a Chinese linguist, a full career as a diplomat, a devotee of yoga, and late in life a new career as a chiropractor. He also published an autobiography, before he retired and moved to Falcons Landing. He graduated from Georgia's Emory University and enrolled for a short, abortive term at the Boston University School of Theology. Appropriately for Jenkins, the divinity school was nicknamed BUST. In his early twenties, a "nervous breakdown," which he described as a "dumb slump," consumed him for many months. A stint as a seventh-grade schoolteacher seemed to be the cure he needed for his nervous breakdown, which he believed was the result, in part, of his "egocentrism."

On advice from a former World War I Army officer, he enlisted in the Army shortly after the attack on Pearl Harbor, anticipating that he was going to enjoy life in the barracks rather than a commission in the Navy. "Clearly, the least fun I ever had in my life was as a buck private in Uncle Sam's Army," Jenkins said. But he eventually adapted to Army life, took flying lessons on his own, and was accepted into an Army one-year Chinese language program at the University of Chicago. There were 165 students in the class. Only twenty of the students, including Jenkins, graduated from the program. Still a noncommissioned officer, he was assigned to the Pentagon. When the war in Europe ended, he found that his language and administrative skills were much in demand. He was commissioned a second lieutenant, eventually mustered out of the Army, and was given a civilian rank equivalent to that of a lieutenant colonel in the same office. He also passed the formidable Foreign Service examination. (Jenkins was one of a hundred who were accepted out of the twenty thousand who had taken the examination that year.)

In 1946, Alfred Jenkins married Martha Lipiatt, a former WAVES (Women Accepted for Volunteer Emergency Service), earned a master's degree in education at Duke University, and was called to service by the State Department. There followed a brilliant diplomatic career that brought him to live in six countries and travel in seventy-nine more. While his area specialty was China, he also served in Washington, Sweden, and Saudi Arabia. He was known as one of the premier military authorities on China and was the only American diplomat to serve in China under both the regimes of Chiang Kai-shek and Mao Tse-tung.

Jenkins collaborated with and rubbed shoulders with such American luminaries as Lyndon Johnson, Richard Nixon, Henry Kissinger, Dean Acheson, Adlai

Stevenson, Robert Kennedy, and a host of others, as well as kings, dictators, and prime ministers.

Characteristically, his autobiography, *Country, Conscience and Caviar: A Diplomat's Journey in the Company of History* was devoted more to his philosophy of life and his assessment of the characteristics of those with whom he served than with a chronology of events. His book indicates more interest in why things happened than a historical chronology and a great interest in his inner self and that of others. The following passages from that book are instructive:

> I loved the Foreign Service, although in three more years I would decide it was time to leave it....Meanwhile, I sought to do what I could under the circumstances about my neglected inner life. First, I began to meditate regularly. I studied several approaches to the art, both Western and Eastern, and adopted an amalgam of my own....Chief contributor in this regard at that time was my association with Maharishi Mahesh Yogi, and the teachings in his *Science of Creative Intelligence.* That association and the related teachings have influenced my later life considerably....I was initiated into TM (transcendental meditation), as was my family....As I practiced the technique, I have to say—to my surprise—that I felt nothing short of gratitude for the teaching. Furthermore, I certainly did not expect the Beatles' guru to satisfy me intellectually, but he did so....
>
> I left the movement when it became more flamboyant, making what charitably can only be viewed as premature claims, and appearing to be more money-conscious than my taste could accommodate. Nevertheless, the teaching is valuable, and Maharishi is a remarkable man. I spent two months with him at his hotel in Arosa, Switzerland, and saw him on numerous other occasions.

Jenkins was posted to the consulate in Tientsen at the fall of Nationalist China to Mao Tse-tung's revolutionary Red Army. In the final months of 1948, most of northern China had fallen to the Communists. The capital, Peking, was surrounded. The Nationalist forces had either been defeated or had transferred allegiance to Mao. The U.S. Marines who had been sent to northern China to repatriate the Japanese and to train and advise the Nationalist forces, left Peking in 1947. The Marines left Tsingtao, the last major city to be taken by the Chinese Communists, in April 1949. Alfred and Martha were living in Tientsin in January 1949 when a reception they were hosting was interrupted by nearby artillery fire. Communist forces had seized the Tientsin airport and were advancing on the main part of the city. Morale of the Nationalists and Nationalist sympathizers was at rock bottom. By mid-January, there was fighting inside the city. Jenkins was isolated in the consulate while his family was still in their home, although they did have telephone communication through a landline that had been strung between the house and the consulate to connect two Marine field phones. These were perilous times for the couple that were described in a letter Martha later wrote to her mother, excerpts of which follow:

> Friday morning there was a lull in the shelling, and we got the baby ready to go out.…We heard a loud siren. We got the baby inside immediately. We had been in about ten minutes when the most awful blast I have ever heard sounded. Our French doors in the dining room leading to the terrace were locked for the winter—and in the Chinese fashion to keep out the cold, cotton had been stuffed in the cracks and white paper pasted over all that. The blast blew open the locked doors and blew all the cotton out of them and out of all the windows on that side of the house. We later learned the explosion involved a huge aviation fuel tank some three miles from the house! The water went off at this time and about a half hour later the electricity went off. Both came on again late that night, so we filled the tubs and a number of pots (with water). We called the men at the (consulate) office.… They just had time to say that they couldn't get home that night, because in addition to 105 mm shells whizzing right by the building, small arms firing had begun in the streets, and grenades were exploding.…Well, here we were, two women with an infant and five servants. Our cellar is only a furnace room with an adjoining room filled with coal, but I decided we would spend the night there.…The next morning we got up about seven.…Carol was on her way upstairs to get one of our coats when Wang, the coolie, came dashing in and said, "Mistress, go to the cellar." He fairly snatched up the baby, Carol's fur coat, her purse, a small suitcase, and ran to the cellar. We were on his heels. We sat there for about ten minutes when a lot of machine gun firing started. Just then we heard footsteps coming down the cellar steps and four men servants and the wash amah ran down and sat on the bed with us. Wang said, "Someone is pounding on the front gate. I think it is soldiers." Then we heard machine gun firing very close, as though it was right in front, and we thought they were trying to shoot the lock in order to get in. Our wall all around the property is not easily scaled. Right across the street is a large school in which Nationalist troops were stationed, so that was probably the actual target.…Then we heard a machine gun right in our garden. We wondered if they would give us a chance to identify ourselves when they entered the cellar, or whether we would just be mowed down!…Pretty soon the servants thought they heard someone walking around upstairs, and they thought it would be better to let them know where we were lest they simply toss grenades into the cellar to clear out any Nationalist soldiers who might be hiding there. The men at the office…said they had talked to the Italian Consul General, who had retreated to his large cellar that was divided in half by a cement wall. The communist soldiers dropped a grenade into one side—fortunately the side where he was not. He had presence of mind enough to dash over to that side,

reasoning they would also try to clear out the side he had been in. They did. He then wasn't sure what to do, so he burst into the open, screaming in Italian, "I am the Italian Consul General, don't shoot!' Of course they didn't understand Italian, but they understood it was not Chinese, and they were only after soldiers. Eleven o'clock to one o'clock was torture. Machine gun bullets were ricocheting off our garden walls, whether from the inside or outside we weren't sure, but it sounded like both. We were sure, however, that rifle fire came over our walls, doubtless from the second story of the school across the street. In the midst of all I was trying to phrase just what I would say to the People's Liberation Army soldiers if they burst in, but I wasn't very good at thinking even in English then, much less in Chinese. I really thought I would never see my husband again....

With puzzling suddenness things became quiet about a quarter to four, so I ventured to stick my head out and go upstairs.... We could come out of the cellar. As I was washing my hands at the downstairs sink Carol came running to me saying there were two Communists in the kitchen. The cook was grinning, offering the soldiers tea, and Wang explained, "This is my mistress, Chin Tai-tai." The soldiers were small of stature, very well dressed, and heavily armed. They said they would have to look around. They went to the cellar and returned to the kitchen where we still were. One said, "You were afraid? No need to be afraid any longer. It is all over." They were polite, but that is all. They left and about five minutes later two more came, this time through the front door. They said they wanted to go upstairs, so I said go ahead, but they then decided not to. A little later Wang told me that there were five soldiers at the front gate, but when he told them this was an American vice consul's house they didn't come in.

So that is how I spent the time during the battle.... I would never want to go through it again, but I'm so glad I didn't elect to return to the States without Alfred, because the agony here, though intense, was relatively short, and it would be worse to separated for a year or so.

Albert and Martha Jenkins left China by ship in late August 1949, just as Chiang Kai-shek and his forces were retreating to the island of Taiwan. Trans-Pacific voyages took a long time in those days, and they arrived in San Francisco on October 8. On October 1, 1949, the Communists had established the People's Republic of China with Beijing, formerly Peking, as its capital under Chairman Mao Tse-tung.

Jenkins with Chou En-lai

Jenkins's next posting was for a very brief stay in Hong Kong and then a two-year posting in Taiwan followed by a tour in Washington as officer-in-charge of Chinese political-military affairs. His next assignment was a complete change of pace. He became the State Department's youngest deputy chief of mission (the number two man in the embassy) in Jidda, Saudi Arabia. It was the only assignment in his career that was not China-related. A 1957–58 tour at the National War College studying grand strategy and the employment of the national resources to advance that strategy was a joy to Jenkins. His student travels with his War College class afforded the forty-two-year-old Jenkins the unique opportunity of a one-on-one meeting with the great eighty-four-year-old humanitarian, Albert Schweitzer, while the class was touring Africa.

Jenkins accompanied Henry Kissinger on three visits to China for discussions with Premier Chou En-lai, and he was with President Nixon on the February 1972 visit that "changed the world." Nixon was the first president to set foot on Chinese soil, and the first to negotiate on the soil of a nation with which the United States did not have diplomatic relations. It was an extraordinary week for America and China. President Nixon was instrumental in generating a new relationship with the People's Republic of China after twenty years of animosity. Nixon met with Communist Party Chairman Mao Tse-tung, but the real progress was made in negotiations with Premier Chou En-lai.

The part Jenkins played in the talks is best described in his reporting of a conversation with columnist Joseph Alsop:

"I said I thought Nixon had 'done the right thing at the right time in the right way.' Martha, in an unabashed volley of spouse-support said, 'Yes. He did it your way!' That was an unconscionable exaggeration, but the kernel of truth, at least, was that it was done in just the way I thought it should be done, and in large measure on the basis of papers emanating from my office, for which I took ultimate responsibility."

Jenkins's shift from diplomacy to chiropractic medicine at the age of seventy was admittedly "peculiar." Nonetheless, as with every other important decision he made during his life, the decision to go to school and practice this form of medicine was the result of deep-seated moral convictions and intellectual probing. Jenkins practiced chiropractic medicine for four years in both one-on-one treatment and in group lectures. Martha served as his receptionist, secretary, and "unparalleled practitioner of goodwill artistry, to say nothing of being my chief sustainer." He lost his life mate of forty-six wonderful years to a genetic heart problem before his move to Falcons Landing.

The thing Jenkins wanted most to see on earth was world peace. In his autobiography, he writes:

> That will happen when nation states, or their successor to them (for they are becoming obsolete), have matured beyond their present level of understanding, accepting that the law of cause and effect is inescapable, operable in *every* circumstance. Like individuals, nations must reap what they sow. Unfortunately, the reaping is too often recognized as, happily, likely to come during the next administration.
>
> With all its many faults, I believe America still holds promise of achieving a significantly higher level of collective knowledge, understanding and awareness—awareness that every thought or act produces results for which responsibility has to be taken.
>
> When will we get better government? When we get a better citizenry that the government must reflect in all its composite complexities. It succeeds right now in that reflection more than most people with their own special interests and limited visions can believe, or stop to think about. We will get better government and a better world when the conscience and the consciousness of the citizens of our country and the world are substantially raised, and almost certainly not before. At least, not in a democracy. It looks like better government is ultimately up to you and me and our neighbor. If we think about it, would we wish to have it any other way?

20

Thomas D. Quinn

Falcons Landing would be a poorer place if it were not for the volunteers providing services to fellow residents who need assistance. There is also a successful outreach program designed to make contributions to the community off the campus.

One of the stalwarts of both the in-house and the outreach effort is Capt. Thomas D. Quinn, United States Navy, (Retired). Tom does his in-house volunteer work in support of the chapel services conducted at least weekly on the cam-

1. This profile is based on a series of interviews with Thomas Quinn beginning January 19, 2005. All photographs are courtesy of Quinn.

pus and in the assisted living operation. He does his outreach work at the National Air and Space Museum Steven F. Udvar-Hazy Center, adjacent to Washington Dulles International Airport. Commonly known as the Udvar Hazy (pronounced OOD-var HAH-zee) Center, the spectacular facility is a companion to the Smithsonian Air and Space Museum in Washington, D.C. A fifteen-minute drive from Falcons Landing, it opened December 15, 2003, with more than eighty aircraft and sixty space and air artifacts on display. But that was just the beginning. The facility will ultimately display more than 200 aircraft and 125 air and space artifacts. The museum includes all types of aircraft, from ultralights and gliders to helicopters and fixed-wing military and commercial aircraft, as well as spacecraft. One of the unusual characteristics of the ten-story high museum is that there are no exhibit galleries, rather, aircraft and artifacts are in open hangars displayed on three levels that open in the center to a grand base that houses the larger space and aircraft.

Tom puts in at least one day a week, normally Monday, as one of 155 docents who guide groups and tours through the museum. He is the only pilot of the 155 who is a veteran of three of America's three major wars of the last century—World War II, Korea, and Vietnam. Tom and his colleagues trained for a year to prepare for their duties. It was not a new field for him, because he had previously served as a docent for twenty-one years at another air and space museum, the "no frills" Paul E. Garber Preservation, Restoration, and Storage Facility, in Suitland, Maryland, where the National Air and Space Museum preserves and stores air and spacecraft in thirty-two metal buildings.

One of Tom's favorite subjects as he leads tours through the museum is the life story of its principal benefactor, Steven Udvar Hazy, a self-made billionaire who, as a thirteen-year-old, fled Hungary with his family, studied economics at UCLA, and became an accomplished aviator. He started the International Lease Finance Corporation to lease aircraft with $150,000 and a bank loan. Today, it is the largest aircraft leasing company in the world.

Tom's docent avocation followed a distinguished combat career as a naval aviator. At the age of eighteen. Tom, along with President George Herbert Walker Bush, was one of the ten youngest naval aviators to serve during World War II.

"Chuck Downey from Chicago was the youngest naval aviator commissioned during the war, as he got his wings a week before President Bush and before he had attained the age of nineteen," Tom said.

Tom was born June 27, 1924, in Queen's Village, New York City, into a middle-class family. He attended parochial schools from the third grade forward, and at eight years of age, met Rose Grogan whom he married some thirteen years later. Tom's father was a deputy chief postal inspector in New York City. The senior Quinn's business was finding and prosecuting white-collar postal criminals and mail robbers. Rose's father was in a similar business with the Pinkerton detective force, providing security at racetracks. The job permitted Rose to "winter in Florida," when her father would be assigned to racetracks in the South during the season. Besides Tom and his parents, his family included an older brother, Joe, who also served in WWII and became a career Army soldier during the Korean and Vietnam wars, and his mother's brother, John Fallon, who lived in the Quinn home.

Tom described his early years:

I never had what is normally considered a formal college experience, but picked up an education in a series of schools while in the Navy, such as Georgia Tech and the Navy Post Graduate School in Monterrey. I went to a college preparatory school, Fordham Prep, for high school. For three years, I had a four-hour bus and subway ride to attend school for five hours; it was a tough grind. In my senior year, I met a neighbor attending Fordham University who drove me back and forth to school, which made life a lot easier. The commute kept me from participating in any of the school's extracurricular activities.

I graduated from Fordham Prep in June of 1942, at the age of eighteen, and enlisted in the U.S. Navy Reserve in July as a second class seaman, hoping to become an aviation cadet. After Pearl Harbor, the requirement that you must have two years of college to qualify for flight training had been waived, but you had to be eighteen to be commissioned. On the first of August, the Navy started the NAVCAD program, but there were more cadets than there were aircraft seats for the classes. I wanted to fly now, so I joined the Civilian Pilot Training Program, an operation wherein the government contracted with civilian colleges to provide ground training. The program took me to Princeton and then on to a farm in Oswigsburg, Pennsylvania, where they had a small airfield, and where we trained in Aeronoca aircraft. We were fifteen to twenty reservists, still on inactive duty, but exempt from the draft. Our goal was to make it to Navy flight school. We had a resident housemother, took our meals there, and lived an extended family life. We soloed and did some cross-country flying. It was mostly routine, but as in all aviation venues, there were some moments of terror.

One came to me as I took off from what had been a potato field in an aircraft that had just been checked. I had about eight to ten hours of flight experience. As I was taking off, a big black cloud emanated from the plane. I got off the ground all right and, at about one hundred feet of altitude, was able to make a turn and get the plane back onto the primitive runway. Upon inspection, we found that there was no oil in the engine. It was so hot that we couldn't touch it for twenty-four hours.

Then, joy to the would-be aviator, I was called to active duty on Christmas Eve of '42 to attend pre-flight training at the University of North Carolina. That meant, I got paid, I had a clean bed every night, and that I was finally on my way to becoming a naval aviator. All this time, Rose was in the College of Saint Elizabeth, in Morristown, New Jersey. We didn't become engaged until her senior year, just before she graduated in June of 1946.

Tom was at Chapel Hill, North Carolina, for the first two months of 1943. In the first week of March, he was transferred to the Naval Air Station at Bunker Hill, Indiana, where he went through four months of primary flight training before being transferred to Pensacola, Florida. He was still an aviation cadet, making fifty dollars a month plus twenty-five dollars flight pay.

Tom's Pensacola stint started with flying the SNV, a Vultee trainer that had the sobriquet, "Vultee Vibrator," because it shook so badly in flight. After instrument training at Whiting field in Alabama, he moved on to advance training at Barin Field in Mobile, Alabama, where they lost so many cadets in accidents, mostly fatal, that it was nicknamed "Bloody Barin." He recounted that time:

> I was commissioned by Admiral George Gallagher October 12, 1943, and was assigned to train in the Avenger TBF, a single-engine, Navy torpedo dive bomber that had a range of about a thousand miles and cruised at a speed of about 153 miles per hour. Subsequently, I was sent to Glenview, Illinois, for carrier qualification off the deck of one of two converted paddlewheelers in Lake Michigan. The Navy had cleared the superstructure of the ships, added a small control tower and installed a flight deck. There were two operations going on aboard the ships; the first was to qualify naval aviators for carrier landings, and the other was to train flight deck crews. The advantage of doing the training in Lake Michigan was that the ships were not vulnerable to German or Japanese submarine attacks as they would have been if they were operating in the Atlantic or Pacific. We never stayed aboard the ship but operated out of and were quartered at Glenview. The deck of the ship was long enough so that you could take off without any assistance but, on landing, we had arresting gear. We qualified for carrier landings once we had made six landings and takeoffs. You could actually get all six landings in a single day. After a bit, the bottom of Lake Michigan was paved with naval aircraft that had failed to make as many landings as takeoffs due to accidents, bad weather, and the like.
>
> The ships would operate on the lake during the day, come to shore at night close to the Navy Pier, and drop anchor. The sailors had a great sport on the wheeler. When they were denied liberty, there was a group that would climb down the paddlewheel at night, swim ashore for liberty in a very hospitable Chicago, and swim back to climb aboard on the wheel again before muster the next morning. Don't ask me how they managed the dry clothes bit going and

coming from and to the boat, but never underestimate the ingenuity of the sailor.

Following carrier qualification out of Glenview, Tom was assigned to the western Pacific with a carrier aircraft service unit (CASU). The unit provided maintenance and supply functions for aircraft going to or coming from aircraft carriers in the Pacific. He went to Espiritu Santo, an island where the Navy Seabees had established a base. He was going to be a replacement for some unnamed naval aviator for some unnamed ship. He was part of a pool of pilots in a replacement draft. Upon arrival, there were neither orders nor aircraft for the replacement pilots to fly.

Tom told of that assignment:

There were four of us on Espiritu Santo who had been together for some time, all of us in the same fix with no assignment and nothing to fly. We heard that at the far end of the runway there was an abandoned TBF. Upon inspection, we found that the Avenger was overgrown with jungle. The authorities told us that if we could get it operational, we could fly it. So we set about getting it back in flying order. We pulled it out of the jungle, and the first time we turned the engine over, we couldn't believe our eyes and ears, it started—it had a full tank of fuel. Nobody knew where the plane came from or how it got there. Can you imagine there being an unaccounted for aircraft today? It must have been left by some aircraft carrier. So three or four of us at a time would take off in the aircraft for hours of familiarization flying, landing, swapping seats, and taking off again. It made us better pilots.

In April of '44, I finally got orders to report to the *Yorktown* where I joined the torpedo squadron, VT-5. The *Yorktown* had been in the Pacific for almost a year. I was a replacement for a pilot by the name of "Pop" Condit who had been shot down in a TBF during the *Yorktown*'s first engagement of the war. He and his crew had made it into a life raft and were taken prisoners by the Japanese. I will come back to Condit a little later in this tale. So here it was almost a year after Condit had been shot down, and I arrive as his replacement. I am just reporting aboard, and the ship will finish its tour in sixty days and return to the States. That would have really meant a short combat tour for me. In the interim, the ship was still committed to some important operations against Palau, the second attack on Truk, and the New Guinea operation. I flew about ten bombing missions against Japanese ships and airfields in those three operations. We didn't fly any torpedo attacks, just bombing missions. The aerial borne torpedo was not a very reliable weapon during World War II, as the torpedoes were technically deficient. We launched torpedoes at 150 feet, 150 knots, and 1,500 yards from the target. A difficult maneuver, as it was done more with "seaman's eye" than with instruments.

Tom on the right, Tom with his two crewmen aboard the Yorktown

The *Yorktown* returned to its home port in San Francisco in mid-1944. En route, they dropped Tom off in Hawaii to report to a rest camp in Honolulu where he spent three weeks in a hotel on Waikiki Beach. At the completion of his stint of rest and relaxation, he was assigned as an instructor in the torpedo training squadron at Ewa, Barber's Point, Hawaii, for four and a half months.

"While I was an instructor at Ewa, lo and behold, who should show up as one of my students, none other than the aviator who had been my primary flight instructor at Bunker Hill, Indiana, the first place I had taken flight training," Tom said. "So suddenly, the tables were turned—he was the student and I was the flight instructor. In the naval aviation culture, flight instructors have a great deal of authority, and they are not always terribly cordial to their students. Nevertheless, we had a pleasant relationship. I didn't try to take advantage of him, although the thought did cross our minds. But he had never harassed me when I was a student, and I didn't harass him."

From Hawaii, Tom was reassigned back to the States to join a squadron at Hyannis, Massachusetts, that was preparing to deploy back to the Pacific. It was composed of a handful of combat-experienced pilots, including Tom, plus about twenty-five other TBF pilots who had no such experience. The squadron was scheduled to join the *Antietam*, which was being built in Philadelphia. It was the same class ship as the *Yorktown*. In the interim, the squadron moved to Edwards Air Force Base, where they practiced night carrier landings.

Tom described the time at Edwards:

> We lost several pilots and aircraft due to accidents during this training period. One of our group was a pilot, Chuck, who came from a pretty tough background, his father having been a rum-runner during Prohibition. One night in a snowstorm, he crash-landed, wheels up, down a row of machine gun butts at Edwards Air Force Base. Incredibly, he and his crew of three walked away from the crash while the plane was perched on top of a fifteen-foot berm. Before the crash, they had called the tower at Edwards and told them that their aircraft was running out of fuel, that the engine was freezing up, and they were about to do a belly-landing. In their next communication, they reported their good fortune that they were on the ground, that no one was injured, and they knew where they were. The tower sent a truck to pick them up. However, the snow was so bad and the visibility so poor, that after picking up the crew, the truck driver lost his way back to the main operations area, and they ended up off the base, in front of a roadhouse.
>
> It's now about one in the morning and the roadhouse is still jumping. The pilot, son of the rum-runner, went into the roadhouse dressed in a flight suit, covered with the mud and the snow from their journey. He was still dazed from his experience. The maître d', or bouncer, met him at the door and asked if he could help him. Chuck didn't realize that he still held a Very pistol in his hand that he had used to signal his crash position with a flare. He asked the man for directions back to Edwards, and the maître d', cum bouncer, wised off to him saying, "Sure, you just go outside, catch a subway, and get off at Edwards Air Force Base." Chuck, just having survived a harrowing experience, was in no mood for sarcasm, and suddenly he was aware of the Very pistol that he held in his hand. He stuck the pistol—while empty, still a frightening thing with a large bore and a two-inch barrel—into the man's forehead and, inclined to stutter when excited, stuttered out some pretty impressive threats. It made a very courteous and cooperative believer out of the man. They got back to the base at about two in the morning with a story that delighted the wardroom for months.

The squadron got new orders in January 1945. They would not join the *Antietam* as originally planned; rather they traveled to San Francisco where they sailed on a troop ship to Hilo, Hawaii, to train with a new inventory of aircraft. The squadron, now fully manned and with a full complement of aircraft, sailed to Saipan were they stayed from May 12 to mid-June. The island had just been taken from the Japanese by the Marines in a fierce battle that cost the Marines 3,000 killed and more than 13,000 wounded.

The squadron moved to a new airfield at Marpi Point on Saipan, which had been the site of a mass Japanese suicide. Saipan had been incorporated into the Japanese domain in 1919, after World War I. Before the Marines' amphibious assault, there were close to 20,000 Japanese and Chamarro civilians on the seventy-square-mile island. The civilians had been told that the Americans, and particularly the Marines, were red-haired monsters who would subject them to horrible atrocities should they be captured. As the Japanese army began to collapse after the Marine landing and fierce battles inland turned the tide against the Japanese, the civilians began to withdraw back to Marpi Point, that terminated in an eighty-foot bluff. Encouraged by Japanese soldiers who were throwing themselves from the cliff, thousands of civilians, men, women, and children followed them, crying "Tenno haiki banzai!" (Long live the Emperor!). Marines tried to stop the mass suicide, but the hapless thousands, seized by mass hysteria, leapt to their deaths, sometimes carrying their children with them.

Saipan was declared secure on July 9, 1944, following a last futile Banzai attack by the Japanese army. Supposedly the island had been cleared of Japanese military by the time Tom's squadron settled in, but there were still Japanese holdouts hiding in the jungles who roamed the American installations like phantoms, foraging for food and equipment.

Tom described that time at Saipan and subsequent attacks on Japan:

> The Seabees (Navy construction battalions) had built a comfortable bivouac area at the airfield that became an enticement to the distressed Japanese holdouts. One night, after we had been there about ten days, I was in my bunk situated just inside the door of the half-Quonset, half-tent shelter I was sharing with other aviators when I was awakened by a sound. I looked up and saw outlined in the doorway absolutely the biggest Japanese I had ever seen or imagined. I had a forty-five under my pillow, but I wasn't about to move to get to it. One of my squadron mates, who was bunked opposite me, saw the apparition as well, and he didn't move a muscle either. The intruder walked partway into the shelter, evidently didn't find anything he needed, and walked out again. Outside of flying, I think that was as close as I had been to cashing

it in during the war, because neither my bunk mate nor I were any match for this Japanese giant.

While we were on Saipan, we were tasked to ferry some aircraft to the Philippines and Okinawa. You remember, I told you about Chuck using the Very pistol to intimidate the maître d' in that roadhouse on Cape Cod? Well, that same Chuck flew one of the aircraft we were supposed to move into Okinawa. Although the Okinawa campaign was long over, the Japanese flew an aircraft onto our Okinawa main operating base the night our pilots were there. During this period, our squadron pilots on Okinawa were given Marine bodyguards. One night, Chuck's bodyguard told him to remove his cap, because it had his insignia on it, which was an invitation for the hostiles to target him. Chuck did as he was told, revealing that he had a streak of white that ran through his black hair that stood out like a beacon. The Marine told him, "You might as well put your hat back on, because you're a dead man either way." Encouraging, wasn't he?

When we finished our training on Saipan in July of '45, our Torpedo Squadron, VT-88, went to the Leyte Gulf in the Philippines, where we finally joined the *Yorktown*. It was a homecoming for me, as the *Yorktown* was the original ship I had joined on my first combat tour in the Pacific. The *Yorktown* had returned from San Francisco, having been provided the maintenance and refitting it required after a lengthy combat tour. Four days after my twenty-first birthday, on 1 July 1945, the *Yorktown*, with my squadron aboard, sailed north, back into combat waters. We weren't aware of it at the time, but we were to be an integral part of the invasion of Japan scheduled to begin on 1 November 1945. Our area of operations was on the Pacific side of the Japanese home islands, while the Army Air Corps operated on the western Sea of Japan side. Our first missions, once we were on station in the Honshu area, were bombing attacks on airfields around Tokyo. We had a pretty good-sized carrier attack group, with about six or seven fleet carriers and about four or five smaller CVLs, and some eight to ten jeep carriers. So it was a really formidable force. I flew sixteen bombing missions against the Japanese mainland during July and up until the end of hostilities on 15 August.

We flew our first missions on the tenth of July against Kasumigaura airfield. I got separated from the flight as we came off our target and found myself in a valley west of Tokyo. As I was making a turn to return, I passed over a Japanese hospital, clearly marked as such. While still in my turn, a 40 mm gun on the hospital grounds fired a single round that hit my right wing, tearing off the aileron. The three of us, the radioman, the turret gunner, and I, were uninjured, but still in one hell of a mess. The turret gunner, a first class aviation mechanic named Terry Tarailies from Mercer, Pennsylvania, who was behind me, was in the worst shape. He was swinging the turret from left to right when it jammed at a tilt of about forty-five degrees, so that he could no longer move it.

It took me a while to get the aircraft under control and, when I did, I realized that the turret was in such a position that the gunner couldn't get out of the turret. He was stuck there, in itself a mighty uncomfortable sensation. Because he was locked in his bubble, I couldn't crash land on water or on land without losing him, I had to get back to the carrier, a hundred and fifty miles away. Although this was his second combat tour, Terry was on his first combat mission with me. He was obviously terrified and never spoke a word on the flight after we were hit.

With the right wing shot up, the only way I could control the plane was to put the stick in the crook of my right arm, reach across the cockpit with my right hand, and grab the throttle. I didn't have enough strength to control the stick with either hand. The right wing was so damaged that it kept dragging me down, and I was fighting it to remain airborne. I wasn't sure I could land it on the ship, but I knew that we had to try if we were going to get Terry out of that glass bubble. But, God forbid, if I had to ditch it, I wanted to be close enough so that we would have help from a destroyer after hitting the water. If I landed it in Japan, we were all going to end up POWs or worse. If I landed it in the water, close to the island, we were all going to end up POWs or not be fished out at all. So we flew the 150 miles back to the ship alone, with me struggling to control the plane all the way.

I was the last bird from the flight to make it back to the ship. The others hadn't a clue as to what had happened to us. When I got to the ship, they knew that I would have to be brought aboard quickly as I didn't have enough fuel remaining to orbit. After they assessed our situation, cleared the flight deck, and gave me permission to land, the landing signal officer, Red Volz, guided me down. Terry, meanwhile, was still immobilized in the turret. In my approach, I dropped the landing gear, and lo and behold, miraculously, the air pressure changed and gave us enough lift so that I could control the stick with one hand and use the other to do what was required for a carrier landing. I was able to get the wounded bird down on the deck of the ship. The third class radioman, Ken Fortier from Concord, New Hampshire, and I were able to walk away from the plane, but we had to chop the turret gunner out with a fire axe. You can imagine the terror that Terry suffered as he was trapped in that bubble in an aircraft that was struggling, and as he watched that flight deck come speeding up toward his glass prison. Terry flew another ten combat flights with me. In most of these, we were exposed to severe antiaircraft fire which began to take its toll on him. After the hostilities ended, he stopped flying. Ken Fortier left the Navy after the war to become a prominent pharmacist in New Hampshire. How young we had all been back in 1945. Terry was the eldest at twenty-two; I came next at twenty-one. Ken Fortier was the youngest at nineteen.

On the twenty-second and the twenty-fifth of July 1945, we attacked the naval port at Kure where we sunk one of their last battleships, the *Haruna*. We were in the general vicinity of the area where the atomic bombs were dropped, and we were told of the bombings soon after the fact. Although we didn't know the reason at the time, we didn't fly from the fourth to the ninth of August because we had stood-down from operations during this critical period. Remember, the first atomic bomb was dropped on the sixth of August, and President Truman sent a message to the Japanese that the second one would be forthcoming if the Japanese failed to surrender. They didn't respond, and the second one was dropped on the ninth of August. We didn't get a response from the Japanese until the fifteenth, and we started flying again from the ninth to the fifteenth of August. We met a great deal of antiaircraft artillery on these missions, but there were few fighter attacks. There was some air-to-air fighter combat, but the Japanese fighters didn't seem disposed to attack our bombers.

The three of us flew ten more combat missions before the end of hostilities on 15 August 1945. We were scheduled to fly what would have been the last raid against Japan on 15 August. The target was the Tokyo Shibaura Electric Company. We had tried to hit it previously but had been turned away by bad weather. We weren't unhappy about this, since this one utility plant was the most heavily defended place in Japan, with five hundred antiaircraft guns defending it.

Nevertheless, here we were again going after the Shibaura target with each aircraft of our squadron carrying a two thousand-pound bomb, the limit of our capacity. At 8:15 am, on a sunny morning when we were within sight of the target, we were informed by radio that the Japanese had agreed to an unconditional surrender. We were eleven miles from the coast of Japan, within sight of the Emperor's palace, when the mission was aborted, and we were called back to the ship. After an almost instantaneous transition from maximum tension to maximum elation we jettisoned our bombs and headed back to the ship.

When we landed, we were told about the Japanese surrender. After four years of war, you can imagine how jubilant we were. The ship's crew partied, and although Josephus Daniels had banned the use of alcohol aboard U.S. naval vessels in 1914, mysteriously, there were enough spirits on board the *Yorktown* to stimulate our celebration.

In 1794, Congress established the daily ration for crews of U.S. naval vessels to be "one half pint of distilled spirits," and if the spirits were not available, "one quart of beer." The ration was changed over time and computed in terms of price or value. For example, in 1847, the ration was three cents of spirits a day. However, in 1914, Secretary of the Navy Josephus Daniels caused General Order 99 to be issued that strictly prohibited "the use or introduction for drinking purposes of alcoholic liquors on board any naval vessel, or within any Navy yard or station.[2]" Sailors have never forgiven him.

Tom described the post-war period:

---

2.   Naval Historical Center, Alcohol in the Navy, 1794-1935, (Washington D.C.) www.history.navy.mil/faqs/faq32-1, 2005

Terry had been emotionally drained by the experience of our first combat flight together and repetitive exposure to intense antiaircraft fire on our subsequent flights. He decided to stop flying. Within a year after we came back to the States and his separation from the Navy, Terry's wife contacted me to let me know that he had been admitted to a veteran's hospital where he died as a consequence of his battle fatigue.

The next order of business was to find the many POW camps around Metropolitan Tokyo and supply food to the prisoners. As soon as weather permitted after the fifteenth of August, we resumed operations. The day after the ceasefire, Admiral [William F.] Halsey broadcast to the fleet that all Japanese aircraft had been grounded—if we should see one flying, we should shoot it down in a "friendly and non-belligerent manner." We delighted in the absurdity of his order.

One of our immediate post-hostility missions was to locate where our POWs were being held and to drop food and supplies to them. The flights produced some of the most gratifying moments of the war for me. However, the weather was not good, interfering with our aerial search. My first POW site search was in the last week of August. I was flying down a street in Tokyo with my wing man when we came to a flat iron building, and I told him that I would take the right side and that he should take the left in our search pattern, and that we should meet outside the city. As we rendezvoused, I spotted this printing on the roof of one of the buildings in a railroad yard on the outskirts of the city, "USS YORKTOWN VT 5 CONDIT." Now this is the squadron I had been in the previous year, and it was Lieutenant James "Pop" Condit's seat I had filled in the squadron. I was elated that I was the one who had found him and fascinated with the coincidence. We showered the site with the "care packages" we were carrying. When I got back to the ship and reported what we had found, one of the squadron aviators, Lt. Bill Thurston, who had been a close friend of Condit, organized a series of flights to deliver messages and as many packages as we thought they could use.

Condit had been shot down during the first raid on Marcus Island in 1943. He and the crew had been picked up by a Japanese ship and imprisoned. This was the first indication anyone had that he was alive. He had been treated roughly, and when Admiral Halsey heard about it, he made arrangements for Condit to attend the surrender ceremony on the USS *Missouri* to face down his captors.

I also participated in that surrender ceremony on September 2, 1945. We were launched for a massive flyover of Tokyo Bay while the Japanese surrender document was signed. When we returned to the ready room after that flyover, we all had the same thought: "Lord, we are glad that in that huge gaggle of aircraft, none of us were killed in a midair collision." It would have ruined our day to have been killed while celebrating our chance to go home.

[Tom didn't meet Condit until years later after Condit had retired as a rear admiral. They met at an aviation convention where Tom was serving as a tour guide at the Silver Hill Restoration facility, and Condit came through on a tour. The meeting took place more than thirty years after Tom had relieved him in absentia and the finding of his POW site. Condit retired in Florida and died in 2004.]

I was told of another gratifying incident through a letter I received shortly after the war from a young soldier from Zanesville, Ohio, who had been a POW in a camp at a grain elevator near Yokusuka, the naval base and shipyard just outside of Tokyo. A survivor of the Bataan Death March, he had found my name on a package that we had dropped on one of the POW recovery flights. He wrote in his letter that for months he had watched a Japanese aircraft carrier being built in the shipyard and witnessed its bombing by our carrier-based aircraft just as the ship was being launched. The bombers hit the ship as it was plunging into the water for the first time, and it just kept sliding and sliding into the waters and never completely surfaced. He wrote that this had been the "best day of the war" for him.

After the war ended and the *Yorktown* returned to Alameda in October 1945, Tom was released from active duty based on the twenty-four service and combat points that he had earned by virtue of his overseas time. He was out of the Navy for seven months and had returned to New York and gone to work for one of the airlines as a reservation clerk. When Rose graduated from college, they drew on Tom's wartime savings and married. Tom missed the Navy. He applied for a regular commission and was accepted at his then-current rank of lieutenant junior grade, losing only about two months on the lineal list, which put him in a different year group, but he was just happy to be back flying again. He learned that he had been accepted back into the Navy when he and Rose returned from their honeymoon. In September 1946, he reported for duty in Norfolk, Virginia, where he served as a catapult and arresting gear officer on a PVE, the USS *Palau*. He recalled:

> I reported aboard the ship at just about midnight on the day I was scheduled to report—just making it under the wire. I was surprised to see not a commissioned officer but a chief petty officer standing watch as officer of the deck, something I had never seen before. I was under the impression that the ship was about to get under way, and I asked the chief if that was the case. He laughed and told me that it was highly unlikely, that he would assign me quarters, that the executive officer would be aboard the following morning, and that he would be able to brief me on the situation. The next morning, the executive officer told me that we weren't about to move the ship anywhere, we were so badly undermanned. He said that they had to borrow crews from three aircraft carriers just to move the *Palau* across Hampton Roads to our current mooring. We were the flagship of the division, and the admiral wanted to be in this position rather than in the Portsmouth shipyards. The

ship was in good condition but had just a skeleton crew, a consequence of the post-war demobilization of the Navy. In 1946, the *Palau* was not unique in this respect, as there were lots of units and ships that couldn't function because they didn't have the personnel. I was assigned to the air department and was one of only nine officers and three enlisted in the department. The normal complement was about twenty-five officers and a hundred enlisted, even before you got the operational squadrons aboard.

In the late 1940s, officers had to either take correspondence courses or sit for exams to qualify for promotion. Tom sat for a week of exams, passed them, and was promoted to full lieutenant. The *Palau* eventually was manned to a level where they could get under way with a Marine fighter squadron with Corsairs aboard. They were operational for about a year and a half, and the highlight of the tour for Tom came at the end of the tour when the ship anchored off Monrovia, the capitol of Liberia, there being no good natural harbors in the country. Tom told of that experience:

> The purpose of our trip was to help celebrate the one-hundredth anniversary of the country's independence, 26 July 1847. Once ashore, we learned that we Americans weren't popular in Liberia, notwithstanding the fact that it had been President Monroe who had been the prime mover for the creation of Liberia as a free African state. There was a Firestone rubber plantation that housed a number of Americans who were virtual prisoners within their compound, which they never left, as they were concerned for their personal security and the sensitivities of their Liberian hosts. We, from the *Palau*, were not prepared for the hostility we met on the streets, where we would be forced off the sidewalks and refused a drink in a bar.
>
> It wasn't all bad, because we learned something about the personal hurt of segregation, we Caucasians being the "segregates" for a change. Of course, there were more than the usual liberty brouhahas, and we had to get some of our crew out of the local jail. The Raymond Construction Company, staffed by some very tough Americans, was also there dredging the Monrovia harbor, and they were most hospitable to us. That stay in Monrovia introduced me to some of the most interesting characters I have ever met.

Following his *Palau* tour, Tom was assigned to a carrier-based anti-submarine warfare squadron, VS 32, for two years. He later served as an assistant safety officer for Air Force, Atlantic Fleet, in Norfolk, where he wrote the first aircraft accident investigator's handbook before being transferred to the Bureau of Naval Weapons where he worked on aviator's survival gear.

"It was during this tour that I became involved with outfitting aviators for high altitude flights," Tom said. "We really didn't know how well we could survive and operate at those extreme altitudes. The Navy was given the responsibility for developing full pressure suits. It was determined that at 37,000 feet, if you lost cabin pressure such as having your canopy blow, your blood would immediately come to a boil. A possible answer was the full-pressure suit. The first people who were to test the gear were civilian contract pilots flying out of Edwards Air Force Base in California. The Air Force was responsible for developing another option, the partial-pressure air suit, which was a modification of the G suit."

The full-pressure suit, developed by the Navy, became the forerunner of the astronaut pressure suit. Tom became known as the Hart, Schaffner & Marx of naval aviation.

"I would go out to California with these suits and try to corral the civilian test pilots to try out the experimental suits," Tom said. "They weren't always anxious to do so, not because they were concerned about personal safety, but merely because it wasn't as much fun as wringing out a high-performance test aircraft. Some of these suits are now at the Udvar Hazy air museum, and I delight in telling the visitors about the background and history of the suits from my first-hand experience."

In the summer of 1963, now a commander, Tom was given command of a radar jamming squadron stationed in Alameda equipped with EA1F aircraft, a version of the A1 attack plane. He was told that there was a serious problem in South Vietnam, because there was no system to control and monitor aircraft flights there. He was tasked to assist in bringing some order out of the chaos in the skies over the country. He explained:

> The tasking changed our role from that of radar jamming to that of intercepting and identifying aircraft by radar from an airborne platform. Our area of operations changed from the eastern Pacific to the beleaguered South Vietnam. So we rigged a system from some old WWII surplus radars and hung them from one side of our aircraft. We went to Fort Ord on the Monterey Peninsula, south of San Francisco, and got some IR (infrared) searchlights from their tank equipment and put them on the other side. Then we procured some warheads from the Sidewinder missile that had an infrared detection system, and we hung the IR system under the aircraft. We then took the aircraft equipped with this mélange of gear up above Tan Son Nhut airfield in South Vietnam, running without any lights to intercept unidentified aircraft in the area.
>
> Since there was no air-control system, all aircraft flying were, in effect, unidentified. We would find the aircraft with our radar and use the IR light to

position ourselves behind the plane. We would then fly alongside the aircraft. The officer observer, the NFO, would shine a white Aldous light into the cockpit of the aircraft or, if that wasn't possible, into whatever window was available and challenge the crew to identify themselves or suffer the consequences. The first month we ran this operation we found 930 unidentified aircraft flying over South Vietnam. A rudimentary air-control system was established that was fleshed out over time. We got the number of unidentified down from the nine hundreds to the two hundreds and then to the one hundreds. In the process, we found out who all these unidentified aircraft were and what they were doing. We estimated that almost 90 percent of them were drug runners. Another 5 percent were Air America, that is, CIA aircraft, the other unidentifieds remained unknown, but who we weren't ready to challenge, or shoot down.

As the squadron commander, Tom was in and out of Vietnam often. This was before 1964, and they were going in country with civilian clothes and on passports. They maintained about five airplanes at a time at Tan San Nhut airfield where the South Vietnamese had set aside a private space for their operation.

"We loved it when we picked up the CIA guys, because they would scream like hell," Tom said. "One night a pilot yelled, 'Turn off that light, or we're going to shoot you down.' Our tower operator at Tan San Nhut told him, 'Unidentified. You identify yourself immediately or the next sound you hear is going to be 50-caliber rounds going through your cockpit.' The pilot accommodated us. We ran that operation for about a year in 1963–1964. I had the squadron until August of '64."

Tom returned to the Pentagon in August 1964 for a four-year tour, then on to the Naval Air Systems Command and to his final tour as Wing Commander of the Atlantic Fleet Carrier Airborne Early Warning Wing (E2 Hawkeye aircraft) with six operational squadrons and a training squadron. He retired from the Navy in 1973. Here's what he said about retirement:

After I retired, I went to work as a defense consultant, but what I was really interested in was to become a Washington, D.C., tour guide. I loved the capital, wanted to know and be able to tell everything about it to our visitors. Then I saw an announcement in the paper that the Paul Garber Aircraft Preservation and Restoration Facility of the Smithsonian was looking for volunteers to attend training to be docents or guides for school tours. That sounded to me that it could be a good introduction to being a Washington tour guide. So I applied for a volunteer job there, was accepted, received six months of training at four hours a week with the training being conducted by the curators and senior docents of the Air and Space Museum. I didn't plan to stay long, but I did volunteer work there for twenty-one years, working every other Sunday. There were between two and four of us docents working every day. We averaged about twenty to forty visitors a day, plus the frequent bus tours and convention crowds. Now I no longer have any association with the Paul Garber facility since it was closed to the public on 1 April 2001 but am completely dedicated to my docent volunteering at the Udvar-Hazy museum, and it is a happy, fulfilling experience.

Rose and Tom Quinn today

Tom and Rose moved into Falcons Landing in August 2002. Their four boys, three girls, and grandchildren are scattered from Alaska to Florida and Wyoming to Massachusetts.

Falcons Landing residents are fond of patting themselves on the back for making such a wise decision as to move into such a comfortable, secure, caring community. The Quinns are no exception, they can boast with the best of them when it comes to their home of choice.

21

Harlan Cleveland

Harlan Cleveland, left, with Secretary of State Dean Rusk, at a NATO
ministers' meeting, circa 1967

One does not acquire the gift of writing trenchant works on the subject of
leadership through academe. It can't be found in studying the psychology of
human behavior or reading biographies of great leaders. These sources may provide the trimmings—some useful tactics of good leadership. To formulate a philosophy of leadership that is worth sharing requires practical experience in the
cauldron of managing subordinates, colleagues, and, sometimes, superiors.
Ambassador Harlan Cleveland of Falcons Landing drew upon his experiences to

---

1.   This profile is based on a series of interviews beginning in March 2004. All photo-
      graphs are courtesy of Cleveland.

write many articles and four books, many of which touch on his philosophy of leadership.[2]

When one asks which events stand out as highlights in his impressive, varied career he will tell you, "They were all highlights." It was a career that included the management of post-World War II relief operations in Italy and China. It included an important role in the implementation of the Marshall Plan. In 1953, he served as the executive editor, then also as publisher, of the *Reporter* magazine. He joined academe as dean of the Maxwell School at Syracuse University. For five years (1969–1974) he was president of the University of Hawaii. In 1979, he was appointed Distinguished Visiting Tom Slick Professor of World Peace at the Lyndon B. Johnson School of Public Affairs, University of Texas at Austin. In 1980, he was the founding dean of the University of Minnesota's Hubert H. Humphrey Institute of Public Affairs. Ambassador Cleveland is also a prominent diplomat, serving as an assistant secretary of state (1961–1965) and as ambassador to NATO (1965–1969). He is the recipient of twenty-two honorary degrees, the U.S. Medal of Freedom, Princeton University's Woodrow Wilson Award, and the Prix de Talloires, a Swiss-based international award for "accomplished generalists."

Despite a lifetime packed with distinction, Harlan believes that it was the early period of his public service, during the decade of the 1940s, that gave birth to his lifelong interest in the art of leadership. This was the decade in which he faced daunting challenges of leadership that set the course for his unique and valuable contribution to the common weal.

Harlan Cleveland was born in 1918 in New York City. "I guess I must not have liked New York," he said, "because the family moved after only three months. My father was an Episcopal priest who served as a college chaplain at such schools as the University of Wisconsin and Princeton. He was an Army chaplain during World War I. He was gassed and later died at age thirty-six, when I was only eight."

Harlan was schooled in France and Switzerland and graduated from Andover in the class of 1934 and from Princeton in the class of 1938. Following Princeton he attended Oxford as a Rhodes Scholar working on a doctorate in comparative politics.

---

2.   Notably: *The Future Executive: A Guide for Tomorrow's Managers* (New York: Harper & Rowe, 1972); *The Knowledge Executive: Leadership in an Information Society*, (New York: E.P. Dutton, 1985).

"However, Adolph Hitler's march into Poland cut my graduate work short, and I committed to an internship in the office of Senator 'Young Bob' La Follette of Wisconsin," Harlan said. "It was during this period that I had the good fortune of meeting, wooing, and wedding another intern, the vivacious Lois Burton, who hailed from Salem, Oregon. As of this writing, we have been married for sixty-four years."

Harlan moved from Senate intern to a staff position within the Farm Security Administration and, with the entry of the United States into the war, he migrated to the Board of Economic Warfare. There he applied his talents to the use of economic force to promote the war effort as an economic analyst.

As a boy, Harlan had suffered an injury to his right eye that denied him service in the military. Nevertheless, he was committed to public service. He was a quick study in his first years in the federal bureaucracy. By 1944, he had acquired extensive experience as a federal executive achieving a solid background in international economics. He focused on the Italian economy and gained valuable experience in directing staff operations that, among other things, advised the Army Air Corps on industrial targeting options. His draft board gave him permission to leave the United States to take a position in Italy. He left for Italy in 1944, the day after Lois gave birth to their boy and girl twins; another daughter, Zoe, had been born two years earlier.

Although still a civilian, Harlan was accorded the courtesies of the rank of a brigadier general. He reported for duty to Gen. Bill O'Dwyer, head of the economic section of the Italian operation. O'Dwyer, a political general and Irish émigré to America, was soon to leave to run for and, in 1946, be elected to the office of mayor of New York City. O'Dwyer's departure and the promotion of his relief, Tony Antolini, vaulted Harlan into the position of the executive director of the Allied Control Commission's (ACC) Economic Section. In the words of Franklin Roosevelt and Winston Churchill, the mission of the ACC was "...to give Italy back to the Italians."

The young staff executive had established his reputation, in large part, by crafting an instant briefing on how the Allies would reconstitute Italy. The briefing was to be used by the administration in Washington to present to Congress. He had only four days in which to produce the report. The report was so well-received that Harlan's reputation was established as the man on the scene who knew the Italian situation.

It is easy to see why Harlan considers this period of his life a threshold. At the age of twenty-six, being neither an economist, nor a financier, nor a political maven, but a self-described generalist, he assumed the responsibility for an operation that was fraught with economic, financial, and political traps. At this early age, he directed the work of fourteen hundred people, including many military officers of the rank of colonel and British brigadier general.

The economic section, under the direction of the young generalist, controlled all imports into Italy, including such basics as coal and wheat from across the Atlantic. The section also directed the operation of the ports. As one might expect, there were obstacles to managing such an enterprise. When it was discovered that they were importing oranges from Florida into citrus-rich Italy, charges flew that they were "carrying coals to Newcastle." But, in fact, Italy's citrus crops had also been a casualty of the war; so, like coal and wheat, also normally plentiful in Europe, even oranges had to be temporarily supplied from North America.

The war in Europe ended in May 1945 and, through the efforts of the United States and Britain, the United Nations Relief and Rehabilitation Administration (UNRRA) joined the effort to restore the Italian economy. UNRRA had been organized in 1943 to provide aid to areas that had been liberated from the Axis powers. Fifty-two countries participated. Nearly four billion dollars were invested in the effort, with the United States providing more than half the funds. The three successive directors general of the operation were all Americans: Herbert H. Lehman, Fiorello LaGuardia and Gen. Lowell Rooks. Now twenty-eight years old, Harlan was offered the post of deputy chief of mission for the Italian UNRRA operation.

"I agreed," he said, "but only if I could also continue, for a transition period, in my job with the Allied Commission, and if I could bring one hundred key personnel from its economic staff into UNRRA. For several months I wore two hats and served two masters—one the United Nations, the other the United States and Britain. These were hectic days, as the team brought into Italian ports three ships a day carrying food, fuel, and agricultural and industrial equipment. The UNRRA effort, building upon what the Allied military government had done, provided the momentum and resources for the 'economic miracle'—the unprecedented rapid recovery of the Italian economy."

UNRRA suspended its European operations in June 1947. Nevertheless, there were still funds available, and there was still work to be done in China; some $650 million in 1947 dollars was devoted to China recovery operations, which would continue for another year. The program was directed by a U.S. Army major general, Glen Edgerton, Corps of Engineers. Edgerton, a former governor of the Panama Canal, was ill, and a replacement was needed. In the spring of 1947, Harlan, now twenty-nine years old, was asked to take over the job, a monumental task. Headquartered in Shanghai, he supervised more than four thousand people (three thousand Chinese and one thousand expatriates) in fifteen regional offices throughout China, working on both sides of the Nationalist-Communist battle lines. The Nationalists were corrupt but cooperated with the program. The Communists, while accepting some aid, were otherwise uncooperative, complicating the administration and accountability of the program.

Harlan, right, Eleanor Roosevelt, left, and Ambassador Charles Yost at a United Nation's Association of the United states of America meeting, circa 1962. (It was Mrs. Roosevelt's last public appearance before her death.)

It was apparent in 1947–1948 that the Nationalist forces were losing the war to the Communist insurgents, and the UNRRA program was reaching its prescribed end. Harlan's assignment lasted less than a year.

He described that period and his transition back to the states:

> I returned to the States in January of 1949, after being overseas for more than four years. The UNRRA program ultimately closed down in March of that year.
>
> During my short time in China, I supervised work being completed on the control of the Yellow River, a project that was "the earth-moving equivalent of building the Panama Canal." I witnessed a 30 percent *per month* hyperinflation of the Chinese national currency. The monetary system was so volatile that I arranged for UNRRA's huge local-currency accounts to be expressed in bales of cotton rather than in Chinese National currency. back in the States, I

quickly returned to the U.S. government. My return to Washington coincided with the final stages of congressional passage of the Marshall Plan for European Recovery, a program I had served from its inception to its culmination. Congress appended to the Marshall Plan a substantial aid package (Title IV) for the Chinese Nationalist government. Fresh from China and a veteran of the UNRRA/ACC programs, I was a logical choice to head the China division of the new Economic Cooperation Administration (ECA) headed by Paul Hoffman. My task was to keep the China aid program afloat and avoid having it distract from the more ambitious European recovery exercise. By1949, after twenty-seven years of civil war, the Communist People's Republic of China had defeated the Kuomintang.

Harlan, right, stands next to President John F. Kennedy; on left is scientific advisor Dr. Jerome Wiesner and the chairman of Reynolds Aluminum Corporation. (This is the last photograph of President Kennedy in the oval office on the day he left for the fatal trip to Dallas, Texas, on November 21, 1963.)

Cleveland's aid program was shifted from mainland China to Taiwan and eventually expanded to "the general area of China," a Far Eastern Program that included South Korea, the Philippines, Indonesia, Burma, Vietnam, Laos, and

Cambodia. In 1950 he was promoted to deputy assistant administrator of ECA. When a new Mutual Security Agency was formed, toward the end of 1951, he was appointed its assistant director for Europe.

And so the decade of the forties came to an end for Harlan Cleveland. What followed was hardly anticlimactic, but it was the forties that shaped the professional career of this talented public servant. It was those first years of his professional life that defined his approach to leadership and imbued him with a lasting interest in documenting the lessons he had learned.

In his 2002 book, *Nobody in Charge*, he offers thirteen "Aphorisms from Experience" on the management of conflict and cooperation that are summarized below:

- No conflict, negotiation, settlement, or bargain is merely two sided.... If you don't get all "sides" involved in the solution, they become part of the problem.

- A third party...is usually indispensable and often lacking. Conflict resolution requires some source of independent elucidation....

- Courage is directly proportional to the distance from the problem.

- Force by itself is not power.

- Creep up carefully on the use of force. Violence is easy to escalate, hard to deescalate....

- Widen the community of the concerned. Problems and their solutions are multilateral....

- Voting is an inferior means of conflict management; consensus procedure usually works better....

- Consensus is not the same as unanimous consent. Consensus is the acquiescence of those who care, supported by the apathy of those who don't.

- Process is the surrogate for substance. People will often clothe their substantive disagreements in procedural raiment....

- Openness has costs as well as benefits.

- Our standards are not the world's standards....

- People can agree on next steps to take together if they carefully avoid trying to agree on why they are agreeing.

- Resolving conflict is not always a Good Thing. Some tensions are promising: the global urge for fairness, insistence on human rights, competitive hustling, rising expectations....

Harlan and Lois Cleveland moved to Falcons Landing in July 1996. They had retired from the University of Minnesota in 1988. Their choice emanated from an invitation from Lt. Gen. Whitey Dreissnack that happened to coincide with their own conclusion that, congenial as Minnesota was in every way, "the winters were simply getting too long." They have found their home here to be thoroughly satisfactory.

Harlan with President Lyndon B. Johnson, en route to the president's first foreign policy speech in December 1063, having assumed the presidency after the assassination of JFK.

Harlan continues to write, having published four books and a number of articles on a variety of subjects, but with the focus on leadership. He was president of the World Academy of Art and Science during the 1990s and is now president emeritus. He continues to follow world events, and his views continue to be insightful and relevant. He feels strongly that, as the remaining superpower in the world, the United States still needs to build coalitions in the pursuit of national security objectives. He believes that the advent of nuclear weapons precludes another big war, "because we invented a weapon, an explosion that's too big to use."

As to leadership in the war on terrorism, he said, "this is not a world inter-religious war, or even a religion-versus-religion long-term struggle, but rather an effort to develop new ways of countering non-state enemies." Harlan has written convincingly in *The American Oxonian* and "The Year 2003 in Perspective of the World Business Academy" of the need for a return to American cooperation with its European allies. In the World Business Academy, he wrote: "The United States is still, as Dean Rusk used to say, 'the fat boy in the canoe.' When we shift our weight, it makes a disproportionate difference. The fat boy has been shifting his weight a lot lately, often without much notice to the other passengers. And the boat we share with our European allies is taking on dangerous amounts of water."[3] Harlan currently is writing his memoirs.

---

3.   Cleveland, Harlan, "Year in Perspective 2003" Vol. 174.23 *World Business Academy*

22

Harry Mangan

Photo courtesy of Harry Mangan

It was December 1941. The Japanese attack at Pearl Harbor on the seventh had crippled the American fleet. A series of well-planned, coordinated, Japanese amphibious assaults had been launched against American forces in the Pacific. The Washington Naval Treaty of 1922, in which the United States had agreed not to fortify its Pacific holdings in exchange for a Japanese promise to limit its shipbuilding, meant that only the island fortress, Corregidor, opposite the Bataan Peninsula, and some of the islands in the entrance to Manila Bay were fortified. The Japanese advances were swift, as the small garrisons of Marines and soldiers on Guam and Wake were overcome on December 10 and 22. Hong Kong fell on December 22. Singapore, thought to be impregnable, fell on February 15, 1942. American and Philippine units would hold out against overwhelming opposition for five months on Luzon in the beleaguered Philippine archipelago.

From the time of the annexation of the Philippines, the United States had maintained a military force in the islands that was partially integrated with indig-

---

1.   This profile is based on a series of interviews with Harry Mangan commencing February 2005.

enous units, but they were far from ready to resist the assault of the Japanese juggernaut.

Before December 7, there were three components of the Philippine defense that bolstered Washington's confidence that the country could be held. One was the leadership of General Douglas MacArthur who had come out of his 1937 retirement as chief of staff of the Army, to organize, train and equip a Philippine defense force. The second was the belief that U.S. sea power would dominate the Pacific and shield the islands from a hostile incursion. The third was the belief that airpower would dominate the battlefield, and that the United States had sufficient air strength, particularly with the proven capabilities of the B-17 Flying Fortress, to counter any Japanese threat. With thirty-five B-17s and 107 P-40 fighter aircraft in the Philippines, the Army air component was formidable; it constituted the largest number of American aircraft outside of the States.

While the confidence in MacArthur's military leadership was not misplaced, he had no opportunity to exercise his strategic genius in these first few days of the war. On March 12, on the orders of President Roosevelt, he and his senior staff withdrew from the Philippines to Australia, where they would continue to prosecute the war. General Jonathan Wainwright assumed command of the remaining forces on Luzon and was ordered to "fight as long as there remains any possibility of resistance."

The U.S. Pacific Fleet had been badly damaged at Pearl Harbor, yielding control of the waters around the Philippines to the Japanese.

The U.S. Army air component was dealt a crippling blow in the early hours of the war. The first word that Manila had of the attack at Pearl Harbor and that the United States was at war with Japan came in the early morning of December 8 (due to the time zone difference). The Japanese pilots of the Imperial Eleventh Air Fleet struck the American main operating base at Clark Field in the Philippines with twenty-seven twin-engine bombers just nine hours later. The Japanese found and destroyed two squadrons of B-17s, still on the ground, and a number of P-40s preparing to launch. They had a similar success at another airfield in northwest Luzon. Half of the entire fleet of American aircraft in the Far East was lost in these first raids.

Second Lt. Harrison Mangan of the U.S. Army Air Corps was thrust into this melee on November 20, seventeen days before Pearl Harbor. As a member of the Twenty-Seventh Bombardment Group Light, he embarked aboard the SS *President Coolidge* in San Francisco, destined for the Philippines. It was a comfortable trip for the officers of the Twenty-Seventh, living three to a state room and eating well. The enlisted had fewer, but nonetheless, comfortable amenities. The short stop they made in Hawaii was festive.

The Twenty-Seventh had been activated in early 1940. They had trained at Barksdale and Hunter Field, Georgia, and tested in the September 1941 war games held in Louisiana, the largest ever to be held in the United States.

Upon landing in the Philippines, the group, which consisted of three squadrons of airmen, checked into Fort McKinley on Luzon—without aircraft. The Army Air Corps had experienced difficulty assembling the fifty-two Dauntless Douglas A-24 dive bombers assigned to the group, and they had sailed in separate shipping. The aircraft were held in Hawaii and, to the dismay of the pilots of the Twenty-Seventh, they never reached the Philippines but were diverted to Australia.

Fort McKinley was a reception center in the middle of an active Filipino community where there were an abundance of grog shops, a golf course, and a Jai-Alai Club, among other amusements. The group organized squadron softball teams and played for a group championship. The senior officer present, General Wainwright, had to remind the group that there were standards of dress and discipline that had to be maintained, but otherwise, their introduction to the Philippines was most pleasant. At the end of November they were able to borrow some old, decrepit B-18s from another air group, which gave them an opportunity to get their requisite flight time. The aircraft were marginal, and the pilots of the Twenty-Seventh were learning the foibles of the B-18. However, they were prepared to go to war with these B-18s and had them loaded for a bombing attack on Japanese installations on Formosa when the strikes were called off.

The group got the news of Pearl Harbor at 4:30 AM on December 8, and they were stunned. They had no aircraft to fly, and there was no enemy in sight, so they carried on their normal duties in a half stupor. The first Japanese bombings of the Philippines came the same day, and there were several false alarms at Fort McKinley. The first raid on the Twenty-Seventh Group came at 4:30 AM the following morning, sending the crews to cover in a ravine about fifty yards from their quarters. The raids became a nightly affair, and the officers started sleeping outdoors in the cover and earthworks they had improvised. Detachments of the Twenty-Seventh were sent to nearby airfields for duty. The group took its first casualty with the death of a private first class who was killed by a Japanese bomb while manning a machine gun during an air raid. There were only four guns available to cover the triangle of three installations: two airfields and Fort McKinley. The guns were so busy that at times they got too hot to fire. It was a turkey shoot for the Japanese bombers. The group commanding officer, Maj. James "Big

Jim" Davies, was concerned that the valuable personnel assets of the Twenty-Seventh would be lost, and he started looking for options to keep the officers and men in the war.

As the situation on the ground continued to deteriorate in the Philippines, final defenses were being drawn by the Far East command. The airmen of the Twenty-Seventh gave up hope of ever being provided aircraft, and the majority was assigned duties as infantry, fighting a delaying action across the Bataan Peninsula and on Corrigedor. For a period, Second Lieutenant Mangan served as commanding officer of his squadron. In the first five days of the war, they had been through thirty-five Japanese bombing raids. The Japanese had landed in force on both the east and west sides of Luzon and were closing on Manila, which fell on January 2, 1942. The forces defending the Bataan Peninsula were overrun, and on May 6, Corregidor was taken. The airmen were marched sixty-five miles north to Camp O'Donnell, a Philippine Army camp. More than two-thirds of the group was killed while defending the Bataan Peninsula as infantry or during the Bataan death march. Between five and ten thousand Filipinos and about six hundred Americans died during the March as a result of malnutrition, injuries, and sometimes because of the malfeasance or cruelty of their captors.

By June 9, organized resistance to the Japanese had ended. The only forces remaining to carry on the fight were the American-Filipino guerillas, operating in such places as the island of Mindanao.

There were some notable Twenty-Seventh Group exceptions to the fate of the Bataan defense and the Death March. One was Lt. Damon "Rocky" Gause, who made a miraculous escape from Bataan to Corregidor to Australia in a 3,200-mile sea voyage in a fishing boat with another American. Gause had been captured with others of the Twenty-Seventh but escaped from his Japanese guards by over-powering one of them and killing his captor with the guard's own knife. It was not the last enemy he was forced to kill in his escape. He swam the three miles from the Peninsula to Corregidor, where he joined the defense forces as the leader of a machine gun squad. After Corregidor fell on May 6, he found a small boat and started to sail to Luzon when an enemy fighter aircraft sank his boat. He swam to the island, clinging to flotsam from the boat. He found his way to the island of Mindaro where he and an Army captain procured a battered twenty-two-foot sailboat with an ancient diesel engine that they sailed to Australia, island hopping along the way to include a stop at a leper colony at Busanga. Half starved and dying of thirst, Gause was eventually picked up by an Australian boat and flown to General MacArthur's headquarters, where he reported to the general. Still barefoot, he saluted and "reported from Corregidor." It is reported that MacArthur's response was, "Well, I'll be damned.[2]"

At least two army pilots of the Twenty-Seventh were evacuated from Corregidor on the submarine *Seawolf.*

Harry Mangan and sixteen other pilots flew out of the Philippines before the fall of the Bataan Peninsula in four of the few aircraft available. The intent was to fly to Australia to marry up with their fleet of A-24s, to fly back to the Philippines, and rejoin the group to battle the Japanese.

On December 16, the Australia-bound cadre of seventeen pilots was briefed by the group commanding officer, Major Davies, and told that they would fly out of Nichols Field the next morning at 3 AM. The plan was to island hop their way to Australia to marry up with the group aircraft. They were told to pack no more than thirty pounds of gear and prepare to be gone for about ten days. They didn't get much sleep the night of the sixteenth. Nichols field was a mess, reeking with the stench of broken gas mains, bodies of the natives, and dead animals strewn in the rubble of the surrounding village that had been bombed by the Japanese. Harry was to fly out of the Philippines in a battered aircraft.

"It was a DC-2 and a half," Harry said. "Later on, the aircraft became the DC-3, the old Gooney Bird of World War II. The only difference was that the tail on this airplane didn't have a dorsal fin, and it had a slightly different rudder, and it had much smaller engines than the eventual DC-3 had. It had been shot up by the Japanese bombers at Nielsen Field, just outside of Manila sometime after the eighth. But we made it flyable. There were thirteen of us aboard when we flew it to Mindanao, one of the southern, more primitive islands of the Philippines. We made the last hours of the flight with only one engine operating."

The other aircraft in the flight included two B-18s. In some cases, the aircraft were new to their pilots or copilots, but they learned quickly. The 2,500-foot runway was pocked with trash and craters from the bombings. They positioned a mechanic with a flashlight at the end of the runway who blinked signals as to when to take off. Once airborne, it wasn't a comfortable ride for the passengers, who weren't prepared for the cold in cabins that were sometimes riddled with holes.

Harry described the trip:

---

2.   Nathaniel Gunn, "Pappy Gunn, The story as 'Pappy' told it to his son Nathaniel," http://home.st.net.au/-dunn/ozatwar/pappygunn.htm

Our trip from Mindanao had taken us first to Tarakan, Indonesia, an island off the coast of Borneo where the Dutch had an airbase where we could refuel. Flying along the island chain that is Mindanao, headed for Tarakan, we sighted a Japanese aircraft carrier and held our breath, hoping that they would not launch aircraft to intercept us. Somehow we slipped by them. After refueling at Tarakan, we next flew to Macassar (now named Ujong Padang), where there was another Dutch airfield, and on to Kupang, Timor. We left Tarakan and Macassar just before they fell to the Japanese. Then on to Darwin, Australia, where the C-39 made a ground loop landing, which greatly impressed our Aussie friends.

From Darwin, a Quantas Airways Short Flying Boat took seventeen passengers with a crew of five to Brisbane. We were at maximum capacity, and all but five seats had been removed to accommodate us, as we laid or sat on the bare deck of the flying boat. Even though we were experienced airmen, the flight was so rough that nearly all hands got sick. The flying boat landed at Townsville on Halifax Bay, and we found a city that had gone to sleep. The highlight of our stop there was finding newspapers that provided us with our first accounts that we had received for a long time on the progress of the war. Our next stop was Rockhampton, where we refueled before flying into Brisbane, landing in the Brisbane River on Christmas Eve, near armed ships of an American convoy. We were a sad looking lot walking the streets of Brisbane in our filthy uniforms, with our gas masks, tin helmets, pistols and combat gear, next to the Aussie population in their crisp uniforms. We must have been a stark reminder to them that there was a war in progress. Unfortunately, the senior American present in the area, a colonel, stumbled onto us, and his expression said it all. I have said that Jim Davies was a movie version of a pirate, but that day we all looked like the real pirates walking the streets of Brisbane

Douglas A-24 Dive Bomber
Source: USAF Museum

The fifty-two A-24s awaiting us were known as the "Blue Rock Clay Pigeons." They arrived in Brisbane, Australia, in the Pensacola Convoy on 22

December, the same day we arrived in Darwin. The A-24s were actually Navy aircraft, SBDs, dive bombers that had been converted for Army use.

We hauled our aircraft to Amberley and Archerfield airdromes. I went to Archerfield. We began assembling our A-24s and readied them for flight. They were in sorry shape; the instruments were bad, the engines burned oil, and the tires were in poor condition, amongst a host of other problems. The planes had been crated carelessly and had suffered in transit. We worked twenty-four hours a day, seven days a week to put them into shape. We couldn't get some of the basic parts and things we needed, such as armament, trigger motors, solenoids, practice bombs, ammunition, and gun mounts, but we begged, we filched, we fabricated, and we improvised.

We had to reorganize our squadrons, integrating the personnel who had come in with the convoy with the seventeen of us aviators who had come out of the Philippines. At this point, there were only about nineteen of us accounted for out of the original four hundred officers and men of the Twenty-Seventh who had been in the Philippines. During this assembly and organization period, we conducted a dive-bombing school for the newly joined pilots. It was intensive schooling that was badly needed for those who had just joined us. Once in a while, we might get into town for a little rest and relaxation, but not too often, for these were busy times, and we were eager to get back to the Philippines.

We were planning our return to the Philippines when Singapore fell. While General MacArthur would eventually return to the Philippines, the Twenty-Seventh would not. As a matter of fact, the group was soon to be disbanded and reactivated in the United States, to commit to the European Theater of Operations. But it was not before we engaged in some serious combat.

The Japanese were coming south down the island chain rapidly. They soon took Java, where we had positioned one of our three squadrons, and it was lost in a matter of days. We flew our first combat missions in the Battle of Macasser Strait.

Macassar Strait off Borneo was the site of what many consider to be the first major battle of the war for the United States armed forces. It took place between January 24 and 27, when Allied air and naval forces struck the Japanese invasion forces that were landing in Java. With a small, badly outnumbered force of B-17s and A-24s, reinforced by Allied aircraft, the Twenty-Seventh acquitted itself well but was unable to stem the Japanese push south.

Harry recalled:

> We had positioned another squadron as far north as Dutch Timor that had to be withdrawn to save it from the fate of the Java squadron. So we ended up with the two remaining squadrons of Group Twenty-Seven in Darwin. Through attrition, we gradually became quite a small group.

The Japanese bombed our airfield at Darwin, and so we moved the group to a small airfield at Charters Towers, in northern Australia. We sent one of the squadrons up to Port Moresby in New Guinea. At this point, we were approaching the spring of 1942, and we were augmented with aircraft that we had flown earlier in Savannah, Georgia—A-20s—and with some new planes, B-25s, just off the Douglas production line. So we had a group with A-24s, A-20 Havocs, and B-25 Mitchells. We had a hell of a problem with training, transition, and maintenance with these different planes. It was a real polyglot of a unit. Fortunately, we were an experienced unit in an organization that dated back to World War I. It almost makes you cry when you think of the quality airmen we had who, in a series of unfortunate events, seemed always to be in the wrong place at the wrong time.

Once we had our aircraft operational, we started flying combat missions in the Java-Borneo area. We suffered a number of losses and near losses. One of our A-24s had been shot up with the oil line severed. The engine started coughing, indicating that it wasn't going to last long. The pilot, Launder, found an airfield in the Java chain where he was about to land until he saw that the aircraft parked there had the insignia of the Rising Sun painted on the wings. He was able to lift out from his landing run and make it out over the ocean where he and his gunner had to ditch into the water about eight miles north of the Japanese airfield. They made it to land and walked fifty-eight miles around the west coast of Bali, staying just ahead of the Japanese. As they approached small villages in their flight, the villagers would come out to greet them, serving tea and bread. At one of the villages, Launder asked if they had any beer, and the village elder sent one of the young men off to find a brew. A half hour later, an exhausted Balinese runner arrived with a hot bottle of beer under each arm. After their fifty-eight miles trek on foot, they were provided bicycles, but they were so spent from their adventures that they could only ride them when going downhill and otherwise just pushed them along. They finally arrived at a fishing village on the northwest coast of Bali where they found a boat and a crew that paddled them to a Dutch outpost on Java. There, they were fed, given money, and transported back to their unit.

In March 1942, the group fell heir to some dormant B-25 bombers that had been assigned to the Dutch air force and had not been used, because the Dutch didn't have enough pilots to man them. Unfortunately, the Dutch had not been told that they were to lose their aircraft to the Twenty-Seventh. As a result, the transfer was clumsy, and the Dutch hid many of the spare parts for the planes. But the transfer was made and the planes were ferried to Charters Towers.

Harry continued:

> As we flew across Australia on one or more of our missions, we found how efficient their grapevine was, for the Australians seemed always to be able to

anticipate our arrival before we got there and knew what our next stop would be.

General MacArthur was so impressed with the acquisition of the B-25s that he wanted to make a show of force against the Japanese. So we were ordered to fly back into some secret airfields on the island of Mindanao where we would operate against the Japanese in the area.

On April 11, 1942, three B-17 Flying Fortresses and eleven of the B-25s took off from Charters Towers, flew to Darwin and thence to the Del Monte plantation on Mindanao in the Philippines. The extra fuel tanks that were fitted on the aircraft for the 1,500 mile Del Monte leg of the flight were removed there, and the aircraft were refitted for carrying bombs. Harry was the pilot of one of the B-25s named the *Lounge Lizard*. The B-25 had much greater capacity, speed, and range than did the A-24.

He described flying the B-25:

> Carrying some much needed drugs for the Americans, we flew to Mindanao from Australia, nonstop, a 1,500 mile trip. It was the longest and most daring mission the U.S. Army Air Corps had ever undertaken. On April 11th, at 1 AM, the flight took off with three B-17s and eleven B-25s. We flew a flight pattern that avoided Japanese-held areas. Colonel Davies led the first flight of five B-25s. The last ship landed in darkness after an eight-hour flight from Darwin.
>
> The Americans and Filipinos had constructed a couple of secret fields at Merrimac and Valencia Mindanao, with protective revetments carved into the jungle. You could land on the grass fields and taxi right into the jungle cover, so that the aircraft couldn't be seen. It was really Hollywood stuff, operating right in the middle of the Japanese-controlled area. Bombs and fuel had been pre-positioned there. We operated out of those fields for three days running strikes against Cebu and Davao and against Japanese shipping in the area until we used up all the bombs and fuel that had been stockpiled. On the final, fourth day, we gathered some forty people who had been in Bataan and on Mindanao and were valuable to the war effort for their special skills. Some of them had escaped from Bataan in Philippine dugout canoes. We put them aboard our aircraft and flew them to Australia. We had a stowaway aboard, a Sergeant Jeffries, as well as a Chinese Army colonel, and a United Press reporter, Frank Hewlett.
>
> We hadn't lost a single plane in this bold operation, while damaging the Japanese-held docks at Cebu and Davao, sinking three transports, damaging four others, and shooting down three seaplanes.
>
> We brought some critical people out of Mindanao, and we showed the enemy that we could go on the offensive. It was one of the early daring, offensive actions of the war, but we didn't get much recognition for it, because it

took place about the same time as the Doolittle Raids on Tokyo that grabbed all the headlines. One person has said of the operation that its success was due to nine-tenths surprise and one-tenth good luck, which is true.

The Doolittle raids were conducted against Tokyo and Nagoya, Japan off the aircraft carrier *Hornet*. Lt. Col. James H. Doolittle launched the flight of sixteen B-25B medium bombers off the carrier, which was six hundred miles from the targets.

The remainder of that year we operated in the South Pacific out of Port Moresby in New Guinea, with B-25s and A-24s. We participated in attacks on a Japanese invasion fleet off the coast of Java, and flew missions over New Guinea. Throughout our operation in the Philippines and in Australia, we had this wonderful commanding officer, James H. "Jungle Jim" Davies, initially a major and our operations officer, who fleeted up to become the commanding officer when we got orders to the Philippines. He was the picture of a pirate. He was a big man, who carried a parrot on his shoulder. He could have starred in adventure movies. But, he was the ideal CO, who looked out for us and was a great combat leader. We would have never made it through those times without him. He survived the war, stayed in the Air Force, and became a general officer.

In November 1942, having been awarded the Silver Star and Distinguished Flying Cross, Harry was ordered back to the United States and assigned to Barksdale to train B-26 crews destined for the European Theater. His return gave him the opportunity to marry Margaret "Maggie" Spears, whom he'd met in high school in Fayetteville, N.C.—a great Christmas gift.

After the war ended, we were in the throes of demobilization. By this time I was a major, and I was assigned to take a unit of P47s and B-25s to Chile to replace the Italian and German aircraft that they had been using. You will recall that they supported the Axis throughout the war, and their aviation inventories came from those allies. The idea was to encourage a new alliance with us, and our supplying them with replacements for their aging arsenal was a part of the program. We stayed there for a year training them in the aircraft they had purchased. My contacts were a Chilean of German descent and another, a Chilean who had fought on Franco's side in the Spanish Civil War. They were most receptive. Their attitude was, "If you guys beat the Germans, you must be pretty good. We are happy to have you here." After my short Chile tour, I attended the Air University in 1948.

Following the Air University, Harry's career was typical of a senior Air Force officer to include several tours at the Pentagon. In 1954, he went to Carswell Air Force Base to check out in the B-36 Peacemaker, which Harry described as "a monster of an aircraft with six turning and four burning" (i.e. six Pratt & Whitney engines and four General Electric jet engines). He had two tours flying B-36s at Carswell Air Force Base in Texas and Ramey Air Force Base in Puerto Rico. Harry went back to school at the Air War College in 1959, then on to Albuquerque in the nuclear weapons program. He retired in 1965 with twenty-seven years of service, having served twelve years as a colonel. It was the culmination of an exciting career, with days of angst, camaraderie, pride, and grief. There was the time in the early days as the Twenty-Seventh was just forming when, on a test flight in an A-20, an engine failed on takeoff, and he crash landed in the Red River in Northwest Louisiana.

Of the twenty-three Army Air Corps people from the Twenty-Seventh Group that left the Philippines before the fall of Baatan and Corregidor, only eleven eventually returned to the United States a year later. The remainder were lost to the war by November 1, 1942. One of those who were captured on Corregidor, not from the Twenty-Seventh, was Harry's stepfather, Col. Marshall Quesenberry, who survived the Bataan Death March and spent the rest of the war in a Japanese prisoner of war camp, returning after the war "a complete wreck."

After retirement from the Air Force, Harry began a new pursuit:

> Initially, following retirement from the Air Force, I thought that I would like to work in the aircraft industry but found that it really didn't excite me anymore. I had always wanted to paint. I had never tried it but, at the age of 51, I thought I would give it a stab. I attended the Corcoran School of Art for a year on the GI Bill where I started working in oils. I didn't feel I was getting much out of the instruction, so instead of formal schooling in art, I began going to workshops around the country where I became interested in watercolors. Over the years, I have tried all the mediums—oil, pastels, watercolors, and acrylics, and Lord knows what else, but I kept coming back to watercolors, which is the only thing I do now.
>
> These workshops were held in pleasant places that Maggie and I enjoyed. They were most instructive in that all you did and thought about was painting. It was intense instruction, total immersion, often in the company of a nationally known artist. I spent quite a bit of time with well-known artists, such as John Pellew, Tony Van Hasselt, and Tony Couch. During these workshops you would start with breakfast in the morning, paint until noon, have lunch, and return to your painting until dinner. After dinner you would assemble to critique your work. It was a full day devoted to learning. You would do it all over again the next day, for a week. The classes are normally

limited to no more than ten or twelve students of varying capabilities, from the little old ladies who were there just for the ambience to the accomplished painters. In terms of age, the groups ranged from about twenty-five to sixty-five. We were in New Hampshire in the fall and in Florida in the winter. It was not only artistically rewarding but a barrel of fun. The workshops could be expensive, depending on where they were held, but, for us, they were always worth the investment.

We worked hard at it, but it was not hard work. I work exclusively in watercolors now, but I can't say that I belong to any school of art. My style is what I have picked up along the way, an amalgamation of the instruction and experience that I have had. A retired combat Air Force artist, John Pike, was a great inspiration. The thing that helped me a great deal in sketching was the mechanical drawing experience I had at The Citadel in Charleston, South Carolina. I was supposed to be studying to be a civil engineer, but other than mechanical drawing, I wasn't very good at it. My good grades in mechanical drawing raised my grade-point average, so they didn't have to throw me out of school. If you are going to paint well, you have to know how to draw.

I became involved in the art industry as an associate in a chain of art stores in the Washington, D.C., area and then worked in the Gilpin Gallery in Alexandria. I joined the America Art Associates in Maryland and the Hill Art School in Arlington, Virginia. We were in the commercial side of art for about twelve years before I retired for the second time to devote all my energies to watercolors. We were pretty successful selling my work and winning some art competitions. We then retired for the third time and came to Falcons Landing in 1996.

I was grateful to have the opportunity to live at Falcons Landing and found the community to be so generous that I wanted to give something back. I thought that a good way to do it would be to organize some art classes, and that was the genesis of what we now call "Harry's Hangar," a studio devoted to our residents, painting under my tutelage. Painting is ideally suited for retired people who have the time, the energy, and inspiration to try it. We have groups of four to ten regulars who participate, meeting one or more times a week in our well-equipped workshop. We have had some twenty-five to thirty people participate in our art programs at the Hangar over the years. Most of them started without any experience at all, and they have become quite good at it.

Of course, there are some of our residents who have never come to a class who are very good artists, Nomie Terry for one, Mildred Printz, and Jerry Scally among others. Mildred, for example, is a graduate of the National School of Fine Arts in Washington, D.C. She had a successful career as a commercial artist in advertising and has received many awards working in many mediums with her favorite being watercolor. We have had a couple of shows here locally, and we have galleries of our works that are displayed along the walls in the halls of the apartment buildings, rotating the artists' works from one side of the complex to the other. We have had some sales in the auditorium that have been well-received. There are residents who have never drawn or painted before that have developed into some impressive talents including, Helen Smeltz, Doris Oller, and Bill Stone, to name but a few. Having started from scratch myself, I think I find it easy to relate to those who are beginning students of art. Military service is a good foundation for teaching of any kind. We have all had experience of that sort, whether it is checking someone out in an aircraft or instructing in a classroom.

Harry is the son of an Army officer. His father, Walter David Mangan, graduated from the U.S. Military Academy in 1916 and was in an Army unit that chased Pancho Villa over the harsh U.S.-Mexican border territory between 1916 and 1919. While serving on the border, Walter Mangan met and married a rancher's daughter, and Harry was born in Nogales, Arizona, at a little Army camp called Stephen D. Little. His father was stationed at Fort Bragg, North Carolina, when Harry met his future wife, Maggie. In December 1941, Maggie, then a student at Coker College, was told that her fiancé, Harry, was missing in action. She assured her family that he was not, because she had "just received a V-letter from him." (V-mail letters were written on forms that could be purchased at stores and the post office. The letters were photographed and the film flown from overseas to the mail center closest to the recipient where it was then reproduced for delivery. The process reduced the weight of the letter by 98%.)

Harry and Maggie Mangan now have three sons and four grandchildren. One of the sons is a professor at the University of Toronto, another is an advertising executive in Richmond, Virginia, and the third works for a systems management firm in Northern Virginia.

Harry is typical of the residents at Falcons Landing in that he is a survivor who has led an exciting and perilous life. While the tempo of his life may not be what it was sixty years ago when he was flying combat operations in the South Pacific, his pace of life remains active, and he continues to be productive and make major contributions to his community.

23

Francis E. "Bud" Rundell

Francis E. "Bud" Rundell was commissioned from the Military Academy out of the extraordinary class of June 1943. In normal times, when the 568 cadets of that class were sworn in on July 1, 1940, they would have become the class of 1944. However, at this point in World War II, after the Japanese attack on Pearl Harbor on December 7, 1941, and Hitler's declaration of war on the United States, the need for graduates to man the officer corps of the Army dictated that their cadet status be compressed into three demanding years of instruction and training rather than four. The story of the June class of 1943 has been told splen-

---

1. This profile is derived from a series of interviews over several months commencing in 2004. All photographs are courtesy of Rundell.

didly through a series of personal and professional profiles in a book titled *Still Loyal Be,*[2] the brainchild of its editor, Bud Rundell.

Following are some numbers concerning the 568 cadets who entered the ranks of the academy in June 1940. Five hundred and fourteen graduated and were commissioned second lieutenants. Of the graduates, 208 (about 40 percent) passed the flying physical and opted to join the Army Air Corps. The remainder were assigned to other branches of the Army. Four of the cadets were killed in training flight accidents before graduation and commissioning. One cadet was killed in a training accident at Fort Dix. Fifty-seven of the graduates, or 11 percent, were killed in action during World War II, the highest number of such fatalities of any West Point class. Giving testament to the hazards of the military profession in routine exercises and flight operations, eleven commissioned officers from the class died in training accidents during the war. Four of the class died in combat in Korea, and one died in Vietnam. Thirty of the class, including Bud Rundell, became prisoners of war.

Of the cadets who entered the academy that year, only 142 were eighteen or younger, only fifty-five had come directly from high school, and some 340 of the 568 had already attended some college. A surprising figure is that 113 had fathers who were serving in the military, including forty who had fathers who were West Point graduates. One of these legacies was Bruce Arnold whose father was Henry "Hap" Arnold, then commanding general of the Army Air Corps, who presented the diplomas to the newly commissioned officers at their graduation ceremony.

The class was oriented toward military careers. Ninety percent of the survivors of World War II eventually retired from the Army or the Air Corps with twenty or more years' service or with a physical disability. Bud Rundell was one of those who had a full career in the Air Force. The class produced an unusual number of senior officers that included one general, thirteen lieutenant generals, thirteen major generals, and eighteen brigadier generals. Significantly, the class also produced a distinguished resident of Falcons Landing, Bud Rundell who, with his wife, Nancy, has made substantial contributions to a variety of public service ventures to that community.

---

2.   Tom Carhart, *Still Loyal Be* (Better Impressions, 2003).

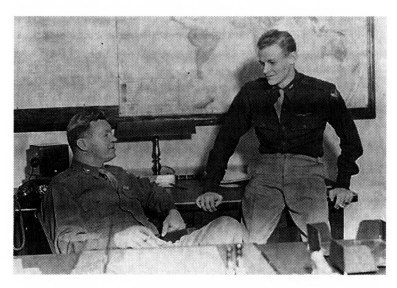

Bud and his father, 1945

Bud was born to Francis E. and Beatrice Hawley Rundell in 1921 in the Panama Canal Zone at Empire, a forward cavalry post in the jungles. Bud's father retired from the regular Army after World War II as a colonel. As a military child, Bud traveled from Army post to Army post, from Wyoming to San Francisco to Texas to Hawaii to Maryland. He graduated from Baltimore Polytech Institute and attended junior college in the Panama Canal Zone from 1939 to 1940. Bud won an appointment to the U.S. Military Academy and entered West Point in July 1940. He captained the swim team and won his wings while at the Academy.

Bud's first assignment following commissioning was to a three-month indoctrination course in the B-25 bomber. He hoped to transfer to the P-38 fighter aircraft. But circumstances dictated that he would fly the B-17 that he described as being a "grand old crate, but somewhat like riding a tricycle after learning how to ride a bicycle."

"We grew to love the old Flying Lady, particularly after hearing tall tales of how much punishment she could take in combat and still make it home," Bud said. The B-17 Flying Fortress is one of the most publicized American aircraft ever built. A prototype was first flown in 1935. After Pearl Harbor, a crash program was initiated to build them by the thousands until May 1945 when a total of 12,726 had rolled off the production lines at a cost of about $276,000 apiece. This four-engine aircraft served with U.S. forces in every combat zone in World War II, but is best known for its daylight strategic bombing of German industrial targets. It had a range of 1,850 miles and a ceiling of 35,000 feet. Bud's appreciation of the durability of the aircraft would soon be validated.

Bud was promoted to first lieutenant eleven months after commissioning. After a rigorous training routine in the States, he was assigned a crew, checked out a B-17G just off the production line, and flew to England as a replacement in the U.S. Eighth Air Force. While the first twelve combat missions could not be called a piece of cake, it was the unlucky thirteenth he recalls so vividly:

> On the night of 20 November 1943, my B-17 crew, stationed at an airfield in England, received a mission briefing. Our target was Merseberg, Germany, a heavily defended industrial city with a synthetic fuel center on the Saal River, just west of Leipzig. It was to be a special mission for our B-17G "Mickey Ship" as, for this mission, it would be equipped with a radar dome in the place of the ball gun turret. Routinely, there would have been a crew of nine in our aircraft. However, because room had to be made for special radar equipment, the ball turret gunner did not make this flight. The navigator was Sec. Lt. Rene P. Champagne while the tail gunner was Staff Sgt. Robert E. Ice. (This gave rise to the boast of our group that we were the only crew in the Army Air Corps that had champagne and ice aboard for every mission.) Breakfast on the twenty-first was at 0230, and we were served fresh eggs—not a good omen.
>
> It seemed we always had fresh eggs instead of the routine powdered variety before a tough mission. We often wondered if the cook knew the target assignment before the crews learned it later at the preflight briefing.

At dawn, the crew took off and quickly climbed to 26,000 feet. Bad weather forced them down to 17,000 feet by the time they reached the Merseberg area. As they bounced below the layer of clouds, they became easy targets for the German antiaircraft (flak) gunners.

Bud recounted:

> At the first burst of flak, our bombardier called for the last oxygen check before bombs away. All crew members checked in positively. The crew acted as a team to get the plane to the target and home safely, but the bombardier was in command during the bombing run. He was responsible for making the trip successful. He manipulated the famous Norden bomb sight that tied into the autopilot that flew the plane while the pilot and copilot kept hands off the controls until bombs away. This was true for bombing by individual aircraft. It was found to be (even) more effective in "pattern bombing" to have the whole formation drop bombs when the lead ship released its bombs for two reasons: first, the best bombardiers were selected to be members of the lead crews, and second, the effect on the target when all bombs exploded together

was greatly enhanced. Since the deputy leader was responsible for dropping his bombs at the exact best time if the leader had a problem and couldn't release, the rest of the squadron would automatically follow his lead on when to drop their bombs.

Red-centered flak bursts appeared at the nine o'clock level. We could tell that these German flak batteries were the more effective type with radar-assisted aiming and altitude-sensitive fuses that could be set accurately for the altitude of the target aircraft. "Them flak gunners ain't pfcs, they're master sergeants!" joked our flight engineer and top turret gunner. His humor helped relieve the tension just a bit.

Flak was visible on all points of the clock now, and often there were red-centered black puffs.

Just before the signal "bombs away" was given, the aircraft was hit and then hit a second time. The number one engine was afire. Bud could not see number two for the obscuring fire. He dove out of the formation as he hit the fuel-shutoff switch to the two disabled engines on the left wing. By great good fortune the flames were extinguished. Bud and his copilot managed to bring the aircraft out of its diving turn, but they were flying with only the two engines on the right wing. He said:

> I was the only one injured. A piece of shrapnel had torn through my flight jacket and ripped open my left forearm, the metal lodging in my jacket just above my heart. I climbed down to the bombardier who dressed the wound, stemming the flow of blood, and I returned to pilot the aircraft.
>
> The B-17 was badly crippled, its tail section was askew, the bomb bay doors were full of holes, and the instrument panel was useless. Notwithstanding our efforts to maintain level flight, we were slowly losing altitude. The situation deteriorated as we spotted a German ME-109 fighter giving chase. Good fortune provided us with a cloud bank that gave concealment and escape from the German fighter. We continued to lose altitude. To give the aircraft more lift, we threw everything overboard that was not bolted down or essential to flight. Two crew members even threw their parachutes overboard! Ice was building up on the wings.
>
> I had been hit before, which gave me confidence that we could survive this crisis. A month earlier, my plane had been hit by shrapnel while I was flying as deputy lead for the 614th Squadron against a target near the Polish seaport of Stettin. The shrapnel had crashed through the copilot's windshield striking the instrument panel, triggering the salvo switch which released our bombs prematurely, but the aircraft was otherwise intact, and I had flown the plane back to our home base. There, I was met by the group commander who asked why I had dropped my bombs five seconds before "bombs away." My being the deputy leader, if the leader can't drop his bombs on a target, the deputy

leader is supposed to activate his salvo switch. He excused me but told me that half of the formation dropped bombs when I did, and the bombs landed in a lake five seconds before the other half of the formation hit the target.

But this time, while still over Germany, Bud was going to have to ditch the aircraft. He searched for an emergency landing site. The crew prepared for an emergency landing, employing procedures practiced many times before. Bud knew that it would have to be a "wheels-up, flaps-down" landing to avoid dipping a wing into the ground. They slid into an open field, spun about as a wingtip struck a mound of dirt, and miraculously slid to a halt, relatively intact.

"On landing I was thrown from my seat, and I bumped my head on the windshield," Bud said. "At any other time I probably would have been knocked out, but I didn't feel any pain and wondered if it was because I was dead."

Bud counted noses as he dropped his six-foot-two frame out of the aircraft—all accounted for. He looked back at the large tail that was so descriptive of the B-17 and was shocked to see that the whole assembly was resting about twenty feet behind the rest of the fuselage. Thankful that this breakup had not happened before the crash, he realized how much damage a B-17 could take and still keep flying. A thermite grenade was thrown into the radio room to destroy documents and the aircraft. Once clear of the aircraft, they removed their flight suits and destroyed all papers they believed might be useful to the Germans. The nine men then split into teams of three anticipating that they would be more difficult to track if traveling in smaller groups. However, traveling in hostile country, with few escape and survival resources, all nine were quickly captured by local German forces. Bud told of the capture and subsequent treatment:

> The three of us were driven to a German home guard headquarters in a village near the crash-landing where we were fed. At this point, our captors were relatively benevolent. Soon a note of black humor was introduced as an older noncommissioned officer burst into our holding quarters. The man, clad in an immaculate green uniform, was wearing a spiked helmet that must have been a relic of World War I. He was shouting, as if speaking louder would make us more likely to understand his German. The situation became humorless as he became frustrated at our not being able to understand him. He unholstered a Luger pistol and shoved it in my face. I was sure I was about to be shot, but the helmeted German moved away and waived the pistol at the door, ordering us out of the building into the dark, cold night. It was absolutely black, and there was complete silence. I knew that the German guard was standing behind us with his pistol. It was the most frightening moment of my life. I could sense the pistol just an inch away from the back of my head. We stayed

that way in absolute silence and complete darkness for at least five minutes that seemed much longer. Finally, the guard yelled for us to march.

We marched to a small building that served as a village jail where the three of us were locked in the only cell. We spent the frigid night huddled together for warmth. The following morning, we were taken out of our cell and, to my amazement, the sergeant in the spiked helmet afforded me the tokens of respect of a commissioned officer to include clicking his heels and rendering a half bow. They loaded us onto a truck, and we were taken to the Luftwaffe interrogation center in Oberursel, eight miles northwest of Frankfurt. I managed to transition through the interrogation ritual providing only the requisite name, rank, and serial number, withstanding a number of sophisticated interrogation ploys used by the interrogators. However, I was held in solitary confinement for a period of ten days while undergoing detailed interrogation on three occasions. While I was not physically maltreated, I was fed only one slice of bread and an ersatz cup of coffee three times a day plus a thin soup for dinner.

I ultimately joined twenty-five other American prisoners, and we were transported to a POW encampment. Prior to leaving for the camp, each of us was given a Red Cross food parcel and was permitted to feast upon American chocolate bars and smoke American cigarettes—a real treat!

The twenty-five American prisoners were transported by train to the site that would be Bud's prison until the end of the war, Stalag Luft 1.[3] The Stalag was situated at Barth, a small town on the Baltic Sea, twenty-three kilometers northwest of Stralsund. The term *"stalag"* is derivative of the German *stammlager* a conjunction of *stamm* (family) and *lager* (camp). Some family camp!

Stalag Luft 1 was opened in October 1942 as a British camp, but by January, 1944, 507 American Army Air Corps officers were detained there. By the time of the liberation of the camp by the Russians, there were 7,717 Americans and 1,427 Britons at the camp. By 1944, more than 3,500 American planes had been shot down over Europe.

The camp had an L-shaped appearance following the outlines of the bay on which the camp was situated. When Bud arrived, the gates were kept open during the day, but after the spring of 1944 the gates remained closed at all times. Around the compound at strategic intervals there were twenty-foot watchtowers manned by two German sentries armed with machine guns and equipped with

---

3.   Greg Hatton, "STALAG LUFT 1 American Prisoners of War in Germany," prepared by Military Intelligence Service War Department, November 1, 1945. http://www.b24.net/pow/stalag1.htm

searchlights. There were two rows of concertina barbed wire surrounding the Stalag.

Bud described life in the POW camp:

> The barracks contained three tier wooden bunks with wood-chip mattresses. Lighting was poor. From 9 PM to 6 AM the shutters were kept closed, permitting little ventilation. I was quartered in a barracks that held about 250 prisoners divided into ten rooms. Each barracks in the Stalag was organized as a squadron. The highest-ranking member of the barracks was assigned as squadron commander. The commander selected three men as his staff, and the four of them had a small room separate from the open squad bay. One of the staff was designated the adjutant, one the Red Cross rations officer, and one the German rations officer. The adjutant was responsible for the administration of the squadron to include the accounting for all the prisoners in his unit and conducting the daily muster at the morning formation. I was soon designated the squadron adjutant in a unit where the commander was a friend of mine. The work as adjutant was not difficult but did keep me busy, which was a welcome diversion from the dreary life of the prisoner. Prison camp was most difficult for those who refused to engage in the squadron activities or accept responsibility for squadron affairs.
>
> There was a separate building for the latrine and cold water wash basins. Toilets were long benches with holes over large barrels that captured the waste. While mustaches were permitted, camp policy prohibited the growing of beards. Shaving in cold water was painful, but we Americans managed to adhere to the policy. During my confinement, the senior American officer was Col. Hubert Zempke, an ace who was well known to the Germans as well as to us Americans. The British and American prisoners chose to be administered separately, but each in a military hierarchy. After the Normandy invasion, there was a concerted, but unsuccessful, effort by the Nazis to convert senior officers in the Stalag to the German point of view, employing what they hoped would be a mutual fear of the Russians.
>
> During the first few months of my incarceration, the treatment of the prisoners was considered to be fairly good. However, following an April 1944 meeting of the Protecting Powers (that oversaw the welfare of prisoners of war), the treatment became more severe. There were a number of shootings of prisoners but not at our camp. More prisoners were placed in solitary cells for punishment, and the Red Cross was denied access to them. The German commandants were disposed to inflict mass punishments, limiting freedoms to an entire barracks for sometimes the most minor infractions by an individual.
>
> In 1944, when I first arrived at Stalag 1, the German food ration was 1,200 to 1,800 calories per man per day. The ration was gradually cut. By the end of our confinement it was down to 800 calories. Red Cross rations, when available, were supposed to be issued at the rate of one parcel per man per week. The parcels were cardboard boxes of a single cubic foot. They included five

packages of twenty cigarettes, a one-pound can of powdered milk, a half-pound can of Spam, jam, jelly, instant coffee, salt, pepper, soap, safety razors, toothbrushes, and other items of health and comfort. The Red Cross also sent playing cards, chess sets, books, and musical instruments, as well as food parcels. Our most popular food item was the "D bar," a thick piece of chocolate, six inches in length, three inches wide, and half an inch thick—Nirvana. But there were long periods when the Red Cross rations were not delivered, and the German rations were reduced. The normal daily meal provided by the Germans in good times was about six small potatoes, a fifth of a loaf of bread, margarine, perhaps marmalade, a small ration of horsemeat, a bit of cabbage, parsnips, beets, or turnips, tea or coffee, and a bit of sugar. The bread came in heavy, long loaves, and it was rumored that up to 10 percent of the contents was sawdust. The slicing of the bread into equal portions was an art reserved for a designated bread slicer selected from the ranks of the prisoners. Each room would elect a cook who would prepare the meals on the tops of coal-burning stoves. If the cook was good, he was a celebrity. If he was bad, we replaced him.

The Red Cross cigarettes were the basis of the monetary exchange system within the camp. Cigarettes were also used in barter with the guards to secure foods such as onions to make our rations more palatable.

We published a clandestine newspaper. The news was gathered with the help of an unauthorized radio that had been fabricated by some talented prisoners. The *Pow Wow*, a one-page paper, was typed and reproduced with a mimeograph machine. The paper would be delivered to the group adjutant who would read it each evening to the assembled prisoners in each room. I burned my copy after reading it. If I had been caught with it, I was supposed to eat it.

There was one bathhouse with ten showerheads to accommodate nine thousand of us. It also was used as a delousing facility. My squadron had access to the shower once every two weeks using our Red Cross-issued soap bars. One minute of hot water was administered followed by two minutes of a cold rinse, three men to a spigot. If a louse was found on any one of us, all members of that room were given access to the shower for a full three minutes of hot water. The policy made the appearance of a louse a cause for celebration. The clothing of the men from the louse-infested room was run through an autoclave which guaranteed clean clothing for the crew but also guaranteed shrinking of the material. Bed linen was supposed to be changed once a month, but it seldom happened. There were no garbage disposal facilities other than an incinerator. Two British physicians and six medical technicians provided rudimentary medical service. An American captain physician arrived in March of 1944.

Historians rate the morale of the American and British prisoners as being generally good. However, there were difficult times during periods when rations were below sustenance levels.

In April 1945, as the war was drawing to a close, the senior American officer had several conversations with the German camp commandant who wanted to use 1,500 American prisoners as hostages to escort the Germans to the west to surrender to the Americans. The Germans were intent on avoiding their capture by the Russians. The senior officer demurred, and the commandant relented to avoid a showdown with the prisoners. On April 30, the Germans turned out the lights in the camp, and the guards marched out of the compound in formation, without closing the gates. The senior American officer formally took charge of the camp and organized an American military police force to maintain order. The watchtowers were now manned by Americans who faced outward rather than into the compound. Overnight, Bud became an MP. On May 1, reconnaissance teams were deployed to make contact with the Russians. The Russians liberated the camp but made no effort to return the prisoners to American or British jurisdiction. A senior American and two British airborne officers were selected to make contact with Allied forces. The party made contact and flew to England where the Americans reported to the Eighth Air Force Headquarters. Arrangements were made to evacuate the prisoners by air. Bud recalled:

> After VE (European Victory) Day we 10,000 *kriegsgefanganens* in Stalag Luft 1 were evacuated by B-17s flying to Camp Lucky Strike, Normandy, France. From Normandy we were flown to Rheims for delousing and issue of clothing, shaving kits, money (script), and a B-4 bag. The next stop was at Camp Lucky Strike. There, I found that all our crew members had made it back safely to Allied control, a very rewarding sight, although the enlisted crew members looked haggard and in worse condition than those of us from Stalag Luft 1. The camp was set to receive about 50,000 POWs, and over 120,000 showed up. The chow lines were actually a mile long. We were fed twice a day, but some of us would eat and immediately go to the end of the line again. We heard that three ex-POWs died from overeating. Two days after arriving, we heard some noise outside the tent, and there was General Eisenhower climbing up on a platform to give a short talk to us. I was surprised and impressed and thought it above and beyond his duty as the Supreme Commander to informally address a scruffy crowd of noncombatants in addition to his busy schedule.

The return of the prisoners to England was completed on May 15, 1945. Bud's first stop in England was Deanethorpe where he informally rejoined his 614th Squadron:

> I was able to drink some real Scotch whiskey with my buddies. After a wonderful few days' reunion with my 614th squadron mates I was politely told I must go to the POW center in London and await transport to the States. After about a week in London doing nothing much, being assigned to a hospital barracks while medics checked us POWs for mental as well as physical condition, I was ordered to board the USS *United States*, a large, luxury cruise ship converted to a troop transport. As the commander of a compartment full of troops (Bud had been promoted to captain) I chose a top bunk (bunks were stacked seven high) near a fan because I'd heard how hot below decks got. The fan turned out to be an exhaust fan, and many of the troops were seasick or didn't bathe, or both, for the six days we were couped up in that hot, crowded compartment. Ugh!

Bud returned to full duty in the States and was assigned to a special studies group at Headquarters, U.S. Army Air Force at the Pentagon in Washington. In the fall of 1946 he attended a course on radiological safety in preparation for duty at Kwajalein Atoll in the Marshall Islands of the western Pacific. While there he served as a radiological safety advisor working with U.S. Navy crews who would clear ships that had been exposed to radiation after the Bikini Able and Baker nuclear weapon tests.

> I returned to the States from the western Pacific in early December 1946, just in time to see the Army–Navy game with a pretty girl named Nancy Torlinski. She made a big hit that day in her WAVE officer uniform in the middle of a hoard of Army guys yelling for the Cadets to sink the Navy. I was promoted to major in February 1947, and the pretty WAVE officer and I were married June 26, 1947, just a few days before the Armed Forces Unification Act. We beat them to the unification process in that this was a joint service marriage ceremony that featured my father, an Army colonel, Nancy's father, a Navy captain, Nancy, a Navy officer, and me, now an Air Force major. Nancy is still pretty after fifty plus years of marriage and two daughters.

Bud and Nancy leave church after their June, 1947 wedding

Bud's subsequent career in the Air Force and industry was hardly anti-climatic. He served in a number of responsible positions in missile programs, moving from base to base. Bud was the program manager during the development and production phases of the supersonic "Hound Dog" guided missile. The missile was carried by the B-52 bomber to attack primary targets with its nuclear warhead. For another three years he was the Headquarters Air Force Minuteman Guided Missile Program officer in the Pentagon. For another two years he was head of the armament laboratory at Eglin Air Force Base, Florida, and he spent three years as assistant director of the Supersonic Transport Program in the Federal Aeronautics Administration, which completed his career in 1972.

After retirement and while employed as a civilian, he and Nancy lived in Iran from 1976 to 1978. Bud assisted the Iranian Air Force Headquarters in the determination of their aircraft and support equipment. He found the Iranians to be compatible and found that they liked working with Americans. Nancy, an accomplished author, wrote of their lives in Iran in a widely read book *Iran: Front Row Balcony.*[4] Upon return to the States, Bud worked for the TRW Corporation for ten years and for another ten years at Anadac Company, supporting Navy shipbuilding programs.

Bud and Nancy are comfortable at Falcons Landing and are among the most active in resident volunteer programs. They both have given much to society in their military careers, and they continue to give generously of their time and talents in this community.

---

4.   Nancy T. Rundell, *Iran: Front Row Balcony* (McLean, VA: Felsun Press, 1981).

24

Hal Naylor

Colonel Hal Naylor, U.S. Air Force, (Retired) recalls:

> I rolled out of my sack to winter darkness on a cold morning of 9 February 1945 at an air base in England. We had stopped the German winter offensive popularized as the Battle of the Bulge. But the war raged on. The storms impeded progress as the Allies mounted the final major attack across Europe in pursuit of the Nazi forces retreating from the Ardennes.

1.   Portions of this profile have been taken from Hal Naylor (as prepared for publication by Beauchamp, Darwin), *Falcons Landing News*, January 2000, pp14-16. Photographs are courtesy of Naylor.

We were briefed on our day's mission. The 602nd Bomb Squadron of B-17 Flying Fortresses would join in a group raid on Paderborn, a rail and road junction in northern Germany, situated between the cities of Essen and Berlin. Our primary target was the railroad yards. It was not a deep mission. We would not need auxiliary fuel tanks, so the bombers would be lighter. We were routed out over the English Channel, straight into the target, and through the German air defenses. Our return flight would be less hazardous, over the Baltic and North Sea coastlines.

I leaned into the bitter wind as we made our preflight inspections. My heavy bomber was the *Atlanta Hurricane*, a romantic allusion to my beautiful sweetheart, Jane.

The control tower fired the flare signaling engine startup, and we soon were taxiing for takeoff. The *Atlanta Hurricane* seemed frisky as it was running much lighter than usual. The bomber leaped off the ground and started to climb like a homesick angel. I had the feeling that the aircraft was tugging at the reins. The squadron and group rendezvous went smoothly. The B-17s slid into place in the bomber stream. My crew and I were starting our ninth mission and had no inkling of the crises that awaited us.

Once over the channel, and having climbed through the overcast, I noticed that the number two engine (left-hand, inboard) had developed an oil leak and had begun to backfire. I shut down that engine. I found that we could stay in formation flying with only three engines, due in part that we were carrying a lighter load than usual. I would hate to abort and lose credit for the mission. (Mission credit was received only if you dropped bombs on the target.) I spoke with the navigator over the intercom and learned that we were less than an hour from the IP (initial point) from where we would begin the bomb run. I made the decision. We would push on to the target.

We reached the IP and made the turn for our bombing run. There were black puffs of ack-ack (anti-aircraft) fire in the midst of the squadrons preceding us. Flak suddenly blossomed around our 602nd bombers. The bombardier opened the bomb doors ready to drop in concert with the lead bombardier. Then all hell broke loose!

The *Atlanta Hurricane* gave a tremendous shudder. A direct hit literally blew the number three engine apart. I looked out the right side window to see the number three engine propeller, with a long section of the crankshaft still connected, spin out ahead of us and down out of sight. I went for the feathering button, but stopped, realizing that it was to no avail because the engine was gone. Then, incredulously, I saw the number three prop spinning back up, in a horizontal spin. It slammed into the number four engine, tearing it out of the wing, shaking the entire aircraft. The number four engine turned inboard and fell away, dicing up the wing in its fall. The number four engine had broken away cleanly, as if with the stroke of a knife. The number three position trailed wires, tubing, and hoses, flapping in the slipstream as fire and smoke bloomed and fuel spewed from the damaged wing.

I was desperate. I straight-armed the throttle of the remaining engine to full power. My senses all seemed to be heightened as I responded to my training in emergency procedures. I flipped the salvo switch to dump the bombs. Amazingly, all the instruments reported good news. The bombs had been jettisoned, and the Bombay doors were closed. But conditions quickly deteriorated. A pulsing fire emanated from the remains of the number three engine. It flared in orange brilliance from the bottom of the right wing. I was flying a bomber that was on fire, with a single, over-boosted number one engine. We were several thousand feet below and a mile behind the squadron formation. We were losing altitude rapidly. I trimmed the aircraft as well as possible to fly on the one engine. Thankful that the controls were still responding, I gently turned to a westerly heading. Perhaps we could make it to an Allied-controlled area for a bailout.

The number one engine was screaming at full emergency war power. Nevertheless, we were losing altitude at close to 1,000 feet per minute. I took a deep breath. The technical order claimed that this engine could sustain maximum power for one hour before failing. We were counting on it.

A chatty P-51 pilot pulled up off our right wing. He reported that we had severe damage plus fire throughout the starboard wing. I knew this. I also knew that we couldn't stay airborne much longer. I instructed McHorse, the navigator, to plot a course that would bring us to an escape route to the channel for disabled aircraft. I ordered the crew to move to bailout positions at the main entrance door at the rear of the fuselage. I stayed on the flight deck, standing with my knees braced between the pilot and copilot seats so I could watch the burning wing. I tentatively adjusted the autopilot to maintain an uncertain heading, fighting against torquing, unsymmetrical power, and a heavy drag.

I realized that the *Atlanta Hurricane* was dying. The altimeter read 14,400 feet. It was time to go. I rang the bailout bell. Just to make certain that the crew got the alert; I went aft to the walkway over the bomb bay and looked through the fuselage. The crew members were leaving the aircraft, plunging out into space. I suddenly remembered that I had left a picture of Jane on the control wheel. I bolted back into the cockpit even as the big bomber began to nose down in a slow turn. I grabbed the photo and dropped down into the forward emergency exit. McHorse was kneeling over the hatch, attempting to pull the cable to release the pins and jettison the cover. The pins had rusted. Between the pins and the force of the slipstream, the hatch wouldn't budge. I climbed onto Mac's back to add weight against the hatch, but no dice. We were running out of time, and the aircraft's descending turn became steeper.

Then a major portion of the right wing burned off the fuselage. The aircraft whipped over and began to spin. Miraculously, the change in forces popped the hatch door open, and Mac and I tumbled out together. I passed under and outside of the left horizontal stabilizer. I counted three and pulled the rip-cord. The chute stripped out of the chest pack and spilled past my face. The opening jolt ripped my electrically heated flying boots off my feet. I didn't notice it until we hit the ground.

I was in the clouds when the chute opened. I could hear the sound of the air passing through and around the chute. In the distance, I could hear the sound of the *Atlanta Hurricane*'s death scream. It faded as she wound up in a tight spin followed by a mighty explosion. It was a relief to see her go. The thought of a heavy bomber rampaging through the clouds was frightening.

When I dropped out of the bottom of the clouds I could see Mac's parachute forty or fifty feet below me and the burning plane below him. It was so quiet that when I hollered at him, I could hear him answer back. I asked him if he was okay, and his reply was that he was. Soon I could hear the fire and the 50-caliber rounds cooking off. The crash was below, and I was drifting toward it. I tried steering the parachute by slipping it to the right by pulling on the right riser, but the canopy partially collapsed so I didn't do that again. I didn't realize how close to the ground I was until I saw one of *Atlanta Hurricane*'s main landing gear wheels, and how big it was. I flexed my knees and hit the ground. I landed just short of the fire. Mac floated across the crash, but the heat and the rising air gave him a boost to the far side of the crash. We were about one hundred feet apart.

Hal and his navigator had landed about ten miles away from other members of the crew. The Germans focused their search for the downed American airmen not in the vicinity of the aircraft, but in the area where the remainder of the crew had landed.

"We had landed in a potato patch with forests on three sides," Hal said. "We scooped up our parachutes and went deep into the nearest woods, where we sat down to take inventory of our situation, and debated what to do. I had twisted my knee on the landing, so Mac scouted up a walking stick for me."

The two inventoried their escape kits. They had dehydrated potatoes, meat, biscuits, an inedible chocolate bar, a small can of Sterno, waterproof matches, and hard candy. Most importantly, there was an escape map and a compass.

"My most pressing problem was my cold wet feet," Hal said. "Mac collected some firewood and started a small fire. The warmth of the fire was the most pleasant thing that had happened to me all day. There was snow on the ground, and my socks were wet from the walk to the woods. So I cut two panels from my parachute and wrapped one around each foot, mukluk style, and hung my socks near the fire to dry."

Mac had left his rosary in the plane, so he and Hal daringly returned to the burned-out, smoking hulk. Mac climbed through the wreckage, retrieved his ground flight jacket and found the rosary in one of the pockets. After burying what remained of their parachutes, the two downed airmen set off looking for an east-west road.

"We had been briefed to avoid young and middle-aged Germans," Hal said, "since they were probably Nazi sympathizers, and if we needed assistance, to contact only elderly and religious types who would be more likely to help us.

"It was somewhere around midnight when we came upon the edge of a town. It was eerily quiet. We couldn't detect any activity. We found an open Catholic church and cautiously made our way to the warmth of the shelter. We laid hidden on the floor of the church, between the pews."

Hal and Mac hid in the church hoping that they might be able to contact someone who would deliver them to one of the clandestine German groups that sheltered downed airmen. Such groups operated under the constant threat of discovery and retribution by the Gestapo. There was a German network that guided downed airmen through the country to points where they would be picked up by Allied aircraft or boats. There were two escape routes, one through northern Germany and the other through Spain. In a remarkable coincidence, they had stumbled into one of the few places where they could find such support.

Hal recalled:

> After a few hours, I heard the front door open. It was still dark outside, but it had to be near dawn. I peered from my hiding place to see a little old man wearing a Roman collar carrying a flashlight. He disappeared behind the altar and soon some light came on in the church. The priest came out from behind the altar and appeared to be preparing for Mass. I decided to take a chance and show myself. I slowly stood up with both hands over my head and repeated "American *fleiger*, American *fleiger*," which was the extent of my German, and I soon learned that he didn't speak English.
>
> Of course, the old priest was startled. He looked down at my feet wrapped in the parachute panels and must have thought that I was seriously wounded. He looked around carefully to ensure that no one was watching us and then motioned me to follow him. Mac remained hidden under the pews. The priest took me behind the altar, down a flight of steps, into a kitchen-like room. He left me there. After a short while, I returned to the empty chapel to get Mac, and we both returned to the kitchen.

Following the scheduled Mass, the priest returned to the kitchen, introduced the two airmen to a woman who was preparing breakfast, and they sat down to a meal of potatoes, bread, and something of a mush. The old priest returned some time later with a package that he presented to Hal that contained an old pair of

U.S. Army boots. They fit well enough, and Hal and Mac were ready to start on their long escape through Germany.

"For the first time, I started to feel that we had done the right thing by surrendering to these people, and that they were going to help us and not turn us in to the German authorities," Hal said. "That very night, we were turned over to a guide, and we started on our first night's walk. We said our thank-yous, received hugs and good wishes, and the three of us left the church into a cold night."

The next few weeks ran together into cycles of walking at night, sleeping during the day, eating whatever was made available, and following orders, as Hal and Mac were passed from anonymous guide to guide. Hal recounted:

> Mac and I would discuss the hard conditions suffered by these people and our gratitude for their willingness to share what little they had and risk their lives for us. After all, just a few days before, we had been bombing them and their cities. But they hated Hitler for what he was doing to their families, their lives, and their country.
>
> Some days we would be housed in basements of a house, some days in attics, and sometimes in barns. Our hosts were all hospitable, some more than others. Some hosts would try to talk with us. Others acted as though we weren't there. We knew that it was death on the spot by the Nazis for any host that was caught helping downed Allied airmen. I have always regretted that we were unable to exchange names and addresses with our hosts, but for their safety, and ours, it was out of the question. I often wish that I was able to go back to them after the war to thank them for saving our lives at such personal risk.
>
> We had been in Germany for five or six weeks, walked about a hundred miles under very difficult circumstances, when we finally came to our rendezvous point. I will never forget that night. Our guide explained to us that he was going to take us to an airfield that was once a German Luftwaffe training site. He would hide us behind some bushes, and a Royal Air Force Dakota (the same aircraft as the American C-47) would come in about 9:00 PM, land going left to right, turn around, and take off in the opposite direction without stopping. The rear cargo door would have been removed. We were told that we should jump up from our hiding place, run out onto the field, and climb on board through the cargo door.
>
> At 9:00 sharp, we heard aircraft engines; they sounded like they were coming in low, but we couldn't see a thing. Although they were flying without lights, I could see the fire coming out of the exhausts of the engines as the pilot throttled back for the landing.
>
> The Dakota rolled past Mac and me and soon made the 180-degree turn to start the run in the opposite direction for the takeoff. The plane was moving slowly when we jumped out of our bushes and started running for the

cargo door—and so did about twenty other Yanks, all downed U.S. airmen, who, unbeknownst to us, had also been hiding behind bushes.

As I ran along the side of the door, a big Brit reached out and grabbed my arm and yanked me aboard. We were all trying to climb up into the cabin of the plane to make room for those who followed. When the Brit had the last man aboard, he signaled the cockpit, and we were airborne. I think we were flying before any of us could catch our breath from our runs, get off the deck of the plane, and find a place to sit. In a few hours, we would be back in England.

But they were scheduled to land within the perimeter of the Greater London Defense Area, a dicey thing, for the perimeter was ringed with a defense system that offered a "safe route" to the airfields that was changed every night. There were hundreds of hydrogen-filled barrage balloons tethered with steel cables capable of shearing off wings of intruding aircraft. However, the Dakota was brought safely home by a competent pilot who threaded his way through the maze.

The remnants of the parachute that served as Hal's footwear while evading capture in Germany are now festooning the ceiling of the Falcons Landing lounge. The white silks provide not only decoration but a conversation piece as well. And the girl, Jane, in the photograph that he retrieved from the cockpit before bailing out of the bomber, was his young wife whom he had married in November 1944, a month before he joined the Eighth Air Force in England. Jane and Hal celebrated their sixtieth wedding anniversary here at Falcons Landing.

Hal was born and bred a Southern Californian, born in Upland and raised in Ontario. He attended Chaffee High School and Chaffee College and was called into service while in his sophomore year in college. He had an early interest in aviation that was cultivated by an Army pilot whom he had met at March Field. The pilot invited him to attend a Saturday morning parade at the field and gave him a tour of the flight line. Hal was hooked. In December 1942, he joined the Army aviation cadet program with the understanding that the Army would permit him to finish the two years of school he had left before graduation. It didn't happen that way. Three months later he was called up for active duty. Hal's joining the Army was a difficult thing for his father and mother, who were members of the River Brethren Church, a Christian sect that opposes war.

Hal's first duty assignment took him to Lincoln, Nebraska. He completed flight training in April 1944. He met Jane in Miami in August 1944 and was fortunate to secure her Atlanta telephone number, which he still remembers (Main 4484). Twice, while flying through the area, he called that number through the Atlanta tower to make a date. During an emergency evacuation of aircraft while under threat of a hurricane, he was fortunate to draw Atlanta as a three- to four-day haven for his aircraft. That was long enough for him to work his charms with Jane to win a promise of marriage. Now you know the derivation of the name of his B-17, the *Atlanta Hurricane.*

Hal Naylor, front row left, with his crew, Navigator Claud McHorse is
second row right.

Hal flew his first combat mission in December 1944 and was on his ninth mission when he bailed out of the fatally crippled bomber. He rotated back to the States after VE Day. The Army permitted him to return to and complete school immediately after the war. He subsequently flew C-54s and supported the Berlin Airlift from a field in the States.

Hal flew the SB-17 air rescue aircraft while he and Jane were stationed in Japan. Arguably, he may have flown the first combat flight of the Korean War as he flew the SB-17 from a Japanese air base to Kimpo Airfield in Korea to evacuate the embassy staff before the rapidly approaching North Korean armies on June, 26, 1950. (At 11 AM on the June 25, North Korea had declared war while launching tank and infantry attacks all along the thirty-eighth parallel. The first major aerial duel took place a year later when more than forty MiG-15s attacked a B-29 formation, shooting down two bombers. Eleven of the MiGs were destroyed.)

Hal had a varied career in the Air Force, which included a tour at Lehigh University while assigned to the Reserve Officer Training Corps program, a tour as the inspector general of the Thirteenth Air Force, one at Clark Field in the Philippines, and a tour of duty in Vietnam. Hal retired in Oregon in 1970, but that was not the end of his adventures.

He and Jane had a yen to live in a houseboat. While serving in Strategic Air Command under Gen. Curtis LeMay, for whom he has the greatest respect and admiration, he was stationed at Little Rock, Arkansas, where there were facilities for such living. They purchased a houseboat in Saint Petersburg, Florida, and took a six-week course in sailing. They set sail from Saint Petersburg, through the Gulf, and up the Mississippi in their craft the *TDY Little Rock*. En route they joined another live-aboard boater, who was also headed for Little Rock.

In Little Rock, Hal and Jane renewed acquaintances with Roland and Marlene Perry. Hal and Roland had been in the same class at flight school and had served together at Little Rock Air Force Base. The Shepherds were a third Air Force couple living at Little Rock at that time. At dinner one evening, the Perrys and the Shepherds told Hal and Jane about the wonderful potential they saw in Falcons Landing. The Naylors moved into the community in July 1996. Through sheer coincidence, the Perrys and the Naylors came to share the same duplex, and Jerry Shepherd, now widowed, lives in one of the apartment buildings. The Naylors, the Perrys, and the Shepherds were charter members of Falcons Landing.

When Hal flew that fateful mission over Paderborn, there was a young German woman, Hildegard Carter, who was living but twenty-five miles away in Kassel. It was from another perspective that she lived and suffered through the agonies of the allied bombings. She was to be widowed during the war, bear her daughter Lorie, and subsequently marry an American Army Air Corps flight surgeon. She was widowed a second time, and she too was destined to live at Falcons Landing. But, that's another story.

25

Epilogue

There are several prominent themes that emerge in these profiles of Americans who are living at Falcons Landing in the autumn of their lives. They are themes of courage, sacrifice, perseverance, faith, and patriotism. The virtues of devotion to duty and willingness to sacrifice themselves for the common good run through the stories of these veterans of American challenges, whether they met the challenges abroad in the skies, seas, and fields of combat, or at home, holding families together and sustaining our domestic and democratic systems. We witnessed the courage of a soldier who captured an enemy tank while afoot, was captured by his enemies, and escaped while under fire from pursuers. We witnessed the dedication and the compassion of a sailor who, on D-Day at Normandy, loaded his small craft with wounded and delivered them to the care of medical authorities while under intense enemy fire. We witnessed the skill of an Air Force pilot who performed what seemed to be impossible, landing a crippled aircraft backwards. We shared the experience of deprivation, hunger, and cruelty suffered by prisoners of war. We read the stories of the diplomat who reconstituted the economies of the countries of our allies and former enemies. They are impressive histories of impressive Americans.

Residents of Falcons Landing are people of distinction and accomplishment. While they have enjoyed success in their careers and their duties, few were born in privileged circumstances. Their successes are a credit to their talents and fortitude, as well as a credit to the American system that permits and encourages those with little to achieve much.

Doctor Herman "Hank" Gensler of Falcons Landing is characteristic of his generation. He is a product of the trials of World War II and the opportunities that were offered to veterans of that war. His is an example of how those born with little can rise through the pyramid of our society to make substantial personal and professional contributions to the American system. Grandfather Gensler, a baker, was once considered a wealthey man in Poland but had lost everything during World War I. A deeply religious but barely literate man, he consulted with the family rabbi about coming to America and was advised that it was not a wise thing to do, because his children were likely to become Christians in that alien land. Nevertheless, he came to Brooklyn alone in 1923. He wasn't joined by his family for many months, until Grandmother Gensler arrived with their children.

"As a young child, my immigrant parents and I lived in a tenement in Manhattan," Hank recalled. "Once a month, we visited my grandparents, taking the Second Avenue El which crossed over the river to Brooklyn on the Brooklyn Bridge. When the Statue of Liberty came into view, my mother would order me to stand at attention, salute, and recite the 'Pledge of Allegiance' as loudly as I could. It usually generated appreciative applause from the other passengers. I was a shy child, and the attention embarrassed me. However, my mother, being so grateful for being in this country, would tell me. "Herman, America is a Golden Land. You are so lucky to have been born here. You must show respect."

Residents of Falcons Landing can give testimony to the verity stated by Hank Genzler's mother, "America is a golden land. You are so lucky to have been born here." They show not only their respect, but, through their lives, their devotion to this great country.

978-0-595-37174-7
0-595-37174-4

CPSIA information can be obtained
at www.ICGtesting.com
Printed in the USA
FFOW03n1519030418
46149786-47312FF